Social Work Research

Social Work Research

Ethical and Political Contexts

Heather D'Cruz
and
Martyn Jones

SAGE Publications
London • Thousand Oaks • New Delhi

SAGE Publications Ltd
1 Oliver's Yard
55 City Road
London EC1Y 1SP

SAGE Publications Inc.
2455 Teller Road
Thousand Oaks, California 91320

SAGE Publications India Pvt Ltd
B-42, Panchsheel Enclave
Post Box 4109
New Delhi 110 017

British Library Cataloguing in Publication data

A catalogue record for this book is available
from the British Library

ISBN 0 7619 4970 4
ISBN 0 7619 4971 2 (pbk)

Library of Congress Control Number: 2003115347

Typeset by C&M Digitals (P) Ltd., Chennai, India
Printed in Great Britain by The Cromwell Press Ltd, Trowbridge, Wiltshire

Contents

Acknowledgements

This book has emerged from our teaching of research to social work students, mostly undergraduates, of whom many regard research with the proverbial fear and loathing and as an unnecessary diversion from their study of 'real social work'. Hence, the approach taken here heavily emphasizes the importance of research for social work as another way of achieving the emancipatory aims that we espouse as a profession. The conceptual approach and many of the exercises have been used in our classes with some success. The beginnings of this book rest in the print study materials (*Social Work Practice Research A: Study Guide and Reader*, © Deakin University) that are used in our teaching of social work research to undergraduate students. We hope that these will be of interest more widely to other social work students. We would like to thank our students for their inadvertent influence on our ideas for this book.

Additionally, we would like to thank various colleagues who have provided their expertise in many ways during the process of writing the book. We would like to thank Helen Modra for locating some of the websites that appear in Chapter 3, and Marion Churkovich and Christine Oughtred, Librarians at Deakin. University, for their prompt and efficient assistance in locating references for us. We are also grateful to Linda Briskman and Struan Jacobs who have generously given their advice and feedback on some chapters.

Finally, we also acknowledge the patience and forbearance of our significant others (feline, in Heather's case, family and canine in Martyn's!) during the chaos that has existed in our lives while writing this book.

Heather D'Cruz and Martyn Jones
June 2003

ONE Research, social work and professional practice

Introduction

There were many reasons for us to write this book. The title – *Social Work Research: Ethical and Political Contexts* – encapsulates what we see as important aspects of social work research, ones that are fundamental to achieving the emancipatory aims of social work rather than yet another set of techniques to be either mastered or avoided. However, we have an ongoing questioning attitude – how is research an essential part of social work and how can it be both ethical and political? We hope that these are questions that you, too, will consider as you read and use this book.

We show how social work research is another social work method or approach, in addition to the more well-known case, group and community work that are seen as 'traditional' or, for some people, 'real' social work. Therefore, we show how social work research, along with other practice approaches, can realize the emancipatory goals and objectives of social work. Furthermore, we make links between social work research and direct service approaches, looking at how one can inform the other – how research can improve practice and practice experiences can influence what and how we research. This book also makes links with perhaps another poor relation in the social work repertoire of approaches – that of social policy as practice. For this book, we take the approach that practice as direct service to clients may inform important research questions about the effectiveness and appropriateness of policies that shape social work practice and service delivery. Social work research is also an important way of contributing to social work theory and knowledge. Finally, we hope that, as a result of reading this book, you will start to appreciate and understand social work research and even become passionate about it!

The aims of this book

The aims of this book and the approach taken are a way of addressing some of the fears and misconceptions that may exist among many social work students and also practitioners with regard to research. The general aversion to social work research is almost a standing joke, coming from knowledge of our own student days, much shared knowledge by social work educators and our own experiences of teaching social work research.

This general 'attitude' has been well captured by Dr Epstein (1987: 71), Professor of Social Work at Hunter College in New York and a teacher of social work research:

> No other part of the social work curriculum has been so consistently received by students with as much groaning, moaning, eye-rolling, bad-mouthing, hyperventilation and waiver-strategizing as the research courses.

As Marlow (2001: 2) notes, this phobia about research is not only restricted to students but also includes social work professionals, to whom she addressed the following statement:

> Social workers often express … suspicion and even a phobia about research. Have you ever skimmed over articles in social work journals because you were intimidated by the language and the displays of results? Have you ever shuddered at the thought of undertaking a research project? If so, you are not alone. Because research is typically associated with mathematics, you may not be enthusiastic about applying what is perceived as a cold, impersonal approach to human needs and problem solving. After all, most social workers want to work with people, not numbers.

By the end of this chapter, we hope that you will recognize the importance of research for social work practice. By the end of the book, you should be able to read and critique some of the social work research literature and have some ideas as to how you might answer some of the questions that may arise for you in your professional practice.

We teach research to social work students because we believe that social work practice is more likely to be effective when social workers are able to draw on and evaluate previous research. We hope to encourage and assist social workers to conduct their own research to answer those questions arising in their practice that cannot be answered by the existing literature.

As Marlow (2001: 2) goes on to write:

> When you are equipped with the knowledge and skills to apply research methods, you will also know how to answer many of the questions that arise in your role as a generalist social worker, such as these:
>
> - Are my visits to Mrs Garcia really helping her cope with the death of her husband? What is her experience of the grief counselling?
> - How effective is programme X in providing services that support and protect victims of domestic violence? What are the experiences of the clients receiving these services?
> - What are the needs of adolescent fathers in City Y? What is it like to be a teenage father in City Y?

We would add, how effective and appropriate is this or that policy in addressing the problems that particular groups may experience? Examples of policies include (un)employment, income support, child welfare and health. You will no doubt know from your own lived experience and/or from your social work practice that many policies are less than effective in changing the disadvantaged circumstances of many people – and some may even appear to worsen the problems they purport to address.

Apart from informing practice and policy change as an immediate concern, research also contributes to social work theory, as generated from practice. This differs from the view that theory (as 'top-down knowledge') is imposed on practice or, even worse, separate from or irrelevant to practice. The connection between 'theory', 'practice' and 'research' is emphasized by Fook (1996) in *The Reflective Researcher*. The generation of social work theory from practice, as a reflective approach, positions the practitioner centrally within the research process, represented as an ongoing enquiry into everyday social work practice:

> a reflective stance questions the ways in which theory, practice and research and the relationships between them have been formulated. ... theory and research do not necessarily precede practice ... but ... theory is often implicit in practice and is unavoidably integrated with it. ... Any useful theory therefore needs to be modified by and responsive to the uncertainties of practice. Any approach to understanding social work should necessarily integrate theorizing, researching and practising. A process of reflection on practice might thus involve the potential for theory development, research enquiry and practice improvement. (Fook, 1996: xiii)

Finally, social work research can meet political objectives, of addressing broader social, organizational and cultural differences manifested as inequalities and 'interlocking oppressions' (Yeatman, 1995) associated with gender, race, ethnicity, culture, class, disability, age, sexual preference and even geographical location. In sociological terms, these are known as 'structural inequalities', which social work has a key role in addressing, by promoting social justice. Social work research can play a significant part in social change by focusing on personal and collective experiences of structural inequality and recommending strategies for change. However, to achieve appropriate recognition from decisionmakers, we must make sure that our research is of high quality and intellectually rigorous.

What is research?

In our experience, many social work students (and practitioners) reject research because of particular images they have of it and researchers. Before reading any further, you may like to spend a few minutes on the exercise below. This exercise is intended to exorcise any demons associated with the word 'research' and explore ways of engaging with what you might enjoy about it.

Exorcising the demons and becoming enchanted with research

1 Write the word 'research' on a piece of paper. Underneath it write down all the 'scary thoughts' that come to mind when you think about 'doing research'. Now write down any positive thoughts you may also have in a separate list.

2 Next, think about how you will approach the following task. You think you may be eligible for some welfare, education or housing benefits (for example, social security, money to assist you to study, rent assistance) provided by the government or private organizations. How will you go about finding out about what is available and whether or not you are eligible to receive these benefits? Write down the steps you will take.

3 Now think about another process you used to find out more about something you had limited knowledge of previously. Write down what you did to find out about it.

4 Look at the headings or descriptions you have given to the processes of enquiry in these two examples. (Remember, we are looking at what you did – that is, the *process*, not the specific *content*, of the enquiry. The aim is to be able to see some equivalence between the steps we take to solve problems of limited knowledge as everyday practices and those linked with the more formal processes called 'research'.)

5 Do you see any ways in which you can translate the headings you gave to your processes of enquiry into the more formal language of social research? You may be familiar with some of these formal concepts already. Alternatively, you may want to browse through the later chapters in this book where these concepts appear. Don't worry if these connections are not immediately apparent. They will become clearer as you engage with and reflect on what we discuss in later chapters. We also encourage you to discuss your ideas with peers and friends.

6 Now write down the word 'enquiry' and the positive and negative meanings associated with it. How might the word 'enquiry' be related to the word 'research'? How might you 'control the demons' (if you have any) and maximize the positive meanings associated with the word 'research'?

7 Keep these thoughts as a starting point against which to review your engagement with this subject as you read and use this book.

When you have completed this exercise, compare your thoughts with those of sociologist Connell (1975, in Wadsworth, 1997: 6):

Research is something that anyone can do, and everyone ought to do. It is, simply collecting information and thinking systematically about it. The word 'research' carries overtones of abstruse statistics, and complex methods, white coats and computers. Some social research is highly specialized, but most of it is not; much of the best work is logically very straight-forward. Useful research on many problems can be done with small resources, and should be the regular part of the life of any thoughtful person involved in social action.

If we take up Connell's idea that research 'is simply collecting information and thinking systematically about it', you might find that you have done exactly this in the exercise above. Although we might not think of it as such, research is one activity that many of us are engaged in every day. Perhaps we use phrases such as 'trial and error' or 'making enquiries' or 'finding out about', rather than 'research'. We may not even conceive of our actions as being research, but it is the process rather than conscious intent that determines whether or not we are engaging in research.

The connections between social work research, practice and theory

While the exercise you have done and the above quotes suggest that research is 'seeking knowledge for a purpose', we want to extend this to incorporate the ethical and political dimensions that are essential to social work research. Everitt et al. (1992: vii) refer to this as 'research-mindedness', by which means research and practice can be interrelated within 'certain intellectual and profes-sional principles'. The three principles of 'research-mindedness' are summar-ized below and will be revisited in different ways in subsequent chapters:

- a participatory/developmental model of social work, as opposed to a social control model
- anti-oppressive values
- a genuine partnership between practitioners and those whom they serve (Everitt et al., 1992: vii).

You might notice that these valued principles for social work research are not at all different from those informing other areas of social work practice. Therefore, as applied to social work research, the principles mean that clients are not treated as objects whose knowledge gained from lived experience is exploited, particularly when they are often vulnerable and relatively powerless. Instead, these principles validate different bases of 'knowing', which are shared and made explicit as much as possible in the interaction between 'researcher' and 'informant'. Subjectivity, as personal experience and worldviews, is also valued and understood as being integral to knowledge gained in the research process. Taken together, you might begin to see some validity to our earlier claim that social work research is another method that can help achieve social work's emancipatory objectives.

Table 1.1   The relationship between research and practice (Marlow, 2001: 25)

Practice	Research
Forming partnerships	Using participatory methods
Articulating challenges	Deciding on the question
Defining directions	Developing the question
Identifying strengths	Collecting the data, sampling and design
Analysing resource capabilities	Organizing and analysing the data
Framing solutions	Research writing
Activating resources, creating alliances and expanding opportunities	Utilization of research findings
Recognizing success and integrating gains	Evaluation of research

Marlow (2001) has another way of conceptualizing the connections between social work research and practice. In Table 1.1 (Marlow, 2001: 25) summarizes 'the relationship between research and practice'.

The main aim of Marlow's (2001) discussion of the relationship between research and social work practice is to minimize what may intimidate us about social work research by showing how it often relies on knowledge, skills and processes that are already familiar to social work practitioners. Like Everitt et al. (1992), Marlow emphasizes 'empowerment-based practice' (Marlow, 2001: 21). She says that both social work practice and research follow particular stages or phases in which similar objectives may be achieved on behalf of client groups. However, Marlow names these stages differently, depending on whether they are associated with 'research' or 'practice'. We would comment that we do not necessarily see research (or, indeed, practice) as a set of neatly sequential stages or phases. Instead, we know from our own experience and that of others (see, for example, Arber, 1993a: 32–50; Mason, 1996) that human behaviour and interactions are rarely so tidy and predictable. However, in dissipating fears about social work research, Marlow's approach is very helpful.

Professionalism and research in social work

As well as understanding research to be a crucial component in the practice of social work, whether that be in direct service provision or policy development, it can also be seen to be significant when it comes to the question of professionalism. In many respects, controversies that surround claims of professionalism on the part of social work are played out in the way research is or isn't held to be relevant and necessary. Of course, these controversies are very much concerned with the place of knowledge and power in professions. As such, they also point to the need to examine the ethical and political dimensions of research and explore the implications for different kinds of professionalism to which social work might lay claim.

For some, the link between research and professionalism in social work has been very clear:

> If the purpose of the craft of welfare professionalism is to strive towards human well-being, justice and equality, then intellectual work and research is fundamental to reveal the structures and mechanisms that generate and maintain inequality. (Everitt et al., 1992: 3)

The effective pursuit of equality is seen as dependent on a properly informed analysis prior to action. While social values and goals still drive the professional agenda, research enters as a vital part of the professional repertoire in directing efforts towards these ends. Moreover, the reference points that can come from research are construed as important in sustaining purposeful action that might otherwise become diverted or misplaced:

> Research-minded practice is concerned with the analytical assessment of social need and resources, and the development, implementation and evaluation of strategies to meet that need. It is not constrained by organizational or professional boundaries ... The taken-for-granted becomes subject to critical scrutiny. (Everitt et al., 1992: 4)

Research as an antidote to the 'taken-for-granted' is a common theme in discussions of its contribution to professionalism. Whether it is preparedness to 'think the unthinkable' or show 'uncommon common sense', research is presented as a safeguard against practice becoming a matter of routine or proceeding on the basis of unexamined assumptions.

If we consider research in terms of its capacity to invigorate and inform professional behaviour, then we might begin to list some of the ways in which this could become manifest. O'Connor et al. (1995: 222–3) offer some examples of the contributions of research in this respect, which are to:

- add to the sum of our knowledge
- address a specific issue of concern
- find out what our clients think of our services
- ascertain social needs in a particular area
- develop a submission
- influence policymakers
- organize people
- translate individual needs into a social voice
- give hidden and unheard people a voice
- change the ways in which things are done
- develop and test new interventions.

Running through these ideas about research and professionalism is the assumption that knowledge generated as a result of research can challenge existing practices and policies and help keep the profession up to date by continually improving its services for the public good. The suggestion, then, is that professionalism, and the survival of a professional group, is dependent at least to some degree on being responsive to new and changing situations and innovative in the form and nature of the expertise it claims to offer.

The human services professions, however, have themselves been subject to many contemporary contextual changes. These include changing welfare regimes, new systems of public management, transformations in communications and information technologies, the impacts of globalization and internationalization, influence of new social movements and post-colonialism, and so on (O'Connor et al., 2000). Consequently, they are confronted with sustaining a viable professionalism both in respect of the clientele they claim to serve and their organizational locations. It is important to contextualize the contribution of research as it occurs in each of these respects.

The introduction of performance management strategies within the public services generally, for example, now requires compliance with predetermined standards. These standards will have variously to do with criteria such as efficiency, quality and effectiveness. The production of such standards may or may not have been informed by studies that have sought to evaluate programmes and performance. Professionalism in this context could then well become associated with the appropriation of research to generate standards by means of the systematic evaluation of a given programme or performance. Professional behaviour would then be monitored for compliance with these standards, such that research knowledge has become part of the organizational governance system.

The growth of interest in evidence-based practice within human services is a further example of the way in which professional, organizational and policy agendas can combine to develop a strategic direction for research and practice that supposedly meets a number of needs. For some, evidence-based practice represents an overdue coming of age for the social work profession, one in which it can legitimate its place not so much by exhorting social values (or ideologies) but by the irrefutable evidence of its effectiveness and utility (Sheldon, 1998). For others, evidence-based practice is an unavoidable and not unattractive pathway to gaining credibility for the profession with key stakeholders and a necessary development in sustaining and promoting its contribution (see Sheldon and Chilvers, 2000). A fit has also been noted between the liberal individualism that underpins both contemporary public policy and those professional activities most amenable to being evaluated on 'hard evidence' (Howe, 1997).

The emergence of centres, institutions and networks devoted to the cause of evidence-based practice in social work and human services marks a significant trend in the configuration of research and practice. In her appraisal, Trinder (2000a) notes how the approach has attracted both 'champions and critics' and examines a series of practical and conceptual issues that arise in pursuit of practice based on research evidence. These include the feasibility of generating an evidence base to inform practice, privileging of certain kinds of evidence, impact that disseminating research findings may or may not have on practice, policy and decision making; scope or otherwise for evidence-based practice to be responsive to consumer concerns and so on.

Trinder herself asserts that 'research is an inherently political process' (2000a: 237). In recommending that the 'definition of evidence should be broadened' and the 'claims of evidence-based practice should be narrowed' (2000a: 237), she is adopting a position very similar to the one taken in this book. In order to realize the potential of research evidence and align this with practice and policy improvement, it is important for professionals to develop an understanding of the political and ethical dimensions of generating knowledge. As we shall see, this includes, much in the way Trinder (2000a: 237) suggests:

> a greater degree of reflexivity amongst researchers, reviewers and practitioners to think about what assumptions about the world are taken for granted and what questions and answers are not addressed or precluded by particular pieces of research or particular research designs.

Processes for generating and managing knowledge within the organizational and policy spheres of public services are significant for understanding the emerging relationships between professionalism and research (Jones, 2004). Of course, new technologies are texturing these processes in particular ways and becoming part of the emerging politics and ethics of knowledge and research. Meanwhile, concurrent contextual changes are substantively affecting definitions and purposes of professionalism with regard to its relationship with service clientele. When hierarchical models of professional expertise are aligned with colonizing patterns of Western society, new versions of professionalism are required if the credibility of the human services within an anti-colonialist context is to be sustained (Ife, 2001). This, too, has immediate consequences for the understanding of research politics and ethics, if research is to remain a constituent and vibrant feature of the new professionalism. An appreciation of diverse paradigms (ways of knowing) and methodologies (ways of building knowledge) can assist the contribution of research to the kinds of critically aware professionalism required to meet the array of contemporary challenges for social work.

Critical thinking, reflexivity and research

Research, it has been suggested, involves 'thinking systematically'. As we undertake research, we engage with an array of information that arises from our interaction with books, journals, files, databases, participants, colleagues, agencies and so on. The orderly generation and processing of information demands of us an intellectual discipline that extends our everyday capacities for doing just that. An important aspect of this intellectual discipline concerns critical thinking.

There are several traditions of critical thinking in Western societies, all of which have implications for the conduct of social work research and practice. Perhaps the most dominant has been that associated with philosophical branches of argumentation and reasoning:

> Critical reasoning is centrally concerned with giving reasons for one's beliefs and actions, analysing and evaluating one's own and other people's reasoning, devising and constructing better reasoning. Common to these activities are certain discrete skills, for example, recognizing reasons and conclusions, recognizing unstated assumptions, drawing conclusions, appraising evidence and evaluating statements, judging whether conclusions are warranted; and underlying all of these skills is the ability to use language with clarity and discrimination. (Thomson, 1996: 2)

This variety of critical thinking has found its place in social work research as a result of attempts to introduce the tenets of 'scientific reasoning' into the ways practitioners might appraise knowledge in everyday practice. Gibbs (1991) suggests, for example, that reasoning might be improved by learning how to spot common fallacies and 'confounders'. Some common fallacies invoked are the appeal to experience, authority, tradition and the uncritical acceptance of documented ideas or testimonials by practitioners or clients regarding the effectiveness of particular methods. Similarly, the attention to confounders is seen to provide a safeguard against drawing dubious conclusions about the relationship between interventions and outcomes by highlighting flaws in causal reasoning. Logical thinking and formal scientific method become the way to advance the state of knowledge in practice.

Other traditions have influenced the approach to critical thinking and, particularly, the development of such capabilities:

> Being a critical thinker involves more than cognitive activities such as logical reasoning or scrutinizing arguments for assertions unsupported by empirical evidence. Thinking critically involves our recognizing the assumptions underlying our beliefs and behaviours. (Brookfield, 1987: 13)

One finds here greater attention to personal and cultural factors and wariness of too narrow an approach that would divorce the operations of rationality from the humanity of the thinker. To this extent, 'critical thinking involves a reflective dimension' (Brookfield, 1987: 14). The reflective process invites the exploration of experiences, meanings and interpretations, without which the creativity of imagining and acting on alternatives is seen to be severely limited.

The added dimension now current within critical thinking concerns the place of critical reflection and reflexivity. In attending to processes of thinking, critical reflection is also concerned with 'the thinker' but locates subjectivities particularly within socio-political contexts. There is still very much a hunt for assumptions, but now to do with how they shape the way we construct problems, needs, issues and so on, and a critical appraisal of what those assumptions might tell us about the contexts and histories of which we are a part.

While such explorations take us into personal, experiential realms, they imply the capacity to become not just more self-aware, but socially self-aware (Fook, 1993: 156–9). Within this approach, our contributions to knowledge-building via research would be seen as embedded within the everyday construction of sets of beliefs and practices ('discourses'), where claims to legitimacy have to do with the subtle and not so subtle exercise of power. Here, the concept of reflexivity assists in sustaining a sense of agency (a capacity to act purposefully) within this complicated process of knowledge construction.

Reflexivity works with the idea that knowledge 'is made rather than revealed' (Taylor and White, 2000: 199). In practising reflexively, we become directly concerned with 'the constructedness of all claims, including our own' (Hall, 1997: 250 cited in Taylor and White, 2000: 199). Such a view accentuates rather than dilutes our responsibilities as knowledgemakers. It requires us to consider how power is exercised in the knowledge-making processes in which we engage. Furthermore, locating ourselves within these operations of power is seen as an intensely moral action. Reflexivity suggests that we cannot find refuge from moral responsibility by following principles of good research practice. The principles are not inviolate, but sustained by the success of the discourses in which they are embedded and are there to be continually scrutinized. Meanwhile, research practice necessitates the interpretation and reconstruction of principles amid competing imperatives, occurring within complicated and contradictory social contexts that more often than not render simple rule-following redundant.

This kind of approach to research can make life difficult. It is a cautionary antidote to the false certainties sometimes evident in research textbooks that seem to imply we can learn how to do research by learning a new set of techniques. Of course, the plethora of techniques that have become part of research tradition within Western societies are there to be learned and their associate skills acquired. Yet, research cannot be spared the debates that have entered into the examination of social practices. In as much as we conceive of research as being a social practice concerned explicitly with the generation of knowledge, we will have to contend with difficult questions concerning the political and ethical dimensions of our knowledge making.

Social work research as a social practice

If we were to make social work research itself the subject of research enquiry, what are some of the questions we might pose? We might find ourselves asking some of the following, for example:

- Who carries out research?
- Who decides what is to be researched?
- Where do the resources (time and money) for research come from?
- What permissions are obtained in order for research to proceed?
- What in practice do researchers do?
- Who reads reports of research?
- What influence does research have?
- Who benefits from research?

By asking questions such as these, we are led on to enquiries concerning the social organization of research, political economy of research, professionalization of research, sociology of research knowledge and so on. In other words, we can view social work research as a social practice. How we understand it as a social practice will depend very much on the perspectives we employ.

Viewing research through a liberal lens, for instance, we might understand the social role of the researcher as that of an independent investigator who follows certain codes of conduct and professionally endorsed techniques to produce new knowledge. This knowledge is then put at the disposal of others (policymakers, practitioners, industries, communities) to act on or not as they see fit. Viewing research through a radical lens, we might construe the researcher as being a social actor whose activities are party to the reproduction and/or transformation of existing social relationships of exclusion or inclusion, domination or oppression. Both processes and outcomes of knowledge production are then considered contributors to social change, and actions weighed accordingly.

As a social practice, we would expect networks to form among like-minded researchers and movements to develop that advocate for their preferred approach to research. It has been commonplace to refer to the 'paradigm wars' that have beset social research in recent decades (Reid, 1994). The emergence of evidence-based practice in social welfare has triggered another site of antagonism. User movements have been pursuing the agenda of empowerment in social work research (Beresford and Evans, 1999). Indigenous groups have increasingly promoted consciousness of the colonial history of research, with implications for not only greater cultural sensitivity but also a fundamental rethink of the tenets and methodologies of Western research practices (Tuhiwai Smith, 1999).

In some respects, this suggests that social work research is beset by a series of dilemmas and the erstwhile researcher has to determine where they stand on a number of political and ethical issues before they can proceed. In a cogent critique of 'critical' social research, Hammersley (1995a) has warned of the pitfalls of conflating the pursuit of political goals with the activity of research and, particularly, questions the philosophical presuppositions of those who seek to change oppressive social structures by means of research praxis.

However, in accentuating social work research as a political and ethical practice, this book presents a rather different way forward. We shall be echoing the sentiments expressed by Fook (2000, 2002), who has argued for an open, inclusive and flexible approach to social work research. Our approach tries to take cognizance of the complicated, changing and uncertain contexts with (and within) which research occurs. Admitting diversity into our practices creates greater possibilities for effective and responsive research. As Fook (2000: 2) puts it:

> A rigid, or even loose, commitment to one type of perspective, be it positivist, qualitative or deconstructive, does not seem to provide the flexibility of thinking needed to work in changing circumstances.

Yet, as Fook also points out, this could lead to the idea that anything goes and, consequently, she defines a crucial issue: 'can we develop an approach which allows us openness, but also builds upon and uses established methods of working?' (2000: 2). As we shall try to show, inclusivity in research is not the same as a free for all or even an eclectic outlook. Rather, it sees all perspectives and methods as a product of time and place and lacking intrinsic properties that could determine whether or not they are right and appropriate in isolation from the contexts of their application. Embedding themselves and their research practices within emerging and contingent contexts, the critical researcher adopting an inclusive approach will understand knowledge and skills in research as resources to be 'used in a meaningful yet flexible way to suit the situation at hand' (Fook, 2000: 2). Such judgements of suitability will engage the researcher in political and ethical as well as technical considerations, but in none of these domains can the researcher rely on pre-existing sets of principles or rules to tell them what is to be done.

The organization of the book

The book follows sequentially the major stages of the research process. The eight chapters emanate from the following key questions.

- What is the relevance of research to social work?
- What do I want to know more about?
- How might I answer my research question?
- How do I make sense of my data so that I can answer my research question?
- How do I pull all this together and communicate it to others?

This chapter has explored conceptions held of social work research and suggested an alternative framing as social enquiry. It has introduced the relevance of research to social work and suggested how it is integral to the historic missions of the profession. This first chapter has also outlined the political and ethical dimensions of social work research and developed these by considering research as a social practice concerned with knowledge making. Chapters 2 and 3 discuss, broadly, the use of research in social work. Determining a focus for research and a research question(s) for our enquiry represents the beginning of the process. This is followed in Chapter 3 by a consideration of how knowledge is located in perspectives on, and assumptions about, the world, with particular practical, ethical and political implications.

Chapters 4, 5 and 6 look at the matter of answering research questions. This starts with a consideration of methodology, which concerns the ways in which we might go about making knowledge. Chapter 5 discusses the more practical task of creating an appropriate plan or design for pursuing research question(s). Chapter 6 examines specific methods for collecting and generating data. In both conceptualizing and conducting research, the political and ethical aspects are emphasized.

Chapter 7 addresses the issue of sense making in research. In drawing links with the theoretical and methodological considerations considered earlier, this approach to analysis aims to ensure proper integrity of the research. The final chapter discusses how research is reported and disseminated. It assumes this is not a neutral exercise, but that communication needs to pay due regard to the perspectives and positions from which reports are, for example, read and written. The book concludes with a last look at research as social practice and the challenges of being a critical and inclusive researcher.

Putting it all together

Social work research is both simpler and more complicated than is sometimes imagined. Considered as an informal process of social enquiry, it is not so far removed from what we find ourselves doing every day when faced with a novel question or situation. If we think of social work as an occupation that is, by and large, dealing with the novel, then we can see how its practitioners find themselves engaging in processes of enquiry as an integral part of their work. In that sense, research is familiar territory, already part of our professional and personal worlds, even if we haven't labelled it as such.

The complexities of research arise as we formalize our processes of enquiry. We have available to us a rich resource about the doing of research that offers us more rigorous and systematic ways of building knowledge. However, we need to remain conscious that the knowledge we generate by using these more formal approaches represents particular ways of knowing. Opening the doors of research means accessing discourses that have a certain currency in securing legitimacy for claims to knowledge and truth. In the chapters to come, we shall be introducing accumulated bodies of teaching concerned with building knowledge by means of research practices. Beyond this, however, we shall be presenting research as a social practice, politically and ethically laden, which carries a special responsibility for those who choose to pursue it. We shall, therefore, be extending the idea of a critical researcher, presenting this as someone who is able to draw flexibly and inclusively on a range of research practices according to their appreciation of the situation in hand and the social dimensions of their knowledge making.

TWO The research question

Introduction

Reduced to its simplest, research is about answering questions. Of course, research goes about producing answers in particular ways, ways that are per-suasive and credible to research communities and the populations they serve. Yet, this is perhaps a peculiar manifestation of a rather fundamental form of enquiry – generating information to throw light on pressing questions.

In this chapter, we shall be examining the question setting that occurs in research, especially social work research. While coming up with questions may seem a rather self-evident process, we don't have to probe far to see that there's more to it than might at first appear. We will look at different kinds of research question, the role that questions play in research and the various facets of formulating questions, including the review of relevant literature. The discussion will conclude by attending to the social contexts of question-setting. To begin, we shall consider what might be the impetus for research.

The impetus for research

There are many ways in which research questions might arise. In social work practice research, it is often the needs or issues that confront us in the course of our work that prompt ideas for research. Then, some personal experience of ours may come into play to give us a special interest. Thus, our imagination might be caught, for example, by any one or more of the following suggested by Wadsworth (1997: 16).

- people are disagreeing strongly about some course of action or issue
- some problem is crying out to be solved
- there's a threat to something we want to keep and we need to be able to say why we think it is valuable
- we just have a feeling that something's not as good as it could be
- everyone else is looking at such and such and I thought it might be worth looking at, too
- I desperately need some information to reach a particular decision
- complaints have been received about the way we work
- something's working well for a change and we'd like to know why!
- there's a possibility of something new but we don't know what would be best.

You might like pause here and spend a few minutes considering the questions listed below.

Prompts for research

- Have you had any ideas about topics or issues that you think should be researched?
- What prompted these ideas?
- Can you identify with any of the prompts Wadsworth suggested above?
- What other prompts would you add to this list?

Sometimes, the image of the researcher is of a dispassionate enquirer who can examine a topic with what we may feel is the requisite neutrality. While open-mindedness is undoubtedly a desirable quality to bring to any piece of research, Alston and Bowles (1998: 29) are convinced that personal interest is also vital:

> Whatever the path by which you become involved, it is critical that *you* are interested in the topic. Research requires much time and effort. Unless you are curious and interested in the area you are about to research, there is little point in devoting your valuable time and energy (and those of other people) to it. (emphasis as in original)

Clearly, our personal interests will reflect our biographies and identities to some degree. If we are to see variety and breadth in the areas that become the subject of social work research, then we need to consider, among other things, what diversity exists among social work researchers. For example, Marlow (2001: 43) has argued that there has traditionally been a 'predominance of studies conducted by white, middle-class men, resulting in an inherent bias in the types of research questions'. She urges that human diversity issues be taken into account in decision making about questions for research. Similarly, she considers the 'bias' that can exist within agencies, illustrating how 'an agency's homophobic attitudes may result in ignoring the needs of lesbian clients' (Marlow, 2001: 45).

We shall be examining a range of factors that contribute to the generation of research questions that translate into research endeavour. However, the crucial point remains that research is a time-consuming activity that commonly occurs over months, if not years. A sense of commitment to, and enthusiasm for, the subject of this enquiry is invaluable in maintaining sufficient momentum to ensure satisfactory completion, particularly during those phases when the research process feels arduous, if not impossible. Evidently, at such moments, researching jointly with others who share that commitment and enthusiasm can prove crucial.

Research questions for social work

Social work occurs in many places, involving a range of people and communities, addressing a mix of issues and needs, utilizing a cascade of theories and methods. Inevitably, questions for research reflect this spread of interests and the 'received wisdoms' (Rojek et al., 1988) by means of which they are construed. Looking for commonalities across these varied interests is a daunting task. One approach is to locate unifying themes not so much in the content areas addressed by social work research as in the broader missions of the profession. Witkin (1995: 427) has put it this way:

> Social work has always struggled with its research identity. Unlike related disciplines such as psychology, sociology and psychiatry, social work has no unique subject matter or methodology ... What the social work profession does have is a unique commitment to a contextual understanding of people, an explicit value base that emphasizes human rights and human dignity, a commitment to serving marginalized and oppressed people, and a mission to foster a more just society.

While this statement might provide a useful framework when considering the focus and conduct of social work research, it still doesn't tell us too much about the kinds of questions that are posed. Some commentators (Marlow, 2001; Royse, 1999) suggest that social work research generally revolves around one (or more) of three strategies: exploratory, descriptive or explanatory. As the name suggests, exploratory research aims to generate knowledge about a relatively under-researched or newly emerging subject; descriptive research to illuminate the features and extent of the subject; and explanatory research to develop explanations of a subject.

If we were interested in the use of the Web in forming self-help groups, for example, and found out that little research had been done on this topic to date, then we might formulate an exploratory question to help define and map its main features. Descriptive questions lead to a more detailed understanding of, perhaps, the extent of Web-based self-help groups, who uses them, what for and how they are run. Explanatory questions would start to investigate the impact of self-help groups on those who subscribe and offer ways of making sense of their success or otherwise.

According to Marlow (2001: 35–40), there are two prime areas where these kinds of questions surface in generalist social work. One is in conducting 'needs assessments' and the other is in regard to 'evaluations', either practice or programme evaluations. Needs assessments are likely to be exploratory or descriptive – assessing the incidence of a particular social issue, for example, or the extent of certain needs. Evaluations are likely to be descriptive or explanatory. They can evaluate either the process (looking at the experience of a service) or the outcome (looking at the effectiveness) of a particular piece of practice or a programme of work.

While these are evidently two significant areas for research in social work, they do not represent all types of questions that can or might be posed. The very notion of 'needs assessment' as a category for ordering research immediately raises the issue of how and by whom needs are identified (Packham, 2000). Moreover, in times when the profession and practice of social work is in transformation, much research effort might well focus on the development of new concepts and models relevant to evolving contexts and tasks (Pease and Fook, 1999). On a somewhat contrasting note, there can also be an emphasis on questions that seek to ensure the utility value of research (Patton, 1997). Shifting ideas as to how social work might define and progress its sense of mission will clearly alter the way in which the contribution of research is viewed and the kinds of questions that then fall within its remit.

Let us look at some examples of research studies that illustrate how the focus of research can differ.

Examples showing how to focus research studies

An *exploratory* study of 'lesbian battering' in the United States included researching the experience of being battered, the frequency and occurrence of battering, and services provided to battered lesbians and lesbian batterers (Renzetti, 1992).

In a study that set out to *describe* social work's role in relation to people in the Grampians, Scotland, who had a diagnosis of personality disorder, Irvine (1995: 125) pursued the following four main research questions.

- How do these clients arrive at the social work department?
- What problems do these clients experience?
- What kinds of work are social workers doing with these clients?
- How are they doing it?

'In what ways does agency work contribute to positive family change?' was the key research question in an *evaluative* New Zealand study of the effectiveness of social services' interventions in supporting families (Sanders and Munford, 2003: 153).

The purpose of research questions

When we think about question-setting for social work research, we do perhaps immediately concentrate on the role questions play in orienting us to certain areas of knowledge. In this sense, attending to our research question(s) focuses our attention on the substantive content area, or topic, of our enquiry.

We can also think about the role played by the question in terms of its place in the processes and structure of our research activity. In a formal sense, research questions are seen as central because they:

- organize the project and give it direction and coherence
- delimit the project, showing its boundaries
- keep the researcher focused during the project
- provide a framework for writing up the project
- point to the data that will be needed (Punch, 1998: 38).

Most people who have attempted even a modest social research project would be able to identify with the experience of 'getting lost on the way' (Punch, 1998: 38). There are many complications and compelling distractions that arise. The research question can provide a relatively constant reference point to help plan and navigate the course.

This said, the impression could be that the researcher determines a question at the outset and sticks rigidly to it no matter what they come across en route. Here, we encounter the issue of how 'tight' or 'loose' an approach to research is being adopted (Miles and Huberman, 1994: 16). This issue has been presented thus:

> The central comparison is between research which is prespecified (or preplanned, or pre-figured, or predetermined) on the one hand, and research which is unfolding (or emerging, or open-ended) on the other ... At [one] end of the continuum, specific research questions are set up in advance to guide the study. It is quite clear, in advance, what questions the study is trying to answer. At the [other] end, only general questions are set up in advance. The argument is that, until some empirical work is carried out, it is not possible (or, if possible, not sensible) to identify specific research questions. They will only become clear as the research unfolds, and as a specific focus for the work is developed. (Punch, 1998: 23, 24)

We shall be looking further into the structuring of research when we consider research design. Generally, however, explanatory research would tend to be found towards the 'tight' end of the continuum and exploratory research more towards the 'loose' end, with descriptive research frequently moving between the two.

Explanatory studies, being informed largely by paradigms associated with 'scientific method', aim for specificity of the research question at the outset. Pursuing this in linear fashion via a controlled series of procedures produces reliable and valid results according to the underlying (positivist) paradigm. By contrast, exploratory studies require openness to what is encountered in the empirical world. In more cyclical fashion, questions are reformulated as the process proceeds and as new understandings emerge from ongoing interpretation and analysis. In the next chapter, we shall be examining different paradigms in detail and seeing how their varying approaches to ways of knowing have contrasting implications for the ways research should proceed.

We have been considering the role and timing of research questions largely in terms of how we conceptualize their place in the research process and structure. In so doing, we have concentrated on the researcher as the key person behind the research question. Clearly, this is only a part of the picture and shortly we shall be recognizing the relevance of other key players (or 'stakeholders').

Nevertheless, by acknowledging the central place that research questions assume, we can begin to anticipate the significance of addressing who does and who does not become involved in formulating them.

Question-setting

The research question (which may indeed have subquestions attached) tells us – and anyone who may ask – what the research is trying to find out.

Sometimes, people will know of a specific question that they wish to investigate. Just as often, the erstwhile researcher will simply be conscious of a general area in which they wish to conduct their research (for example, migration, youth suicide, system abuse). Usually, wherever one starts, the process of question-setting is characterized by a movement between the general and the specific. As a result of this going back and forth (sometimes referred to as an iterative process), we steadily make progress in clarifying just what our research will and will not be trying to find out, though, often, it may feel as if we are going round in circles and getting nowhere! While, ultimately, it is important to gain sufficient specificity to focus the research, it is also necessary to be able to locate specific questions within their broader field of enquiry, as this will assist in connecting the study to relevant literature, current knowledge and ways of thinking.

At this point, you might like to begin developing a research question and seeing what happens when you try to do so. The list below (adapted from Punch, 1998) replicates some of the initial steps involved. You will probably notice, even now, how developing questions takes time. However, given the important role played by a well-formulated question, this is undoubtedly time well spent.

- Identify a subject area for social work research that is of interest to you.
- Generate a list of possible questions for research concerning this subject area.
- Try to disentangle different questions from one another and put them into some kind of order.
- Attempt to develop a focus for a viable research project, drawing boundaries around what will and will not be included.

Now that you have developed a possible question(s) for research, you might like to try checking the words and phrases you have used for their clarity. If a question is to provide a reference point for the researcher – and, indeed, others involved in the research – then its meaning needs to be as unambiguous and precise as possible. It is important that you have (working) definitions for the terms that you have used in the question so it is clear what is meant by them. Indeed, this exercise is very much a part of developing a question and becoming sure about what it is the research will be aiming to find out and what will be outside its scope.

So far, we have been considering how our own knowledge and thinking about the research area will assist us in exploring relevant possibilities for enquiry. Shortly, we shall be looking at how, in reviewing the literature, we draw into the process other sources of existing knowledge. Consultation and collaboration with others (fellow researchers or practitioners, prospective research participants, community or agency representatives and so on) further extends the sources of knowledge and range of perspectives that may contribute to the question-setting process. This can sometimes be formalized to good effect – by establishing an advisory/steering group, critical reference group or management group – at the earliest stages of the project's inception. The involvement of participants and intended beneficiaries of the research in shaping its focus has become a key principle of 'research that creates change' (Munford and Sanders, 2003).

The scope of the project will also be shaped and limited by another set of rather more material and practical concerns. Whether one is applying for funding for the project or working with resources (including time) committed from elsewhere, question-setting commonly involves 'bringing the project down to size' (Punch, 1998: 37). *Feasibility*, then, is a further factor in the equation, with the guiding principle: 'it is better to do a smaller project thoroughly than a larger project superficially' (Punch, 1998: 37).

Feasibility is one of four criteria to be met in question-setting (Williams et al., 1995, as adapted by Alston and Bowles, 1998). The other three criteria ask us to consider whether or not the topic is relevant, researchable and ethical. *Relevance* refers to the credibility the research needs to have in addressing the concerns of the profession and the social work and human services sector generally. The question also needs to be *researchable* in the sense of being a question that has the potential to be answered by the generation of research knowledge. Not all questions are of this nature. Questions that concern moral judgement (phrased, for example, as what 'should' be the case) are posing an issue that cannot be answered by research per se. Last, a research question needs to be consistent with the *ethical* conduct of research. Here, we can think in terms of ethical codes that prescribe such principles as respect for persons, beneficence and justice (Commonwealth of Australia, 1999) as well as broader ethical considerations that stem from an acknowledgement of the cultural and political dimensions of knowledge making (Tuhiwai Smith, 1999).

These criteria once again underline how research occurs in a social context that has to be taken into account if one wishes to see potential topics for enquiry progress from ideas to actions. They highlight, too, how the formation of a research project, while driven by what one hopes is a well-formulated question(s), is inescapably bound up with the political processes of gaining financial, organizational and ethical approval to proceed. Working effectively as part of this social context is integral to question-setting.

There are three key elements to critical research practice in this respect: reflexivity, participation and negotiation. By *reflexively* appreciating one's personal location (one's social position and biography), the interests and assumptions we bring to developing questions for research can more readily be examined and appraised. Enhancing *participation* in setting the agenda for research can begin to unsettle an exercise of power that could otherwise perpetuate oppressive practices. Skilful *negotiation* of research foci with gatekeepers (of funding, permissions and strategic objectives) can create possibilities for research into sensitive and high-risk topics that are of great social benefit.

In developing research questions, then, we find ourselves at the interface between a process of conceptual sifting and the exercise of social practices. The accommodation we might reach between the two can vary and be perceived very differently. For example, policy moves towards increased collaborative research with industry can be viewed as either compromising intellectual freedom or increasing the number of opportunities to make a difference. However, instead, perhaps the crucial issues are to do with who is involved in setting questions for research and who are the likely beneficiaries.

The factors involved in question-setting are depicted in Figure 2.1. One component yet to be fully addressed concerns the important step of reviewing the literature.

Reviewing the literature

We have seen how the matter of question-setting involves moving between the general and specific in order to determine a researchable focus within the chosen field of enquiry. While one might think of developing a question(s) as being essentially concerned with clarifying what the research is trying to find out, the process of reviewing the literature could be seen to represent an attempt to ascertain what is already known about the subject. If we take the traditional view of the purpose of undertaking research as being to add to our knowledge, then we can understand how a literature review is perceived as crucial. According to Royse (1999: 23), 'the necessity of immersing yourself in the literature cannot be emphasized strongly enough. Research builds upon the accumulated efforts of all those labouring to expand our knowledge'.

However, as Punch (1998: 43) indicates:

> It is a matter of judgment at what point to concentrate on the literature. Factors involved in this judgment include the style of the research, the overall research strategy, what the objectives of the proposed study are, the nature of the substantive problem and how much is known about it, how well developed the literature in the area is, and how closely this study wants to follow the directions established by that literature. A further important factor is the knowledge that the researcher already has, especially when the research topic comes from practice or experience.

Existing knowledge doesn't only reside in the literature, of course, and, even when it might, that literature isn't necessarily readily accessible! Existing knowledge, too, will be partial and incomplete in a variety of ways. As well as looking for gaps in the literature, for example, the way in which any such knowledge has been generated may be open to critique from a number of vantage points. Hence, the review process entails more than becoming acquainted with existing knowledge – it requires a critical engagement with the literature.

Figure 2.1   Factors in question-setting

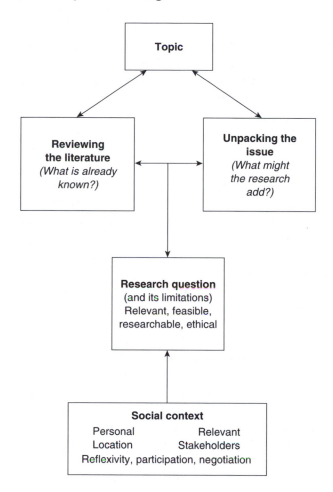

Existing knowledge may present itself in forms other than 'the literature'. You may like to think about the following issues at this point.

Searching beyond the literature

It is common to concentrate on 'the literature' as the main source of existing knowledge and review it when generating possibilities for the potential research area. For any research enquiry, there may well be other sources it would be sensible and desirable to consult as well. Returning to the research questions you developed earlier, consider what sources, other than the literature, you would wish to consult in formulating these questions. Why would you want to do this?

The growth of Internet usage is, of course, profoundly influencing the availability of information. Online access connects us with an ever-expanding range of providers and virtual learning communities. Moreover, in social work research, relevant knowledge may likely be found within professional and user communities. As suggested above, this affects the way in which we think about consulting and collaborating in order to shape our research focus. It may turn us towards less traditional approaches to engaging with current knowledge, such as we find in participatory models of research (Martin, 1994).

The notion of 'reviewing the literature' is, in many respects therefore, in danger of becoming an outdated, rather narrow and not always appropriate means of engaging critically with current knowledge relevant to the substance of our social work research. Despite this, it remains a standard procedure and provides one important means by which the researcher can define and justify their project. Marlow (2001: 51) has suggested that the literature review assists in:

- generating the question
- connecting the question to theory
- identifying previous research
- giving direction to the project.

A literature search goes hand in hand with a literature review. When we search the literature, there are several approaches that we can take. These vary from browsing the library shelves or the Web (generally, a time-consuming approach and not the most efficient or effective) to using bibliographic databases and information gateways. Scanning recent editions of specialist journals can also provide a useful starting point. We might even be fortunate enough to find an article that surveys the literature on our topic. Locating relevant theses can similarly accelerate the process as they often have comprehensive literature reviews and bibliographies. Government documents may well have their own catalogues and gateways, too. However, it is the electronic databases that are increasingly providing the most efficient way of conducting a systematic search of the literature.

Bell (1993: 41–9) highlights a few key steps in planning a literature search:

1 select the topic
2 define the terminology
3 define parameters – language, geography, time period, type of material, sector
4 list possible search terms
5 select sources – library catalogues, computer searching, bibliographies in books, journals and articles, abstracts or theses.

As Royse (1999: 20) suggests, searching databases may result in one of two common problems: '(1) not finding any (or enough) literature on your topic; and (2) finding too much'. A few tips Royse (1999: 21) offers in this respect are given below, with our own input. The matter of little existing literature on a topic might, of course, mean it is an area that has received scant attention to date. In such cases it is often useful to look for parallel studies that may offer beginning, analogous frameworks for consideration.

Tips for when database searching returns too few hits

- Substitute synonyms – for example, try 'adolescent' instead of 'teenager'.
- Think in terms of categories – for example, 'parenting styles', 'disciplinary techniques'.
- Go further back than the last three years – for example, five or seven years.
- Check your spelling!
- Use fewer words – 'parenting' rather than 'parental disciplinary styles' will be less prescriptive.
- Look in a different database.
- Try variations of the keywords – 'juvenile delinquent' *and* 'juvenile delinquency', for example.

Tips for when database searching returns too many hits

- Add keywords – for example, 'suspensions high school', not just 'suspensions'.
- Skim the most current titles to determine if there are other keywords that may eliminate some of the citations that do not interest you.
- Limit the search by language, year or type of publication.
- Skim the titles and/or abstracts for those articles that are themselves reviews of the literature on your topic.

Having accessed material, we become involved in a critical analysis of it. This entails being able to summarize accurately, but reviewing implies much more. Royse (1999: 23) talks of 'reading for a purpose', where the researcher is trying to discover answers to the following questions:

- What do the majority of the studies conclude?
- What theories have attempted to explain the phenomenon?
- What interventions have been tried?
- What instruments have been used to assess the problem?

- What are the gaps in our knowledge about the problem?
- What additional research needs have been identified?

A review, then, examines all aspects of previous knowledge making relevant to the topic and research question. Some gaps will be explicit in the reported studies, a statement concerning acknowledged limitations of a project or proposed areas for future research. However, the gaps will also be a consequence of inbuilt factors that are frequently left implicit, such as the perspectives from which a research question has been framed, the methodologies that have informed how the research has been conducted or the extent to which participants have been involved in shaping the research.

It should be apparent from this that a literature review is very different to an annotated bibliography. The latter comprises a list of texts (mostly books and articles), usually presented alphabetically or under headings, with notes against each separate text. It can provide a useful resource that documents materials and indicates in summary fashion their key features. However, the critical engagement with literature that occurs in a review results in the material being organized in a different form – for example, according to the main themes or controversies that have arisen.

Marlow (2001: 56) suggests that:

> A literature review places the current research in its historical and theoretical context. It describes the background to the study and the relationship between the present study and previous studies conducted in the same area. It also identifies trends and debates in the existing literature.

Hence, when writing the review, Royse et al. (2001: 378–9) advise that you:

- Make sure that the early major or classical studies in the field are included …
- Do not, however, focus so much on the earlier studies that the review of the literature is 'light' on current studies …
- Make minimal use of direct quotations from other sources and, by all means, avoid incorporating long passages from original sources …
- Try to provide a balanced presentation; acknowledge theories or explanations even if you do not subscribe to them …
- Construct the literature review so that the reader can easily follow your organisational scheme and will come away knowing the breadth of the prior research, the gaps in the literature, and the purpose of your proposal or research initiative. Distinguish for the reader the uniqueness of your study or describe how it is similar to others.

There is a certain art in writing literature reviews that, for most, only comes with practice. Perhaps one of the most helpful ways to start is to consult a range of literature reviews written by others, analyse the styles and structures used and consider how well you think they meet the above criteria.

A literature review is commonly situated at the beginning of a research report and will influence the credibility with which the research is viewed. Credibility is likely to be heightened when the process of reviewing the literature has been formative in developing the focus for the research. The writing of it will reflect the clarity of thinking that has helped finally define the research focus and question after the considerable time and effort that has been devoted to this early stage in the overall process.

Putting it all together

This chapter has surveyed various facets in determining a focus for research by setting questions for enquiry. This is a crucial phase in the research process. It shapes what follows, reflects a diverse range of interests and includes assumptions both about worthwhile areas for enquiry and ways in which new knowledge can be generated about them. In making research knowledge, one of the crucial questions concerns who is setting the research agenda.

The processes involved in developing research questions incorporate the intellectual ones of locating new projects in the history of previous studies, the practical ones of scoping an initiative that will be properly resourced and the interactional ones of engaging with key stakeholders (both gatekeepers and participants). All three dimensions face us with distinctive political and ethical considerations. In facing these issues, it is suggested that the critical researcher will need to exercise reflexivity, participation and negotiation. In the next chapter, we shall be looking more closely at how different ways of thinking impact upon what takes place in research.

THREE   Different ways of knowing and their relevance for research

Introduction

In this chapter we explore how preferred or dominant ways of knowing about and understanding the world, social problems and human experience may be taken for granted as the only legitimate ways of knowing. We consider the implications of preferred or dominant ways of knowing for social work research, practice and theory. In particular, we explore these issues as ethical and political dimensions for social work research. We then look at different ways of knowing and how these differences may form the basis of conflicts about 'truth' and valid knowledge. This is especially important for social work. We often conduct research on social issues that may not be valued by political or organizational representatives who may have different perspectives on problems or ways of understanding, explaining or responding to them. Views considered as different from the dominant view or that challenge it may become marginalized or considered as subversive or just plain wrong, thus creating difficulties for bringing about social change.

Paradigms

Different ways of knowing are represented by the concept of *paradigms*. The idea of paradigms and the implications for how we know, what we know and how we act on that knowledge is attributed, in the first instance, to Kuhn. Kuhn's work (1970) on the history of natural sciences discussed how scientists engage in debates about the phenomena that they study in their research and develop as theories (Bryman, 1988). Different beliefs and values about the phenomena being investigated inform the positions taken in scientific debates, which then influence the investigative techniques and theories that are developed.

Here are two formal definitions of paradigms. The first is by Kuhn (1970: 175):

the entire constellation of beliefs, values, techniques and so on shared by members of a given [scientific] community.

A second definition is by Bryman (1988: 4), drawing on Kuhn:

a cluster of beliefs and dictates which for scientists in a particular discipline influence what should be studied, how research should be done, how results should be interpreted, and so on.

While Kuhn's definition of paradigms and their importance was formed in relation to the natural sciences, the ideas associated with it are also seen as important for the social sciences. Social work research, like all research, never happens in a vacuum (see, for example, Feyerabend, 1975; Potter, 1996; Jacobs, 2002a, 2002b, who look at paradigms in relation to the social studies of natural sciences). Instead, a new research project is located within previous research, interlinked theories and assumptions and related debates, discussed in published journal articles and textbooks, in print and electronic media and organizational policies and procedures. Indeed, 'The problems researchers tackle are derived from sociological perspectives which, although in constant flux, have been fashioned through a hundred years of sociological thought' (Gilbert, 1993a: 29).

Social work researcher, Marlow (2001: 7), says that:

> Paradigms function as maps, directing us to the problems that are important to address, the theories that are acceptable, and the procedures needed to solve the problems. ... Paradigms reflect changing values, countering the idea that a fixed reality exists out there to be objectively observed.

Research is also a social process associated with authorized versions of knowledge and linkage within a cultural and professional community of 'knowers' (Gilbert, 1993a; Jacobs, 2002a). In addition to literature, the researcher is also positioned within a network of stakeholders in the community, where there may be various ways of knowing about the problem being investigated. A 'community' with an interest in a particular research project may include a local geographic area or neighbourhood or even an international audience. Such a community also includes professional, organizational, personal and political interest groups. The relationships between individuals and groups within the network are embedded in power that can generate struggles about the research being undertaken because of differences in ways of knowing that may only be resolved by negotiation, compromise and even coercion and subversion ('dirty tricks') if the stakes are high enough.

Being aware of different ways of knowing is fundamental to understanding why and how any research – particularly social work research – has both political and ethical dimensions that cannot be separated from a discussion of techniques or research methods. In fact, although we do discuss methods in later chapters, we do not approach this in the same way as do most authors of texts on research methods. Instead, we address methods as they are located within a set of intellectual assumptions that influence how we explain the problems we choose to research, frame research questions and the research design and the conclusions we draw from the research. In the next section, we look at how and why different ways of knowing are related to politics and ethics. This is followed by a discussion of some paradigms that influence social work research and how paradigms relate to social work research as a political and ethical practice. Finally, we summarize some contemporary debates about paradigms associated with the idea of 'incommensurability' (Blaikie, 1993; Bryman, 2001: 433, 446; Jacobs, 2002b).

The politics and ethics of different ways of knowing

Becoming part of a community of knowledgeable persons happens as a result of processes of training and professionalization. Individuals are socialized by means of education accredited by a professional association into what are considered to be legitimate values, knowledge and practices for that profession. For example, social workers around the world are associated with professional bodies in their home countries that are involved in reviewing and accrediting social work programmes taught at universities.

The implications of professionalization are that only certain people are seen as social workers. This operates to define particular knowledge and practice boundaries between professions, identifying certain people as legitimate practitioners of different professions (Leonard, 1997). Social work knowledge constructed as 'legitimate' within particular social, cultural and political contexts may exclude other ways of knowing that nonetheless have the potential to challenge the dominant view of social work – for example, from indigenous people's perspectives (Tuhiwai Smith, 1999; Bruyere, 1998; Zapf, 1999; Aboriginal Health Council of South Australia, 1995; Lucashenko, 1994; Huggins, 1991).

There are even more profound implications of such knowledge boundaries and processes by which they are demarcated for those people we call 'clients'. Unless social workers can appreciate that professional knowledge also confers the power to exclude other ways of knowing, we risk practising in oppressive ways by disallowing our clients' voices in naming their experiences and proposing solutions to their problems that are relevant for them. This may seem most obvious if we are engaged in providing services directly to clients – for example, via case, group or community work. However, it is also important to remember that, in social work research, the construction of knowledge is not the sole concern. What also matter are the ethical and political dimensions of how 'knowledge' is generated and interpreted. That is, social work research is not solely or primarily conducted as a pursuit of knowledge but also has a political and ethical purpose in keeping with social work objectives to achieve social justice and improve the social conditions of individuals, groups and communities.

Social workers such as Hartman (1990, 1992) have written about 'different ways of knowing' and the 'search for subjugated knowledge' as important for social workers as professionals concerned with addressing injustice and oppression. Hartman seeks to validate the different ways in which social workers understand the world and develop 'practice wisdom'. She extends this to social work's responsibility to give legitimacy to knowledge that has been 'subjugated' by dominant views. Social work research is therefore more than a technical exercise – it has ethical and political dimensions as well.

You may like to take a few moments to consider the questions below regarding the importance of 'many ways of knowing' for social work research.

- Why is awareness of 'many ways of knowing' an important consideration in social work research?
- How can social work help 'subjugated knowledge' to be given space in which to be expressed?
- Think of examples from your own experience where your point of view or perspective on a topic or issue differed significantly from the views of your friends or family members. Think through and write down how these differences were expressed. How were different people treated in the group depending on their views of the topic?

The politics and ethics of research: positioning of the self and others

Another important dimension to different ways of knowing is that of *positioning* of the individual, as social worker and/or researcher. 'Positioning' refers to how individuals connect themselves within the bigger knowledge picture – for example, social work professional knowledge, taken for granted social and cultural beliefs of the wider society or even beliefs associated with identities or affiliations, including gender, religion or ethnicity. Riessman (1994a: 133–8) discusses how 'subjectivity matters' in undertaking social work research as a 'positioned investigator':

> Subjectivity has been a dirty word in social research modelled on the physical sciences ... a source of bias to be controlled in the interest of producing objective, reliable, and valid knowledge. The Doctrine of Immaculate Perception, as Van Maanen calls it (1988, p. 73), is still a rhetorical device. But the old Enlightenment position – the experiencing self is clearly separable from the experienced world – is gradually shifting to a view of subjective experience as part of the world (Polkinghorne, 1988). There is reality outside the self ... but 'the self organizes it and makes it meaningful'. (Stivers, 1993, p. 410)

While not disputing that there is a physical world, Riessman (1994a), like other authors cited by Angen (2000) – for example, Maxwell (1992), Silverman (1993), Altheide and Johnson (1994), Hammersley (1995b) and Wakefield (1995) – distinguishes between material reality and the meaning that is given by individuals to that reality. Later on in this chapter we will look at some case studies where a particular 'reality' was understood in particular ways depending on the positioning or subjectivity of participants. However, in this section, we will continue to explore ideas of subjectivity and positioning of the researcher and others involved in the research process.

Riessman (1994a: 133) discusses how 'contemporary feminist' researchers 'model how subjectivity, both informants' and investigators', can enter methodological discussion in social research'. She cites as examples Ellis and Flaherty (1992); Hollway (1989); Personal Narratives Group (1989) and Reinharz (1992). A collaborative approach to subjectivity and positioning in social research is integral to action research (Reason and Bradbury, 2001), participatory research (Everitt et al., 1992), anti-discriminatory research (Humphries and Truman, 1994) and that which allows colonized and indigenous peoples to reassert their knowledge and agendas where they have been excluded and achieve self-determination (Tuhiwai Smith, 1999).

The researcher as 'the outsider within' (Riessman, 1994a: 135) the research process 'stimulates a distinct angle of vision'. The researcher's inclusion of 'the self as context' allows for 'the interplay, for example, between our categories of belonging – class, race, religion, gender, age – and those of the people studied' (Riessman, 1994a: 135). Like Angen (2000), Stanley and Wise (1993) and Everitt et al. (1992), Riessman (1994a: 135) explains how our subjectivity positions us within the research process and why acknowledging this is important if we want our research to be seen as ethically and methodologically sound:

> We are not robots who collect pure information (Gould, 1981), but humans with emotions, values, social biographies, and institutional locations. They shape the problems we choose, the ways we go about studying them, the eyes we bring to observation, and the relationships we have in the field. Locating ourselves in the work, instead of pretending we're not there, helps readers evaluate the situated knowledge we produce.

The positioned researcher: reflective and reflexive practice

The social work researcher is a practitioner like any other social worker who aims to bring about social change. The importance of both critical reflection (Fook, 1996) and reflexivity (Taylor and White, 2000) in providing ethical and theoretically informed services to clients, for example, in case group and community work, is also essential for social work research. This is because social work research is another approach for achieving social work objectives rather than something that is only relevant to a minority of social workers. Riessman discusses the connections between the researcher's subjectivity, reflective and reflexive practices as being necessary for ethically and methodologically sound research. She says that reflexivity – defined as 'reflection about our interpretive practices' about the social world and events – is as important for research as it is for our work with clients (Riessman, 1994a: 135). Because there is no unbiased knowledge, being 'objective' would mean that the researcher should state his or her assumptions and interests in the research and acknowledge the emotional aspects of the research process. Instead of treating methodology as a set of neutral techniques that are applied in the same way in every context, the researcher instead must acknowledge the actual processes, 'how research gets done'. The researcher's awareness of the actual research process would include the recognition that, unlike its representation in textbooks, actual research is not neat and orderly and problem-free. Furthermore, the researcher's awareness of what is actually going on in her or his research would enhance the opportunities for flexibility in addressing problems that may emerge that are specific to the context. These problems may include the appropriateness of the design and strategies for gaining access to people, places and data (Riessman, 1994a: 135–6).

You may now like to explore your own subjectivity and positioning in relation to social problems and groups or individuals who experience these problems, by doing the following exercise.

Exploring my positioning and subjectivity

Write down how your personal positioning (called subjectivity) matters. This includes your experiences, personal values, affiliations, history and biography.

How might your positioning influence your interests as a social worker? How might you (or do you) perceive particular social problems or group and individual experiences of particular problems? How might your positioning influence your attraction to, or empathy for, particular individuals or groups? How might your positioning influence your aversion to, or avoidance of, particular individuals or groups?

It is quite normal to be positioned in these ways. What is important is the ability to honestly confront these positionings rather than pretending that they are not there because we can do more damage if we are unaware of these influences than if we take them into account. Confronting them allows for change if necessary.

Aside from appreciating our own positioning in relation to social problems and issues, we need to realize that other people also see the world from their own positioning. The recognition of different subjectivities is a starting point from which we can acknowledge and explore the relationships between individuals and groups (also known as stakeholders) who are positioned differently in relation to social problems, knowledge and values. We must recognize that different knowledge and ways of knowing often involve political and ethical struggles. This is especially an issue for social research because we cannot assume that everyone shares our interest in a particular problem or the ways in which we understand and explain it or what appropriate services may be. Some people may be extremely antagonistic to either seeing a problem at all or ways of addressing structural inequalities, preferring to take an individualistic approach that explains the cause of the problem as individual deficiency or pathology. For example, unemployment may be explained as individual failure or idleness or a consequence of various structural issues that affect the availability and distribution of jobs and employers' practices (Edwards, 2001: 137–76). Another example is domestic violence in heterosexual partnerships, which may be variously understood as an individual and private experience for women as victims, an example of individual men's pathology or a consequence of patriarchal societies and women's inequality in relation to men (Gelles, 1987: 26–46; Renzetti and Curran, 1995: 237–43; Hearn, 1996). Thus, research that explores unemployment or domestic violence will be informed by particular theoretical and value positions that will shape the research questions, how they will be investigated and the conclusions related to bringing about change.

In the next section, three case studies taken from Australia, the USA and the UK are discussed. They aim to show how the positioning of different stakeholders in relation to social issues was expressed and with what consequences. They illustrate the political and ethical aspects of knowledge associated with positioning and subjectivity of stakeholders. All participants as individuals or in groups have a perspective informed by particular intellectual and ethical assumptions. The case studies show that knowledge about social issues is neither neutral nor objective and that 'truth' is disputed territory.

Only one of the three case studies is about research per se. The research case study is about an enquiry into the removal by state authorities of indigenous children in Australia from the care of their families and communities and their placement in 'white' foster care and institutions (Human Rights and Equal Opportunity Commission, 1997). The other two case studies relate to social issues that are important to social work – child sexual abuse and 'the Cleveland affair' in the UK (Parton, 1991; Campbell, 1988) and sexual harassment as alleged by Anita Hill against Clarence Thomas in the USA (Morrison, 1993; Hill and Jordan, 1995). However, all are high-profile examples of struggles about knowledge and its 'truth'.

Positioning, subjectivity and stakeholders: three case studies

---

The stolen generations – an Australian case study (1997)

This case study relates to an inquiry by the Australian Human Rights and Equal Opportunity Commission into the policies and practices relating to the removal of indigenous children from the care of their parents and communities. These policies and practices, informed by

---

assumptions about race, were especially associated with the colonization of Australia by English settlers that began in the eighteenth century and were explicit until the middle 1960s. However, despite the changes in legislation and policies beginning in the late 1960s that aimed to establish equal treatment for indigenous people, some stakeholders argue that the new policies and practices did not change significantly, due to the underlying racism and ethnocentrism associated with this 'equal treatment'. The Human Rights and Equal Opportunity Commission released its report in 1997. The report, *Bringing Them Home: National Inquiry into the Separation of Aboriginal and Torres Strait Islander Children from their Families*, relies primarily on personal stories from the people who were removed into care as children and their family members and summarizes the legislation and policies that allowed such practices. The term, 'the stolen generations' was coined to characterize the main theme of these colonialist policies and practices.

This report has become the subject of much controversy that has engaged participants from the Aboriginal community, politicians, members of the public, academics and media, to name a few of the main protagonists (Blainey, 2000; Reynolds, 2000a; Markus, 2001; Horne, 2001: 51–72; Manne, 2001a, 2001b; Windschuttle, 2002). One key topic is the intent of the policies of removal of children. For example, were the children 'stolen' or forcibly removed, was it a compassionate policy of child rescue from deprivation and abandonment or voluntary relinquishment by the mothers? Another topic is the importance and significance of the whole matter within the overall history of the colonization of Australia. Other topics include a dispute about the numbers of children involved: did it 'really' involve 'a generation' or 'only' a small proportion of children, technically 'not a generation'? Also, the credibility of the information presented in the report and the methods used by the Commission to gather the information: did they talk to all 'relevant' people, are personal accounts by the people affected by these policies merely anecdotal and therefore biased, untrue or a version of false memory? Are these stories individually or collectively really a political push by indigenous activists seeking massive claims for compensation? These arguments seem to be captured best by pithy phrases expressed by some factions as a 'black armband view of history', merely a 'blemish' within a generally proud history and by others as a 'white blindfold view' that denies the profound consequences of these policies for indigenous people in Australia (Blainey, 2000; Reynolds, 2000a; Manne, 2001a, 2001b; Horne, 2001: 53–5, 56; Windschuttle, 2002; Yallop, 2003).

You may like to explore in detail some of the debates relating to this issue by accessing the resources listed below. These show how different protagonists are positioned in relation to the topic and how they express different perspectives. Take special note of the language used and how opposing perspectives are responded to. (You may have also noted that my introductory remarks represented a particular political and ethical position.) How do you respond to these debates and why do you respond in particular ways? What are the values underpinning your response?

Resources

A search using www.google.com and keywords that include 'Australian', 'Aboriginal', 'stolen children', 'generations' produced the following reuslts:

European Network for Indigenous Australian Rights, use search to find Cubillo-Gunner test case:
www.eniar.org/news/rightwrong.html

730 Report – 3/4/2000: No Stolen Generation: Australian Government:
www.abc.net.au/7.30/stories/s115691.htm

Newsfactor Network, Brash Web Game Roils Australian Government: John Herron's stance on the stolen generations and Internet firestorm down under:
www.newsfactors.com/perl/story/6885. html
www.newsfactors.com/perl/story/7032.html

World Socialist website: article 'An inevitable outcome: an Australian court dismisses "Stolen generations test case"':
www.wsws.org/articles/2000/aug2000/stol-a21/shtml

Australian Humanities Review: 'Those two little words':
www.lib.latrobe.edu.au/AHR/archive/Issue-September-2000/spencer2.html

The Guardian: 'Howard Government's history rewrite', April 12 2000:
www.cpa.org.au/garchve2/996stole.html

Shame 2000: 'Why the Prime Minister can't say "Sorry"':
www.unolympics.com/reconciliation/sorry.shtml

Native Title Issues: 'What will "sorry" mean for Australia?'
www.erc.org.au/issues/text/sa00.htm
www.anta.org.au/apology/html

E law: *Murdoch University Electronic Journal of Law:* 'Unfinished business: the Australian stolen generations':
www.murdoch.edu.au/elaw/issues/v7n4/buti74_text.html

Gesellschaft für bedrote völker: 'The 100th anniversary of Australian independence: indigenous people are still victims of racial discrimination:
www.gfbv.de/gfbv_e/docus/aborigin.htm

Peace Movement Aotearoa: 'Australian government defends forced removal of Aboriginal children':
www.converge.org.nz/pma/a101199.htm

More websites

For newspaper articles from *The Age, Herald Sun, The Australian* and *Koorie Mail*, on the stolen generations from 21 May 1997 to 26 May 1997 see the Department for Victorian Communities, Aboriginal Affairs website:
www.dhs.vic.gov.au/aav/lib/biblio4.htm

Related Internet links are provided at this site. You can follow these up by clicking on the appropriate subjects.

ATSIC (Aboriginal and Torres Strait Islander Commission)
www.atsic.gov.au

FOX News Channel. Use search facility to find articles.
www.foxnews.com

You can also access media commentaries in *The Age* newspaper by Robert Manne, former editor of the magazine, *Quadrant*:
www.theage.com.au

Clarence Thomas and Anita Hill – a case study of sexual harassment, gender and race in the USA (1991)

The back cover of Morrison's (1993) book, *Race-ing Justice, En-gendering Power*, summarizes the theme of this case study:

The United States Senate hearings in 1991 on the controversial nomination of Clarence Thomas to the Supreme Court, and accusations of sexual harrassment [sic] brought by Anita Hill, disturbed radio and television audiences throughout the world and immediately provoked outraged debate.

In July 1991, President George Bush (Senior) nominated Justice Clarence Thomas to the Supreme Court of the United States to fill a vacancy created by the resignation of Justice Thurgood Marshall, 'the first African-American to serve on the Supreme Court' (Hill and Jordan, 1995: xix). Justice Thomas was also an African-American, described by President Bush as ' "the best person for this position" ' (Hill and Jordan, 1995: xix). Soon after the nomination, 'a public interest watchdog coalition that tracks judicial appointments and opposes conservative nominees, [learnt] that a former colleague of Thomas's ... told a ... classmate that she had been sexually harassed by [Clarence Thomas]' (Hill and Jordan, 1995: xix). The colleague was later identified as Anita Hill. After a great deal of private communication with Anita Hill about the allegations by various parties, including journalists, lawyers, politicians and their associates, a story about the allegations appeared in October 1991 in *Newsday* (Hill and Jordan, 1995: xix–xxiv). The subsequent controversy played out in the media was, at base, over the validity of 'truth' claims by Clarence Thomas (and his supporters) and Anita Hill (and her supporters).

Morrison (1993) and Hill herself (Hill and Jordan, 1995) have edited texts that explore various writers' analyses of race, gender and class, as well as the relationships of power and powerlessness and positioning of stakeholders in the debate.

> The points of the vector were all the plateaus of power and powerlessness: white men, black men, black women, white women, inter-racial couples; those with a traditionally conservative agenda, and those representing neo-conservative conversions; citizens with radical and progressive programmes; the full spectre of the 'pro' antagonists ('choice' and 'life'); there were the publicly elected, the self-elected, the racial supremacists, the racial egalitarians, and nationalists of every stripe. (Morrison, 1993: ix)

Listed below are several sources where you can track the salient points of this controversy. Apart from the *content*, notice *how* what is said is related to the positioning of different stakeholders in disputing the 'truth' about the issue. Be aware of your own responses to what you read, as this is one way of practising reflexivity and awareness of your own subjectivity and positioning.

Resources

A search using www.lexis.com and the keywords 'clarence thomas' and 'anita hill' produced the following results:

'He admitted he lied about Anita Hill – so now he's credible?' (2001) *Southern California Living, Part 5: Los Angeles Times*, Sunday, July 15, 3.

Hinckley, D. (2002) 'Confession of a loose cannon', *Showtime: Daily News* (New York), Sunday, March 10, 19.

Note: The above two articles refer to a preceding article by David Brock that attacked Anita Hill's credibility. The source is Media Watch: http://secure.mediaresearch.org/news/mediawatch/1992/mw19920201 stud.html

Marcus, R. (1991) 'Thomas, allies step up counterattack', *First Section: The Washington Post*, Sunday, October 13, A1.

Heller, Z. (1991) 'Let's banish the boring solemnity of the sex-pest debate', *Editorial page, The Independent* (London), Sunday, 20 October, 25.

Schepple, K.L. (1992) 'Just the facts, ma'am: sexualized violence, evidentiary habits, and the revision of truth', *37 New York School of Law Review*, 123.

Groner, J. (1993) 'Book world: the Thomas–Hill debate: a revisionist's view', *Style: The Washington Post*, Monday, May 3, C1.

Thomas, D., McCoy, C. and McBride, A. (1993) 'Deconstructing the political spectacle: sex, race, and subjectivity in public response to the Clarence Thomas/Anita Hill "sexual harassment" hearings', *American Journal of Political Science*, 37, 3, 699–720.

Other sources

Bhavnani, K.-K. and Collins, D. (1993) 'Racism and feminism: an analysis of the Anita Hill and Clarence Thomas hearings', *New Community*, 19, 3, 493–505.

Fraser, N. (1992) 'Sex, lies and the public sphere: some reflections on the confirmation of Clarence Thomas', *Critical Inquiry*, 18, 3, 595–612.

Hale, C.I., Cooks, L.M. and DeWine, S. (1994) 'Anita Hill on trial: a dialectical analysis of a persuasive interrogation', in S.G. Bingham (ed.) *Conceptualizing Sexual Harassment as a Discursive Practice*. Westport, Connecticut: Praeger, 71–87.

Rucinski, D. (1993) 'The polls – a review: rush to judgment? Fast reaction polls in the Anita Hill–Clarence Thomas controversy', *The Public Opinion Quarterly*, 57, 4, 575–92.

From the Center for History and New Media, George Mason University, USA:

Jill Niebrugge-Brantley, 'A Feminist writes about the Anita Hill–Clarence Thomas conflict':
http://chnm.gmu.edu/courses/122/hill/brantley.htm

'An outline of the Anita Hill and Clarence Thomas controversy':
http://chnm.gmu.edu/courses/122/hill/hilloutline2.htm

From *The American Prospect*:

Jane Mayen (2001) 'Clarence Thomas's revenge', 12 (13):
www.prospect.org/print/V12/13/mayer-j.html

Marietta Higgs and the Cleveland affair – a case study relating to mistaken or correct diagnoses of child sexual abuse in the UK (1987)

In an excellent analysis of the Cleveland affair, Parton (1991: 79–80) describes the precipitating events as follows:

> In June 1987, a local newspaper in Cleveland began to publish stories concerning a large number of confused and angry parents who claimed that their children had been taken from them by local authority social workers on the basis of disputed diagnoses of sexual abuse made by two paediatricians, Dr Marietta Higgs and Dr Geoffrey Wyatt. The *Daily Mail* ran the story on 23 June 1987 with the front-page headline 'Hand Over Your Children, Council Orders Parents of 200 Youngsters', and within days 'Cleveland' had become a national scandal, with the various professional combatants, together with the parents, receiving massive television, radio and newspaper exposure.

The central issue was 'the difficulties of recognition of sexual abuse of children and the threshold of suspicion at which action was to be taken' (Secretary of State for Social Services, 1988, cited in Parton, 1991: 84). In particular, the anal dilatation test that had been proposed as a 'medical advance' in the physical diagnosis of sexual abuse, which Drs Higgs and Wyatt had relied on, was central to 'the explosion of medical argument' (Parton, 1991: 90) associated with the controversy and subsequent inquiry. Dr Marietta Higgs was criticized for her 'unshakeable confidence' in the diagnostic technique and its consequences for the children and their families (Parton, 1991: 104). The resulting furore was in part related to disbelief that so many children appeared to have been sexually abused by their fathers when the assumption was that child sexual abuse, while accepted as a social problem, was less prevalent than such numbers would indicate. Furthermore, there was also disbelief in the claims of sexual abuse against men who were considered to be pillars of the community and otherwise did not fit the image of 'paedophile'.

The Cleveland affair challenged a number of fundamental assumptions related to child sexual abuse. One assumption was that there is an objective way of unequivocally diagnosing child sexual abuse, particularly by means of medical technologies (Parton, 1991). In this case, the anal dilatation technique was called into question by medical professionals who doubted its effectiveness as a diagnostic procedure and other stakeholders who questioned its validity because it appeared to include men who were above reproach, contrary to the image of paedophiles as an aberrant minority.

Both Campbell (1988) and Parton (1991) critically analysed this controversy and the positions of different stakeholders around the social problem of child sexual abuse. Their analyses show how social problems are not objective facts and that ways of understanding, defining and responding to social problems are fraught with controversy as different stakeholders debate what is legitimate knowledge, and what is and is not to be included as a professional and public concern. Furthermore, Campbell (1988) also explored gender relations associated with the controversy.

The resources listed below show the range of positions adopted by different stakeholders and the focus of the debate on the credentials, competence and expertise of Dr Marietta Higgs that encapsulated the main themes. As with the two case studies discussed above, you may like to access some of these resources to explore how knowledge and 'truth' are associated with political processes in which stakeholders are positioned differently. Again, reflexive reading of the sources is encouraged to raise your awareness of your own positioning in relation to knowledge and 'truth'.

Resources

A search using www.google.com and the keywords: 'marietta higgs', 'cleveland' and 'child sexual abuse' produced the following results:

IPT, journal: *Issues in Child Abuse Accusations*, 'Medical considerations in the diagnosis of child sexual abuse' (6 (2) Spring 1994):
www.ipt-forensics.com

The Irish Times article regarding 'mistakes in diagnosis', 'doubt case on one specific physical diagnostic technique used by ... Dr Marietta Higgs':
www.ireland.com

Festival of Light Resource Papers on Child Abuse, Mary Pride, 'The child abuse industry':
www.fol.org.au/papers/child-abuse.html

The British False Memory Society reviews the key issues: 'for investigative reliability', 'havoc and injustice in Cleveland':
www.bfms.org.uk/site_pages/shieldfield.htm

2 March 1989 Cleveland Child Abuse Crisis:
www.stuartbellmp.org/chibus2march1989.htm

House of Commons Hansard Debates for 27 April 1989: 'truly disgraceful regime':
www.parliament.the-stationery-office.co.uk

House of Commons Hansard Debates for 27 April 1989: 'Cleveland?'
www.parliament.the-stationery-office.co.uk

Skeptic Tank Text Archive File, 'rumor' directory, file ns 1060990: 'Dangerous nonsense' may have convinced social workers:
www.skepticfiles.org

Identifying and exploring a case study of your choice

Having explored the particular examples above, you may like to identify and analyse some examples of your own using the guidelines set out below.

Guidelines for exploring your own case study

Follow a particular issue or current event via the print, electronic media and Internet. Some examples include unemployment/unemployed people, single mothers on welfare payments, attitudes to refugees and asylum seekers, attitudes to Muslims and Arabs since the attack on the Twin Towers in New York on September 11th, 2001, and the war on Iraq.

Identify the different stakeholders. Who are they? Is a particular individual's position his or her own or does he or she represent or claim to represent a group? What are the different perspectives on the issue?

Record the language (keywords) used by different stakeholders to debate the issue. How do you think the keywords represent particular values and assumptions about the problem or the people who experience that problem? What may be alternative words used to describe the problems or people identified as problems?

How do these examples illustrate the politics of different ways of knowing about people's problems and how may they be understood, interpreted and represented? How do these examples pose ethical issues for social workers?

Paradigms in practice

So far we have looked at the importance of recognizing different ways of knowing for social work research and noted that our own ways of knowing may reflect bodies of knowledge that are taken for granted as legitimate in our society, such as professional, organizational and cultural assumptions. Furthermore, we are not the sole participants in the research process, but in a relationship with other stakeholders. Before we move on to the more abstract concepts concerning different ways of knowing and their relevance for social work research, we are going to take part in a reflective process to learn how to explore personal positioning and subjectivity, as discussed by Riessman (1994a) above.

Fook (1996) sets out this approach in her chapter 'The reflective researcher: developing a reflective approach to practice'. An extract from Fook, *The Reflective Researcher* (1996: 6–8) appears below. In *The Reflective Researcher*, Fook sets out the steps that need to be taken to reflect on your personal way of knowing within social work and broader cultural knowledge and assumptions.

The reflective process

1 Identify and describe the practice/experience and its context in terms that are as concrete and specific as possible. The practice you choose to describe might conceivably include any activity you perform or experience as a social worker.

2 Reflect on your account.

Fook then provides a set of questions that she has found helpful 'in stimulating a critical analysis' of her work.

- What main themes and patterns emerge from my account?
- Try to differentiate thoughts, feelings, actions, intentions and interpretations. How are they connected?
- What interpretations or explanations did I make and whose interpretations are they? How did my interpretations influence the situation? How did I personally influence the situation? How might the situation have been interpreted differently by someone else or from a different perspective?
- What assumptions are implied in my account and how relevant are they to the situation?
- What are the assumptions about? Practice theory? Human behaviour? Value systems? Political change? Plus other such questions.
- Where do these assumptions come from? Whose assumptions are they? Who stands to gain from holding them? Are they mine and/or what roles/power positions was I assuming in making particular assumptions? Are they conflictual or contradictory?
- What are the gaps and biases implied in my account? What perspectives are repressed, distorted or simply missing or de-emphasized?
- What actions or assumptions reinforce these gaps and biases?
- What type of language did I use? What are the key and recurring terms and what do they imply? What categories/classifications are implied? Are they oppositional categories? Why did I choose to use these terms and what others could have been used in their place? How concrete or abstract was my terminology and what led me to frame my account in this way? What functions are performed by framing my practice in this way?
- What was expected and unexpected and what contradictions are implied?

Below is a case study that serves as an example of how you might apply the reflective process above. It is an intake report from a child protection organization in Australia. The discussion that follows shows how the intake report can be read in different ways that suggest different personal and professional positionings in relation to social problems. While the case study is about social work practice with clients, the reflective process is also relevant to social work research. It shows how, as practitioners, we understand our practice partly from our own assumptions about the world and partly as influenced by professional, organizational and broader cultural assumptions. You may like to write down your own thoughts about the case study to compare them with the different perspectives that are described after it.

A 14-year-old girl reported

... that she is being hit at home:

(1) [date] she was hit with the wooden handle of the broom across the arm, back and behind her right ear ... by mum
(2) [previous night] hit by mum across her face as mum thought she had hit her sister across her face [in keeping with] the [family] rule
(3) a week after the last school holidays ended, dad hit her with a strap across her face ...

Three possible ways of engaging with the above intake report are discussed below. These are not necessarily mutually exclusive, but may instead overlap. The possible ways of engaging with the case have been labelled using formal theoretical concepts and these may be unfamiliar to you. They relate to significant paradigms, which we will be exploring in more detail later in this chapter. You can refer to the section below under the heading 'Paradigms: formal theories about ways of knowing' for clarification if needed at this stage.

One way of categorizing this intake report is as a child protection case. In contemporary child protection policy in many contexts, the main 'clue' that practitioners may draw on for making such a categorization is that the girl described someone (her parents) hitting her (Thorpe, 1994; D'Cruz, 2002). Critics of such an approach argue that this is taking a *positivist* position (for example, Parton et al., 1997; D'Cruz, 1999). A positivist position assumes that there is a direct relationship between the cause (parental hitting) and effects (on the girl's body and emotionally) – that is, a basic professional and often social and cultural assumption associated with 'child maltreatment/abuse'. Furthermore, the context for the hitting would not necessarily be considered as significant in making the categorization of the case type. The intervention would require you to check the truth of the girl's allegations (investigate) and conclude whether there is any substance to the report or not (can it be substantiated or not). The approach requires you to judge the potentially different explanations of what happened, determine who is telling the truth – there can be only one correct and absolute version – and you as a social worker are assumed to be the best person to judge this.

Another possible response to the intake report is that the problem may have something to do with gender roles and responsibilities in families (assumed to be heterosexual in our society) and their consequences for childcare and discipline. This is a *feminist* position (Stark and Flitcraft, 1988; Featherstone, 1996, 1997; D'Cruz, 1998, 2002). The clues might be the girl's identification of her parents as 'mum' and 'dad' or taken for granted knowledge of how families in our society generally are structured. A feminist perspective understands social problems as gendered experiences and therefore the approach explores experiences as positioned and structured by patriarchy and potential inequality between men and women. There are different feminist positions, although all are connected by their understanding and exploration of social problems and experiences as patterns of difference and gender inequality related to patriarchy (Dominelli, 1997: 26–47).

A third possible perspective is that of *interpretivism*. From this perspective, you would be aware that the intake record is a teenage girl's report of examples of her apparently problematic relationship with her parents and find it helpful to know what the parents' views are before taking further action. This does not mean that you do not take seriously what the girl is saying. However, you may consider that, to be able to respond constructively, you need to know more about the circumstances in which the reported incidents occurred and the people involved. This perspective stems from the idea that events and experiences may have different meanings for different people, including your own as reader of the report and possibly as social worker and/or researcher. Each participant is positioned differently in relation to the event and will likely have a different or overlapping explanation of the meaning of 'what happened'. So, a mother's position as primary carer may differ from that of a father who is mainly engaged in paid employment outside the home and each child, depending on age and gender, may offer a different view, complicated by relationships with siblings and parents.

These are only three possible perspectives on the case study and, as mentioned above, they may overlap in practice. For example, you might combine feminist and interpretive perspectives without losing sight of the basic facts of the report and that the girl feels vulnerable in her family.

You may have engaged with the case study differently. This indicates yet another way of knowing, not that you are wrong. Think about your way of knowing and reflect on your assumptions, values and processes of interpretation.

The following list sets out the process by which possible perspectives in relation to the case material may be identified.

1 What sort of case would you say this is? How would you justify this case category from what have you read in the extract? (Alternatively, how do you know it is this type of case rather than another type?)
2 Pick out 'clues' (words) in the intake report that influenced you to categorize the case. How did these clues influence you one way rather than another? When you read the clues, what assumptions did you make about the cultural background of the family? What did the clues tell you about

what is assumed to be normal or not normal in our society about parents, children and families? What do the clues tell you about what is culturally normal (and not normal)? Might there be another way of naming the type of case this is?

3   How would the way you categorized the case influence your intervention as a social worker? Would an alternative case category make a difference to your choice of social work intervention?

4   What might the implications be of your way(s) of knowing, especially in relation to professional power associated with professional knowledge?

Below is another case study of an intake report that you can again use to discover your theoretical perspectives/positioning, following the steps described above.

The police

… called with concerns over Pam's four children. Constable Care said that [when] issuing a restraining order against Pam's ex-[male] partner, Steven, he spoke to Steven's mother, [who] informed him that there was a possibility that Pam's children were being sexually abused by [her] current partner, a 19 y.o. man known only as Claude. [Steven's mother] said that she had also spoken with a neighbour of Pam's who claimed that the children had told her that 'Claude is doing things to us'. [Steven's mother] said that the children had recently been to hospital for treatment for oral herpes. […].

Paradigms: ethical and political considerations

Rhodes (1986), an American social worker, discusses fundamental professional, socio-legal, casework and ethical assumptions that influence practice. Her critiques, discussed in relation to a case study, show how professional knowledge might be oppressive. She suggests an alternative approach that allows 'dialogue about alternative frameworks' (Rhodes, 1986: 19). A dialogue disrupts the assumption that only the person in a more powerful or authoritative position is correct and, instead, offers space for other ways of knowing. Furthermore, 'social workers should acknowledge the diversity of ethical views that confront them and set aside time for examining them. Each social worker must determine her own position …' (Rhodes, 1986: 19). The positioning described by Rhodes in relation to social work practice and theory is also apparent in social work research, as we have discussed above in relation to paradigms and case studies.

We now move on to looking at paradigms from a more theoretical perspective and explore their relevance for social work research. Social work researchers do not all engage with paradigms in exactly the same way. Some, such as Marlow, perceive paradigm differences as 'different approaches to science' (2001: 12). Marlow seems to see different perspectives as 'interesting points of view' that can be advantageous in answering research questions:

> Different types of understanding are based on sources of knowledge including values, intuition, experience, authority and science. The positivist and interpretist [sic] approaches to science can both offer advantages in addressing the different types of research questions asked in generalist social work. (2001: 12)

Marlow's comment implies that different perspectives are also neutral and can be used pragmatically to shape a research agenda, rather than being associated with power, with particular consequences for the research processes and outcomes. In contrast, Everitt et al. (1992) take a political perspective of knowledge (as theory) for social work. They move beyond the pragmatic approach taken by Marlow, who basically sees any approach as justifiable as long as it helps to answer social work research questions. Instead, Everitt et al. (1992: 17) argue that:

> Different ways of knowing and understanding the world make different assumptions about the individual and society, and about their interrelationships. Unless these assumptions are teased out, they may be adopted unknowingly and uncritically by practitioners. And yet these assumptions have implications for practice.

They go on to say:

> If the fundamental purpose of social welfare is the pursuit of justice and equality, then practitioners have a professional responsibility to be alert to the ways in which power operates through ways of knowing. To be in a position to understand and name the needs and problems that others experience is to be powerful. To be in a position where others accord you the right to know and give credibility to your understandings is also powerful. And it is especially powerful to be able to secure, through legal requirement or voluntarily, the engagement of others in a range of mechanisms and approaches, treatments and care plans, on the basis of these understandings.

However, in this book we do not want to polarize the debate between *pragmatism* (where research is a technical exercise in answering questions) and *ideology* (where research is a political approach to social questions). Instead, we argue that 'being pragmatic' involves knowledge of the *political* aspects of the research in question. That is, choice of methods and approaches may be informed as much by political aspects, whereby powerful stakeholders need to be convinced, as by the ethical aspects, whereby social change is the aim. For example, if you consider that a statistical study may have a more convincing effect for government bureaucrats than a qualitative study, you may combine the two approaches, making sure that the research is methodologically and ethically sound while meeting political agendas.

We would probably support Feyerabend's (1975: 18) concept of 'opportunism' in research, explained as the ability to 'adopt any procedure that fits the occasion'. This idea may be positioned within reformist politics, rather than a self-seeking, apolitical and potentially unethical response, where the researcher:

> ... must be able to master *all* forms or aspects of social activity without exception [it must be able to understand, and to apply, not only one particular type of methodology, but any methodology, and any variation thereof] [and] it must be ready to pass from one to another in the quickest possible manner. (Feyerabend, 1975: 18, original emphasis)

Paradigms: formal theories about ways of knowing

In this section, we will look at some formal theories about different ways of knowing that have been proposed by philosophers, sociologists, feminists and social workers. Before we do that, we need to look at some concepts that provide the framework for understanding and differentiating between paradigms. These concepts are cosmology, ontology, epistemology and ethics. Ethics is a concept familiar to all social workers and we have already discussed its relevance for social work research in the sections above. We will look at definitions of the other three concepts below.

Cosmology, ontology and epistemology

If you are a novice researcher and also relatively new to sociology and social theory, these three concepts may be quite daunting. However, do not despair. A response of panic and confusion is quite normal when you first come across such abstract concepts and their definitions. This is mainly because the definitions themselves challenge how we normally engage with and 'know' the material and social world and we hope that they will encourage you to think critically about our taken for granted ways of knowing and being. The most useful advice that can be given, which comes from our own experience, is to persevere with the definitions and think them through carefully, looking for ways in which to illustrate the abstract concepts and their meanings in every-day, familiar examples.

Cosmology refers to ideas about 'the universe as a totality' (Peile, 1988: 7). Cosmology (with ontology, epistemology and ethics) represents the worldview of the researcher or any other participant with an interest in an issue, problem or topic.

Ontology and *epistemology* are connected concepts. Sometimes definitions of epistemology do not make explicit what ontology is (for example, Everitt et al., 1992: 16–34; Bryman, 1988). Thus, for Everitt et al. (1992: 16) epistemology is a 'theory of knowledge' or a way of questioning the assumptions underlying social work theories about needs assessment and social problems, about services, interventions and effectiveness.

Other writers (such as Blaikie, 1993; Peile et al., 1995) provide separate definitions for each concept, some with illustrative or applied examples.

Blaikie (1993: 6–7) defines epistemology (theories of knowledge) and the related concept, ontology (theories of being, of what constitutes the world and reality) as follows:

> The root definition of *ontology* is 'the science or study of being'. … *ontology* refers to the claims or assumptions that a particular approach to social enquiry makes about the nature of social reality – claims about what exists, what it looks like, what units make it up and how these units interact with each other.
> The root definition of *epistemology* is 'the theory or science of the method or grounds of knowledge'. … *epistemology* refers to the claims or assumptions made about the ways in which it is possible to gain knowledge of this reality, whatever it is understood to be; claims about how what exists may be known. An *epistemology* is a theory of knowledge; it presents a view and a justification for what can be regarded as knowledge – what can be known, and what criteria such knowledge must satisfy in order to be called knowledge rather than beliefs. (Original emphasis)

In everyday language, epistemology means how we know what we know and relates to assumptions about social reality. It is a theory of knowledge by which you set out your assumptions about particular problems and what constitutes an appropriate way of knowing about them. Ontology is related to epistemology because it refers to how we understand reality and therefore we will then theorize, research or explain it in particular ways. The section below will show by example how different understandings about what reality is and how this may be known are related to different paradigms, theories or ways of knowing.

To help you with these concepts, in your own words, summarize what 'epistemology', and its related concept 'ontology', mean.

Formal paradigms: positivism, interpretivism and feminism

Peile et al. (1995) in their discussion paper 'Child abuse paradigms: an analysis of the basic theoretical and epistemological assumptions underlying child abuse literature' compare seven different paradigms: positivist, interpretivist, critical, ecological, feminist, postmodern and creative. Three of these paradigms – positivist, interpretivist and feminist – are summarized below in Table 3.1 (in line with Peile et al., 1995). Read the information about the three paradigms carefully, noting the differences between them in terms of assumptions related to a worldview (cosmology), about reality (ontology), ways of knowing (epistemology) and ethics.

Formal paradigms: indigenous perspectives

Research is a dirty word among many indigenous and formerly colonized peoples. Colonization by Western peoples as a result of conquest, war or other

Table 3.1 Three paradigms – positivist, interpretivist and feminist (summarized from Pelle et al., 1995)

Assumptions	Positivist	Interpretivist	Feminist
Cosmological assumptions	The world is predictable, knowable and measurable. Reality can be understood as separate parts	Knowledge is contextual and a symbolic social construction. Events can be explained and their meaning for people uncovered. Parts can only be understood in context	Reality is created by human beings and the central organizing process is gender. The sexual division of labour is implicated in asymmetrics of power [inequality between men and women]. Biology is transformed by turning into gender by political processes
Ontological assumptions	Behaviour can be explained in causal, deterministic ways. It has a mechanistic quality. People are able to be manipulated and controlled	Behaviour is intentional and creative. It can be explained but is not predictable. People shape their own reality	A central feature of identity and social organization is gender, and its reproduction and organization are political/social/ interactional processes located simultaneously in individuals and social structure: the personal is political and the political is personal
Epistemological assumptions	Knowledge arises from experiments and observations. It is grounded in the certainty of sense experience [that we know things through our sensesand no other way] with the aim of arriving at universal claims to truth. Quantitative methodologies are highly valued	Knowledge arises from interpretation and insight and is grounded in empathetic communication with the subjects of the research. In-depth interviewing, participant observation and other qualitative methods are used	Knowledge comes from a commitment to affirming women's knowing, rediscovering links between personal experience and structural inequality, building collective insights among women which deepen their sense of identity, interconnectedness, and extending their analysis of repression and how that repression is internalized. Uses intuition, collaboration and feelings in research

(Continued)

Table 3.1 Continued

Assumptions	Positivist	Interpretivist	Feminist
Ethical assumptions	A separation between knowledge and values. Science produces knowledge. How it is used is a value, ethical or moral question and is outside the concern of science	Values are the subject of research. Moral or ethical relativism [different values and ethics, rather than absolute or single moral stances]	Control and exploitation, whether of nature, women or children, is wrong and damaging of life and relationships and ultimately self-defeating. A new ethics of equality and mutuality is required

forms of violence was, and continues to be, exacerbated by research. Research has included formal scientific and social studies, as well as less formal, but nonetheless significant, practices, such as travellers' tales, explorers' diaries and anecdotes and removal of material artefacts, even human bodies, to Western museums as objects of interest (Said, 1978; Viswanathan, 1992; Gilman, 1992; Fanon, 1992; Weedon, 1999: 178–97). Tuhiwai Smith (1999) critically analyses such practices of colonization in which conquered peoples, their lives, practices and communities were transformed into objects of knowledge by colonizers who created their own versions of knowledge and truth about colonized societies.

The creation of knowledge via colonizers' research practices is aptly summed up by this description: 'they came, they saw, they named, they claimed' (Tuhiwai Smith, 1999: 80). Colonizers' versions of knowledge have become legitimized as truth as a consequence of their formal power and authority. Thus, legitimate ways of knowing are positioned firmly within dominant Western worldviews that are taken for granted as normal. Hence, such normal-ized and dominant worldviews also become invisible while differing views remain marginalized and are required to prove their validity against normative Western ways of knowing. From an indigenous perspective, the paradigms discussed in the sections above are all located within 'Western, white, academic, outsider' ways of knowing (Tuhiwai Smith, 1999: 42), despite the critiques of each paradigm and the differences between them. For example, a class or feminist analysis might challenge psychodynamic or positivist perspectives, but, from an indigenous perspective, all these approaches have their origins within Western worldviews, and the processes of knowledge construction, including classification, representation, models of comparison and criteria of evaluation (Tuhiwai Smith, 1999: 42–3) dominate.

Tuhiwai Smith (1999) gives an excellent example of the processes of knowledge construction in the spatial vocabulary of colonialism in nineteenth-century Aotearoa/New Zealand (Tuhiwai Smith, 1999: 53), that gave legitimacy to the colonizers' ways of engaging with the colonized and their societies, shown in Table 3.2.

Table 3.2   The spatial vocabulary of colonialism in nineteenth-century Aotearoa (Tuhiwai Smith, 1999: Table 2.1, 53)

The line	The centre	The outside
maps	mother country	empty land
charts	London	*terra nullius*
roads	magistrate's residence	uninhabited
boundaries	redoubt, stockade, barracks	unoccupied
pegs	prison	uncharted
surveys	mission station	reserves
claims	Parliament	*Maori pa*
fences	store	*Kainga*
hedges	Church	*Marae*
stone walls	Europe	burial grounds
tracks	port	background
genealogies	foreground	hinterland
perimeters	flagpole	

Tuhiwai Smith (1999: 52–3) explains that 'the spatial vocabulary of colonialism can be assembled around three concepts':

(1) the line, (2) the centre, and (3) the outside. The 'line' is important because it was used to map territory, to survey land, to establish boundaries and to mark the limits of colonial power. The 'centre' is important because orientation to the centre was an orientation to the system of power. The 'outside' is important because it positioned territory and people in an oppositional relation to the colonial centre; for indigenous Australians to be in an 'empty space' was to 'not exist'.

Tuhiwai Smith (1999) explicitly supports research for its political and ethical possibilities by restoring and recovering indigenous people's voices, lost in the process of colonization, to achieve self-determination, emancipation and practical benefits. To achieve these aims, Tuhiwai Smith (1999) proposes 'decolonizing' the research process itself, whereby the relationship between theories, methodologies and knowledge can be transformed into a liberating strategy, rather than maintaining its oppressive practices and consequences. 'Methodologies and methods of research, the theories that inform them, the questions which they generate and the writing styles they employ all become significant acts' (Tuhiwai Smith, 1999: 39). Decolonizing research also involves the 'divesting of colonial power' (Tuhiwai Smith, 1999: 98) and building 'global strategic alliances' with other indigenous and colonized groups (Tuhiwai Smith, 1999: 108) in addition to handing over governance to them.

Indigenous research is central and essential to these political processes and acts of resistance. A 'series of accounts and guidelines' are offered as a 'map' rather than a practice 'manual' (Tuhiwai Smith, 1999: 9).

Critical questions that relate to the political and ethical dimensions of research are also familiar to social researchers who are positioned within feminist (Stanley and Wise, 1993; Olesen, 1994), emancipatory or anti-discriminatory agendas (Everitt et al., 1992; Humphries and Truman, 1994). For example,

Whose research is it? Who owns it? Whose interests does it serve? Who will benefit from it? Who has designed the questions and framed its scope? Who will carry it out? Who will write it up? How will its results be disseminated? (Tuhiwai Smith, 1999: 10)

However, for indigenous peoples, such questions help to decolonize research, by challenging Western worldviews and ownership. The differences in world-views become clearer as a result of questions for indigenous research/ers that relate to a culturally specific and practical context. For example, 'Is her spirit clear?' and 'Can they fix up our generator?' (Tuhiwai Smith, 1999: 10).

Formal paradigms: other perspectives

The paradigms or perspectives discussed above are only some examples among many others. The scope of this book does not permit any more than an intro-ductory mention of these others.

For example, Everitt et al. (1992: 23–8) discuss a range of perspectives, including feminist, psychodynamic and Marxist. It is important to understand how psychodynamic perspectives – derived from Freud's theories of psycho-analysis – have significantly influenced social work theories and practice with individuals, groups and even organizational dynamics (Everitt et al., 1992: 24–5). Psychoanalysis has engaged many social theorists, such as Lacan, and feminists (Rose, 1998; Weedon, 1999) in theorizing identity, subjectivity and gender. However, these analyses are beyond the scope of this discussion.

Marxism is another important influence on social work theories and practice. From this perspective, social problems are understood as inequalities related to social class, as social positions defined by either 'capital' or 'labour' (Everitt et al., 1992: 26–8). Consciousness of class inequalities and their consequences offers an alternative to approaches that pathologize or blame individuals or groups for prob-lems they experience, allowing for an understanding of the dialectical relationship between private and public, personal and political (Everitt et al., 1992: 28).

Additional and increasingly popular perspectives influenced by sociology include social constructionism, postmodernism, poststructuralism and critical theory. You can read about these perspectives, for example, in Denzin and Lincoln's (1994) *Handbook of Qualitative Research*, Reason and Bradbury's (2001) *Handbook of Action Research* and Truman's forthcoming book, *Social Research and Social Inequality*. These are excellent resources because they show, in a depth that is beyond the scope of this book, the links between the theoretical and political aspects of ways of knowing with the more practical aspects of research, including methods. Examples of research that have relied on some of these approaches include Jones (1990) and Saleeby (1994) (interpretive), Trinder (2000b) (postmodern feminism), D'Cruz (1999, 2002) (social constructionism).

Tuhiwai Smith (1999: 143–61) cites '25 indigenous projects' as examples of indigenous research positioned within a 'decolonizing' perspective. These pro-jects include community action, local initiatives and tribal research, as well as indigenous researchers being located in formal institutions and research centres

(Tuhiwai Smith, 1999: 125). Kaupapa Maori research as an example of 'indigenous methodology' that has emerged in Aotearoa, New Zealand, includes particular institutional structures and processes, such as enabling legislation and treaties, the expression of particular knowledge, epistemologies, language and culture, that are political strategies for achieving self-determination (Tuhiwai Smith, 1999).

Paradigms and the idea of incommensurability

The idea of *incommensurability* has two main strands. The first strand is that the differences between paradigms cannot be reconciled. According to Blaikie (1993: 108), paradigms are considered to be competing (rival) perspectives and 'incompatible worldviews' because they are informed by different assumptions about reality and how one knows about that reality. These arguments are probably now clear enough without needing to add anything more, having come this far through this chapter, in which we have discussed different paradigms and the political and ethical issues associated with different ways of knowing.

A second strand to the meaning of incommensurability – one that is perhaps less well known but emerging as an issue – is about the relationship between 'paradigm' and 'method'. Bryman (1988: 118–26; 2001: 433) presents the various arguments of those who argue that there is a link between epistemology and method and those who argue for the opposite position. Notable are claims made by Snizek (1976) and Platt (1986) that a paradigm, as is the case with assumptions, beliefs, values and related theories about reality, has a 'free floating' relationship to 'methods' (in Bryman, 2001: 433).

> ... if we accept that there is no perfect correspondence between research strategy and matters of epistemology and ontology, the notion that a method is inherently or necessarily indicative of certain wider assumptions about knowledge and the nature of social reality begins to founder.

Snizek (1976, cited in Bryman, 1988: 124; 2001: 433) analysed 1434 articles in sociology journals between 1950 and 1970 for their grounding in either 'social factist' (quantitative) or 'social definitionist' (qualitative) approaches. He argued that he 'was unable to uncover an unambiguous pattern linking the grounding of an article in either of these two paradigms with the research methods used'. Platt (1986, cited by Bryman, 1988: 125; 2001: 433), who reviewed historical articles between 1920 and 1960 argued that 'the connection that is often forged between functionalism, which itself is associated with positivism, and the social survey is greatly exaggerated. Instead, 'the two originated independently, and that leading functionalists had no special propensity to use surveys and leading surveyors no special propensity for functionalism' (Platt, 1986: 527, in Bryman, 2001: 433).

In response to Snizek (1976) and Platt (1986), one could argue several points. First, whether or not the paradigms that Snizek explored were the same as the paradigms explored in this chapter and also more extensively by research scholars (for example, Denzin and Lincoln, 1994; Reason and Bradbury, 2001; Stanley and Wise, 1993). Bryman (2001: 446) and Jacobs (1997) argue that the meaning of 'paradigm' is itself not necessarily consistent, even as used by Kuhn himself. Hence, one could say that the paradigms explored by Snizek (1976) were related to different *methods* of data generation, as quantitative or qualitative (in Bryman, 2001: 433), compared with the political and ethical understandings of epistemology, expressed by the paradigms explored in this chapter – feminism, Marxism or interpretivism, for example.

Second, the time period for which both Snizek and Platt conducted their studies would not have been associated with the emergence of paradigm debates that have characterized social science research since the 1970s, particularly with the emergence of feminist sociology and research. This claim may be supported by the even more recent emergence of indigenous perspectives related to new social movements of the 1980s and post-colonial theorizing (Said, 1978; Tuhiwai Smith, 1999). Platt's (1986) claim that functionalism and surveys 'originated independently' and that there is no connection between the two can also be disputed. It could be argued that the normative place of functionalism and positivism in sociology, social science and research from the 1920s to the 1960s would mask the connections between theorizing and knowing and survey methods that were based in 'scientific' (positivist) research strategies.

As to Platt's claim that 'general theoretical/methodological stances are just stances: ... not guidelines with clear implications that are followed in practice' (Platt, 1986: 275, cited in Bryman, 2001: 433), we have argued in this chapter that methodological stances are a set of assumptions about social reality and social problems that therefore influence the conceptual approach taken and the framing of research questions, design and analysis. Bryman (1988: 119–20) has argued that one can conduct a qualitative study, for example, using a participant observation method, but relate to the process of data generation and analysis from either a positivist or interpretivist perspective. Furthermore, as we argue later in this book, a choice of method may be strategic – to engage with political aspects of research and ensure powerful stakeholders are convinced about the issues, for example, as proposed by Jayaratne (1993) and Truman (forthcoming). It is well known that a key strategy used by powerful stakeholders to dismiss research with which they disagree is to attack the methodology (Silverman, 1998) – for example, *Bringing Them Home* (HREOC, 1997; Manne, 2001b) – so strategic choices of method are important.

Finally, theoretical discussions about the relationship between paradigm and method have become more relevant in contemporary times where the sociology of knowledge – particularly as informed by feminism, postmodernism, poststructuralism and post-colonialism – has contested the dominant (and heretofore invisible) positivist, scientific, white-Western-male paradigm. Alternative ways of knowing have created a space whereby all knowledge is seen as political, the positioning of the knower is essential in its creation and marginal groups are given a voice.

The paradigm debate: our position

The view that we take in this book – one that is indirectly supported by many other writers (Everitt et al., 1992; Denzin and Lincoln, 1994; Truman, forthcoming; Stanley and Wise, 1993; Blaikie, 1993; Jacobs, 2002a, 2002b; Feyerabend, 1975) – is that, as social workers, we must be aware of the political and ethical processes of knowledge construction in all aspects of our practice. Social work research is just one of these aspects. If we are to achieve social change as social workers, we are immediately positioned both politically and ethically in relation to social issues and social problems. Therefore, we cannot escape our personal or professional assumptions or goals. Nor can we be ignorant of the broader political agenda that permeates all aspects of public and social policy and that is increasingly informed by research. If, as some would claim, there is a spurious link between paradigm and method, we would argue in return that if a researcher does not consciously relate theoretical, political and ethical positionings (paradigm) to a choice of methods, then she or he is either politically naive or ethically and methodologically unsound.

As we show in later chapters of this book, the selection of design, methodology, data generation and analysis does not consist of random or ad hoc decisions (or neutral methods or techniques), but in assumptions about reality (ontology) and how this may be known and understood (epistemology). Furthermore, it may be necessary to make pragmatic decisions about methods to meet broader political agendas – for example, if key stakeholders are unlikely to be convinced by a wholly qualitative study as they give greater credence to statistical analyses and have particular expectations about what constitutes trustworthy research (Silverman, 1998). However, we also argue that it is necessary for the researcher to make explicit his or her intellectual and ethical assumptions in justifying the methods as a way of demonstrating methodological rigour. We also emphasize the importance of reflexive and reflective practice in social work research to ensure that both paradigm and method are linked to account for the political and ethical dimensions in achieving social change.

Putting it all together

In this chapter, we have looked at paradigms and their relevance for social work research, theory and practice. The main theme has been the connection between different ways of knowing and the political and ethical issues associated with such differences. The idea of the researcher's subjectivity or positioning has been thoroughly explored as being crucial to methodologically and ethically sound social work research. However, the idea of subjectivity has been extended to acknowledge that all individuals or groups with an interest in the research are positioned in particular ways in relation to it.

We have explored some examples of how positioning works in the public domain. We have also shown that positioning of individuals in relation to knowledge is complicated and not confined to single perspectives about the social world and human experiences. Therefore, a social work researcher must not only be aware of her or his own positioning, but also engage in ways that take account of others' positionings to maximize the effectiveness of research.

Riessman (1994a) shows how ways of knowing as personal positioning address diversity and difference, as well as closing the gap between social work practitioners and researchers and between social workers/researchers and clients. She cites England (1994, in Riessman, 1994a: 138) who says, 'We could begin by returning the human voice to our research, welcoming pluralism in experience, method, and interpretation.'

Finally, this chapter has also introduced some key paradigms that inform social work research, showing examples of how they may be applied in practice.

The next chapter looks at methodology. It begins to forge the links between theoretical, political and ethical assumptions (paradigm) and methods by which you would implement a research project. In the chapters that follow, these connections will be explored further by looking at research design, generating data and analysing it.

FOUR   Methodology

Introduction

So far in this book, we have looked at how to define a research question so that it takes into account the required knowledge base. This acknowledgement of existing knowledge is known as a literature review. We have also discussed the importance of being aware of the politics and ethics of knowledge from the start of a research project. The politics and ethics of knowledge includes the concept of paradigms as ways of knowing about social events and experiences and what is (and is not) considered to be legitimate knowledge about these events and experiences. The implications for social work research have been explored as potential ways in which we may oppress or empower individuals and groups who are marginalized in our society and on whose behalf we often claim to undertake research.

In the three chapters that follow this one, we will look at how the research question must be translated into a plan for conducting the research (a set of intellectually and ethically rigorous techniques and processes for generating and analysing data). However, in this chapter, to look at how these techniques and processes are embedded in dominant values and beliefs about what is the best way to know about social events and experiences (epistemology). This is another way of saying that we need to recognize how different ways of knowing (understanding and explaining) social issues may also influence how we explore them in research by using different processes and techniques. This chapter aims to differentiate between research techniques as data-gathering and analytical devices (methods) and the linkage between techniques and the intellectual and value positions that inform them (methodology).

Methodology and methods

Blaikie (1993: 7) defines *methodology* as being:

> ... the analysis of how research should or does proceed. ... It includes discussions of how theories are generated and tested – what kind of logic is used, what criteria they have to satisfy, what theories look like and how particular theoretical perspectives can be related to particular research problems.

Blaikie (1993: 7) defines *methods* as being:

... the actual techniques and procedures used to gather and analyse data related to some research question or hypothesis.

Methods for data collection and analysis are usually differentiated as either *quantitative* or *qualitative*. We will explore this distinction further in Chapters 6 and 7. However, in this chapter, we want to explore the connection between methods and methodology. Here, we extend the discussion about different ways of knowing set out in Chapter 3. In Chapter 3, we presented debates about different ways of knowing and how these may be translated into different methods as legitimate ways of knowing about and investigating the social world and, more specifically, the selected research problem. We will now explore these issues further, first by briefly defining quantitative and qualitative methods and then by locating these methods within discussions about methodology as a set of values and approaches to credible, valid and reliable knowledge.

Quantitative or qualitative methods?

This section briefly summarizes and defines quantitative and qualitative methods as techniques of enquiry and relates them to arguments about different ways of knowing. In doing so, we hope to show how and why a social work researcher ought to be reflective and reflexive when conducting research and why research is more than methods of enquiry.

Quantitative methods are those that relate to quantity or number. Therefore, the data sought will be in the form of numbers and analysed in appropriate ways that allow for mathematical calculations and the generation of statistical rules about the meaning and significance of the results (Bryman, 1988; Silverman, 1998).

Quantitative methods usually involve some form of structured investigation and analysis – such as questionnaires or surveys, interviews, observations, text analysis or statistical collections. Such structured investigation allows for numerical codes and categories to be generated. The numbers of informants (or 'sources') are usually relatively large to accommodate the rules of ensuring statistical rigour and credibility and analytical techniques that rely on statistical tests of significance.

Qualitative methods are those that produce data concerning quality (Bryman, 1988). It is probably easier to describe qualitative methods as what they are *not* – that is, not quantifiable (Silverman, 1998) – because there is no exhaustive list of what they *are*. However, they include an exploration of values, processes, experiences, language and meaning, among other things. The numbers of informants are usually limited, to be able to cope with the volume of data, which is usually in text (words, language) form.

Qualitative methods are usually relatively unstructured or semi-structured, relying on open-ended questions or themes to elicit responses in questionnaires, surveys, interviews, observations and text analysis. Statistical collections are not usually the main form of data sought in a qualitative study. However, sometimes statistics may be the subject of a qualitative study to ascertain the diversity of meaning that may be masked by statistical categories. Qualitative studies may also explore the processes by which statistics are produced by people in various forms of social organization.

For examples of such research, see Cicourel (1974), Garfinkel (1974), Government Statisticians' Collective (1993), Ahmad and Sheldon (1993), Thorpe (1994), Harrison and Cameron-Traub (1994), Thomas (1996) and D'Cruz (1999). These studies problematize the assumption that statistics are 'objective facts' that represent a fixed reality. Instead, statistics are seen as social constructions resulting from usually invisible or taken for granted processes and that knowing how these social processes operate is crucially important to understanding the statistics as representations of reality.

Quantitative or qualitative?
The debates about methods

Choosing whether to use *qualitative* or *quantitative* approaches to research is not a neutral exercise. Instead, each approach is associated with perceived or actual differences that are influenced by particular paradigms or ways of knowing. Basically, the arguments for or against qualitative and quantitative methods relate to judgements about trustworthy research that are informed by beliefs about reality and how one knows about and investigates that reality. Chapter 3 discussed various paradigms, showing how there are different assumptions about knowledge and truth and how good research may be designed within each paradigm.

The debates associated with the trustworthiness of quantitative and qualitative approaches extend discussions about paradigms from Chapter 3. We are now starting to look at how abstract concepts such as paradigms or researcher subjectivity (positioning) have an influence on the more practical aspects of translating a research question into a research design that can be implemented and shed light on the issues of interest in the project.

Many scholarly texts on research methodology – for example, Denzin and Lincoln (1994), Reason and Bradbury (2001), Stanley and Wise (1993), Bryman (1988, 2001) – discuss at length key intellectual and philosophical assumptions and debates associated with quantitative and qualitative research. However, for an introductory text such as this one, we have summarized the main aspects of these debates. A central issue is the perceived or actual differences between quantitative and qualitative methods in terms of ontology, epistemology, values and methods. Table 4.1 (taken from Bryman, 1988: 94) sets out these differences, which are seen as irreconcilable – you are either a quantitative or qualitative researcher. You cannot use both approaches because the assumptions about reality and ways of knowing (as methods) differ so significantly. There are, of course, researchers who combine quantitative and qualitative approaches (such as Mason, 1994, 1996; Tashakkori and Teddlie, 1998;

Table 4.1   Some of the differences between quantitative and qualitative research (Bryman, 1988: Table 5.1, 94)

Aspects of research	Quantitative	Qualitative
Role of qualitative research	Preparatory	Means to exploration of actors' interpretation
Relationship between researcher and subject	Distant	Close
Researcher's stance in relation to subject	Outsider	Insider
Relationship between theory/concepts and research	Confirmation	Emergent
Research strategy	Structured	Unstructured
Scope of findings	Nomothetic (generalizable)	Idiographic [sic]
Image of social reality	Static and external to actor	Processual and socially constructed by actor
Nature of data	Hard, reliable	Rich, deep

Hammersley, 1996, cited in Bryman, 2001: 447; Morgan, 1998, cited in Bryman, 2001: 448; Greene, 2002). However, to be able to successfully undertake 'multi-strategy research' (Bryman, 2001: 444–57), you need to first understand the issues and debates about the differences between approaches. Researchers who have undertaken multistrategy research in a methodologically sound way are aware of the debates about paradigms and able to justify their approach accordingly.

The eight main points of difference between quantitative and qualitative approaches listed in Table 4.1, in summary, show the following.

1   Qualitative research is understood in different ways for its contribution to research design. In a primarily quantitative study, qualitative research has a subsidiary role, being 'preparatory' in developing a more extensive quantitative study (Bryman, 1988: 94–5; 2001: 449–50) or equated with unstructured methods that may be useful for developing more structured 'research instruments', such as interview schedules (Kumar, 1996: 109). While Table 4.1 suggests that there is no corresponding position for quantitative research for a primarily qualitative project, in a later publication, Bryman (2001: 450) discusses how quantitative research may 'prepare the ground for qualitative research' – for example, in a study of media reports of social science research. Additionally, some qualitative researchers may use quantitative studies as a starting point to explore the meanings of the experiences and events that are summarized as statistical patterns, and/or the processes by which the statistics are constructed in social interactions. Examples include Cicourel (1974), Garfinkel (1974), Ahmad and Sheldon (1993), Thorpe (1994), Harrison and Cameron-Traub (1994), Thomas (1996) and D'Cruz (1999).

2   The researcher's relationship with the informants to the research and the topic differs based on assumptions about bias and objectivity. These relationships in the research process are informed by the researcher's images of social reality. As can be seen from Table 4.1, quantitative research is traditionally informed by positivism. It is assumed that the researcher is separate from social reality and, therefore, that it is possible, as well as essential, for a researcher to be objective by separating personal values (biases) from the topic and informants. Qualitative research, if informed by, say, feminist or interpretive paradigms, generally argues that it is necessary to be reflexive and reflective about one's subjectivity and positioning in relation to the subject being researched and informants and their subjectivities. Hence, qualitative research is the preferred approach if informants' experiences about problems or services received are the focus. Furthermore, the researcher is acknowledged as an active agent in constructing knowledge by means of the research process, rather than as an external actor in relation to objective knowledge.

3   Quantitative research has traditionally been informed by positivism and scientific research designs – for example, experiments. Therefore, the aim is to test theory by means of research using hypotheses known as the hypothetico-deductive method (Abercrombie et al., 1988: 116; Royse, 1999: 14–18). The theory drives the research and the aim in the first instance is to disprove the theory – a process known as 'falsification' (Abercrombie et al., 1988: 95, 116; Royse, 1999: 14–18) – by showing that there is no relationship between the variables of interest. For example, if you are running a family support pro-gramme and want to know if it is effective or not, in an experimental design you would want to show that there is no relationship between the programme and the outcomes for families. If your research shows that there *is* a relation-ship, this serves to confirm the theory. Qualitative research, on the other hand, is said to rely on emergent theories – those that come from life or are grounded in human experience. Some critics would argue that it is impossible to produce entirely emergent or grounded theory untouched by the researcher's own intellectual positioning (Stanley and Wise, 1990; Bryman, 1988: 84–5; Denzin, 1994: 508; D'Cruz, 2001: 23).

4   Quantitative and qualitative research are further differentiated according to the degree of structure in data generation. The more practical aspects of data generation will be explored further in Chapter 6. The degree of structure reflects the assumptions about the ways in which reality may be understood (for example, only known by the senses or the value of experiences and intuition) and the best way to generate the data and analyse them. More structured approaches allow for statistical tests of significance to be conducted, which is the main feature of quantitative research. Structured approaches are seen as more reliable, especially where statistics may be valued more highly as hard evidence (Silverman, 1998). Qualitative data tends to be limited by numbers of informants but may be enhanced by depth and richness that is missing from structured studies that rely on very large numbers of informants.

5   The reason that statistical analyses are fundamental to quantitative methods is to allow generalization of the results to the wider population (a nomo-thetic scope). The need to generalize the research outcomes to populations beyond the sampled group is why quantitative research relies so heavily on probability sampling, so that the researcher can apply statistical rules for data quality and generalizability (Arber, 1993b). Qualitative research, on the other hand, does not seek to generalize to populations, but, instead, looks at alternative ways of generating theory about human experiences and the con-texts in which they occur. Hence, non-probability sampling methods are justifiable (Arber, 1993b). (Sampling will be discussed further in Chapter 5, as it is an important part of research design.)

The reflexive researcher: linking paradigm and method

The above summary of quantitative and qualitative research as 'ideal types' and mutually exclusive shows how different ways of knowing (paradigms) might be associated with each approach. Quantitative research would seem to be most closely associated with positivism, while qualitative research might be related to feminist or interpretive paradigms. This argument, which links paradigm to method in an idealized way, may not be practical or politically or ethically possible in real-world research. For example, it may be possible or necessary to combine methods in order to answer the research question in a way that only one approach cannot do successfully (Bryman, 1988, 2001; Mason, 1994, 1996). However, beyond the practical aspects of methodology, it may also be necessary for political and ethical purposes to choose appropriate methods by which to engage stakeholders in the research process to achieve social change (Jayaratne, 1993; Silverman, 1998; Cockburn, 2000; Kaufman Hall, 2001; Truman, 1994; Greene, 2002). Additionally, in practice, researchers may not link paradigm and method if they do not consider the different assumptions about data and how the knowledge generated is validated. For example, some researchers who have used methods traditionally regarded as qualitative, such as ethnographies, have treated the data as objective facts much as survey data may be treated in a quantitative (and positivist) methodology (Bryman, 1988: 93–126; Woolgar, 1982, cited in Fuchs, 1992: 154). That is, the researchers who have generated data by means of qualitative methods, such as ethnogra-phies, but treat the data as objective facts do not appear to work from the alter-native assumptions that interpretivist or feminist researchers might associate with ethnographies. These alternative assumptions might include the influence of the researcher as a positioned investigator and the consequences for the claims and meaning of the objectivity of the data (Riessman, 1994a) and the importance of context in making sense of the data.

The above discussion illustrates that, to make informed choices achieving methodologically and ethically sound research, you need to justify your methodology, making explicit your positioning and explaining the choices of methods. To do this, you need to know what the criteria are for trustworthy research depending on the paradigm. This is important for two main reasons. First, because, as a researcher, you need to know how you are positioned and therefore why you are approaching your research in a particular way. It would be both ethically and methodologically sound for you to then make explicit your positioning as a researcher so that other stakeholders can understand how and why you have conducted your research in a particular way and made the claims you have.

Second, being aware of different criteria for trustworthy research can help you to be strategic so you can choose a design that will convince powerful stakeholders, who may have a different position in relation to knowledge and ways of knowing, without losing the ethical stance you want to inform your research.

In the rest of this chapter, we look at the debates about quantitative and qualitative research. In particular, we discuss the thorny question of how to ensure trustworthy research by applying appropriate criteria to evaluate qualitative or quantitative approaches rather than using the criteria for one approach to assess the other. We also look at how research for, or with, indigenous communities may require additional criteria for trustworthiness, given the overlying political and ethical issues related to colonization.

Finally, we relate social work values and ethics to research as a political and ethical practice as another social work approach for achieving change.

Quantitative and qualitative data – critiques

Below is an exercise to help you develop responses to critiques about quantitative and qualitative approaches. It is designed to get you thinking about different ways of knowing and how different stakeholders may respond to particular approaches. The exercise is also designed to trigger your own reactions and for you to reflect on them as a way of exploring further your subjectivity and positioning as a researcher. The critical statements are derived from various scholarly research texts that discuss such debates (for example, Silverman, 1998; Bryman, 1988, 2001; Mason, 1994, 1996; Stanley and Wise, 1990, 1993; Denzin and Lincoln, 1994; Humphries and Truman, 1994).

Critiquing quantitative and qualitative approaches

1 Read the statements below and repeat the following steps for each in turn.
2 What is your reaction to the statement (emotionally and/or intellectually)? (Note that there is no right or wrong reaction. It is important to be aware of your reactions because they are one

indication of your personal positioning in relation to knowledge and ways of knowing.)

3   Identify the paradigm(s) represented by the statement.

4   Which stakeholders are more likely to make such a statement? Why might they make such a statement? (Consider what their knowledge, political and ethical positions might be. What's in it for them?)

5   To what extent is the statement valid or true?

6   To what extent could you challenge the statement?

7   How might you challenge the statement in terms of alternative assumptions about different ways of knowing? (To do this, you will need to set out what the assumptions are in the statement and what some alternative assumptions might be.)

8   How might you explain your reactions to the statement and the response that you made to it? (Think about what you have learnt, past experiences and so on.)

Critical statements about quantitative approaches

Your data are meaningless because they are only numbers.

It is impossible to generalize about whole populations on the basis of responses provided by a sample population.

How can you control for what goes on in 'the real world'?

There is no truth in the claim that your design and data are unbiased.

There is no truth in the claim that you have succeeded in separating your values from the facts generated by the research.

How can you say that you have been able to measure people's experiences?

Critical statements about qualitative approaches

Your data are anecdotal and do not provide any real evidence of true experiences.

Your data are biased and subjective because your informants are talking about their own experiences.

Your informants are not being objective, they have a vested interest in what they are telling you.

There is no consistency in your data because informants have told their stories in their own way.

You have not used a random way of finding your informants so your research is biased.

How can a few stories be useful to bring about change?

How can one story tell us anything of value? It is only one example.

The above exercise emphasizes how and why it is helpful and ethical to locate and justify methods of enquiry within methodology. Methodology or a statement of assumptions sets out how we as researchers are positioned in relation to the problem in question and how we propose to enquire into, understand and explain it.

In the next few sections, we explore in more detail how the credibility and trustworthiness of research processes and outcomes are evaluated from three perspectives. These perspectives are considered the dominant or most prevalent ones, but we also look at two alternatives. The sections below show that judgements of credibility are not neutral but, rather, associated with perceptions of what valid knowledge is and how social reality may be best understood.

Criteria for research trustworthiness: from a dominant, traditional, rationalist perspective

In this section, we explore four criteria for trustworthy research that are most familiar to researchers as they appear in many research texts, both quantitative and qualitative. Indeed, many researchers cite these criteria to justify their methodology. Critics of research that is controversial may also use them to undermine the claims made by attacking the methodology. These four criteria are reliability, internal validity, external validity (also known as generalizability) and objectivity.

Reliability

A test of good (reliable) research is the replicability of the research process and outcomes (Bryman, 1988: 37–8). The primary concern is about the consistency of research instruments – for example, surveys or observation criteria – as measures of the phenomena that you are seeking to investigate. Any differences that may emerge in the study must be related to the actual phenomena and not to inconsistencies in the research instruments:

> Reliability indicates the extent to which a measure reveals actual differences in the phenomenon measured, rather than differences inherent in the measuring instrument itself. Reliability refers to the consistency of a measure. (Marlow, 2001: 181)

Moser and Kalton (1989: 353, in Kumar, 1996: 140) states:

> if a research tool is consistent and stable, and hence, predictable and accurate, it is said to be reliable. … 'a scale or test is reliable to the extent that repeat measurements made by it under constant conditions will give the same result'.

Marlow (2001) uses the example of a ruler that remains consistent over time (and is therefore reliable) as a research instrument. Similarly, the research instruments that you as a researcher will develop to investigate your question – surveys or observation criteria, for example – need to be reliable over time and place as a way of ensuring the replicability of the results. The idea of replicability as it is related to reliability means that another researcher may want to repeat your study. Therefore, if they use exactly the same research instruments, they should get the same results, which is a way of confirming the trustworthiness of your research and its outcomes.

Sources of error

Researchers using these assumptions about the trustworthiness of their research process and methods seek to maximize reliability by minimizing sources of error (Marlow, 2001; Kumar, 1996). Marlow (2001: 182–3), for example, identifies four sources of error. These are unclear definitions of variables, use of retrospective information, variations in conditions for collecting data and structure of the instrument.

Unclear definitions of variables
In research that values reliability defined as consistent research instruments and replicable processes to ensure replicable outcomes, it is essential to define the variables being investigated. If the variables remain loose or nebulous, then you will not necessarily develop appropriate questions that address the phenomena you are interested in and you may not be sure that you are measuring what you think you are measuring. Furthermore, respondents may interpret the questions in particular ways that, under these assumptions about reliability, are considered to be problematic.

Problems of reliable definitions may be more easily addressed if you are undertaking a scientific study where the variables perhaps lend themselves to clear definition – for example, blood pressure or income levels. However, for social work research, most of the issues of interest are abstract concepts, such as poverty or self-esteem or emotional abuse, that remain controversial as well as extremely difficult to operationalize (define in ways that make them seem concrete and physically real and, therefore, measurable).

Use of retrospective information
Reliability is seen as problematic if you rely on informants' recollections of events or experiences from the past, for example, if you use questionnaires or interviews. Case records also pose such problems because they are not only retrospective but represent a selective recording of case details.

If you are using such material, it is essential to justify intellectually and ethically why you are using a retrospective approach – that is, you cannot conduct a prospective study for ethical, legal or methodological reasons. You must also discuss such limitations as they affect your conclusions.

Variations in conditions for collecting data
One source of variation may be related to whether you have mailed out your questionnaires or are conducting

face-to-face interviews. Face-to-face interviews introduce additional variations. For example, the characteristics of the researcher, such as gender, age and ethnicity, may influence the responses given. The place of the interview is also considered to be a variation that could affect reliability. In research that seeks consistency throughout the process, these variations are extremely problematic and should therefore be minimized.

Structure of the instrument   For a higher degree of reliability, it is better to have structured methods of enquiry (using closed questions in questionnaires or interviews, for example) to control the degree to which informants may inter- pret what is meant by the questions. More open-ended questions that require categories to be developed by the researcher from the free-flowing responses given by informants pose problems in terms of reliability.

Testing reliability

In addition to sources of error, researchers who wish to ensure reliability defined as consistency of their research instruments may test for it using the following approaches recommended by Marlow (2001: 183–4) and Kumar (1996: 141–2). These are test–retest, alternate form, split half and observer reliability.

The first three approaches are different versions of a technique that aims to achieve consistent responses from informants by asking people who are not the actual informants for the research to answer questions that have been developed for a survey or questionnaire. This is usually known as a pilot study. The same set of questions may be asked on two occasions or different but equivalent forms of the questions may be asked (Marlow, 2001: 183). The assumption is that it is possible to develop questions that will generate similar responses if asked at different times and across a group of informants. If the two sets of responses are very similar, this indicates that the questions have a high degree of reliability. Studies that have used such tests of reliability are Hudson (1990) and Teare et al. (1998) (both cited in Marlow, 2001: 184–5).

Observer reliability refers to consistency of observations if more than one person is involved in observations of settings and interactions as a method of data generation. Observers are usually trained in what is to be observed and how it is to be recorded. Additionally, predetermined criteria are used by at least two other people to code each of the observers' responses.

As can be seen, these approaches to testing reliability are influenced by assumptions that there is an absolute reality that can be ascertained by means of appropriately generated data. Furthermore, it is assumed that other researchers who wish to replicate the research will make use of the same research instruments with the aim of testing the replicability of the initial research outcomes also. Questions and observations are therefore understood to be neutral techniques that can generate objective truths by minimizing inconsistencies in how questions are interpreted by informants. It does not consider how context may influence responses.

Internal validity

Internal validity refers to 'the extent to which you are measuring what you think you are measuring' (Marlow, 2001: 185) or 'whether the right concept is being measured' (Procter, 1993: 127). Marlow identifies three kinds of internal validity that the method of data collection (a research instrument) must meet: criterion, content and construct validity (Marlow, 2001: 185–7).

Criterion validity

Criterion validity – referred to by Kumar (1996: 139) as 'concurrent and predictive validity' – is a process of comparison between a research measure that you develop with another measure that also claims to represent the criteria being investigated, such as a scale or standardized measure. If the comparisons are similar, then the indicators that you have developed may be claimed to have high validity.

These types of comparisons establish two types of validity: predictive and concurrent. *Predictive validity* is judged by the degree to which an instrument can forecast an outcome. *Concurrent validity* is judged by how well an instrument compares with a second assessment concurrently done (Kumar, 1996: 139).

Content validity

Content validity – referred to by Kumar (1996: 138) as 'face validity' – 'is concerned with the representativeness of the content of the instrument' (Marlow, 2001: 186). It is 'based upon the logical link between the questions and the objectives of the study' (Kumar, 1996: 138). This means that the questions you ask informants or the themes that structure your observations must be directly associated with the research questions.

Construct validity

Construct validity:

> describes the extent to which an instrument measures a theoretical construct. … With construct validity, we are looking not only at the instrument but also at the theory underlying it. The instrument must reflect this theory. (Marlow, 2001: 186)

This definition shows the importance of the literature review in helping you to develop the practical aspects of your research. However, there are many concepts in social work that may have theoretical explanations, such as aggression, sociability and self-esteem, but may be 'difficult to define and theoretically vague' (Marlow, 2001: 186).

Generalizability

Generalizability is concerned with being able to draw conclusions and inferences about the wider population based on what is found by the research study via a sample of informants or sources. This is particularly important in quantitative studies that use statistical techniques to select samples so that the analysis and conclusions may then be applicable (generalizable), within statistical laws, to the wider population (Marlow, 2001: 8–9; Mason, 1996: 152–3; Bryman, 1988: 34–7; Schofield, 1993. For more on this subject, see the section on sampling in Chapter 5, Designing research).

External validity is related to generalizability. It is an important consideration in group designs, particularly in programme evaluations where you may want to explore or compare the outcomes (effectiveness) of services provided to different, but comparable, client groups (Marlow, 2001: 89). Apart from the sampling approach taken, Marlow argues that external validity or generalizability:

> depends on two other conditions: first, ensuring the equivalency [comparability] of the groups [Is this possible or desirable? Why or why not?] and second, ensuring that nothing happens during the course of the evaluation to jeopardize the equivalence of the groups or the representativeness of the sample [Is this possible or desirable? Why or why not?]. (Marlow, 2001: 89)

Objectivity

Objectivity is a principle that aims to minimize the influences of the researcher's values, beliefs and potentially vested interests in the topic being researched. Someone who is not seen as objective under this definition is described as biased (Marlow, 2001: 6). One aim is to foster an attitude of disinterest as a dispassionate enquirer whose primary task is to search for knowledge as an absolute truth, as an object of discovery, rather than trying to prove what you as researcher believe to be true.

This is clearly an important ethical consideration. However, the principle also seeks to separate values from knowledge. As social workers, we need to consider whether or not such a stance is possible or desirable when the objectives of social work clearly position us in particular ways in relation to disadvantage and inequality. In this book, instead of dismissing or seeking to limit the influence of personal and professional values and ethics in social work research, we argue that the theoretical and ethical assumptions influencing a research study should be made explicit.

Criteria for research trustworthiness: critiques and alternatives

You may have noticed from the preceding section that the four criteria usually cited for ensuring trustworthy research focus on issues such as measurement, instruments, accuracy, predictability, value neutrality and distance between

Table 4.2   Axiomatic differences between the rationalistic and naturalistic paradigms (from Guba and Lincoln, 1982: 237)

Subject of axiom	Paradigm	
	Rationalistic	Naturalistic
Reality	Single, tangible, convergent, fragmentable	Multiple, intangible, divergent, holistic
Enquirer/respondent relationship	Independent	Interrelated
Nature of truth statements	Context-free generalizations – nomothetic statements – focus on similarities	Context-bound working hypotheses – idiographic statements – focus on differences
Attribution/explanation of action	'Real' causes; temporally precedent or simultaneous, manipulable, probabilistic	Attributional shapers, interactive (feedforward and feedback), non-manipulable, plausible
Relationship of values to enquiry	Value-free	Value-bound

researcher and researched (or similar). The assumptions about truth and reality and ways of knowing about reality that inform these criteria are primarily associated with positivism. (If you need to refresh your memory about positivism as a paradigm, or way of knowing, review Chapter 3.)

Many qualitative researchers and scholars who write about theoretical issues associated with research methodology have argued that the parameters for ensuring trustworthy research need to be reconsidered beyond positivism and its usual application in the form of quantitative methods. In a very influential article, Guba and Lincoln (1982) have set out an argument for an alternative way of ensuring trustworthy qualitative research that may be appropriate to perspectives such as feminism and interpretivism. They have simplified the distinctions between positivism and the variety of competing paradigms that we explored briefly in Chapter 3. They make a dichotomy between positivism, which they call 'rationalism' and alternatives, which they call 'naturalism'.

Guba and Lincoln's (1982: 237) table of the differences between rationalistic and naturalistic paradigms is reproduced in Table 4.2. It is an excellent summary of the main differences that inform the criteria of trustworthiness.

Table 4.2 revisits many of the claimed differences between positivism (rationalism) and other paradigms (naturalism) that challenge the assumptions underlying positivism. The main features of rationalism are that reality is single and able to be studied/known in fragments or parts and that those fragments are only what can be known via the senses. Cause–effect relationships are sought, with 'cause' being what happens immediately before the effect (it is 'temporally precedent') or at the same time as the effect (simultaneous). The researcher aims to manipulate one or more causes to study and predict the effects in statistically probable terms. Context is not relevant; generalization is the aim. The researcher should be separated from the topic and informants as values and facts must be separated.

In contrast, the naturalistic paradigm assumes a multiple reality that can only be understood in holistic terms and where context is essential to theorizing. The researcher interacts with informants and the context and it is impossible to be value-free. From a naturalistic position, the idea of causality is problematic, especially in relation to social problems and the effectiveness of services that are provided. For example, is substance abuse by young people a cause of homelessness and crime or is there a more complicated relationship between these three problems? Also, does it necessarily follow that substance abuse, homelessness and crime are associated for every young person? In relation to service effectiveness, how do you know that a parent education programme is directly related to changes in how programme participants parent their children? How do you know that there are not other, unrelated factors (intervening variables) that you cannot control for, as required in rationalist, experimental research?

As you read the above section about 'axiomatic differences', you may have felt a sense of familiarity with the ideas and their discussion. This familiarity suggests that you are becoming accustomed to the concepts and debates that are central to the idea of social work research as an ethical and political practice.

Apart from being aware of the axioms, or assumptions, related to different ways of knowing (paradigms), Guba and Lincoln (1982: 246) identify four obligations that underpin all research, *regardless of paradigm*. These obligations that all researchers must attend to are:

- the truth value of the findings
- applicability to other contexts
- consistency of the findings, assuming similar respondents and contexts
- neutrality as far as representing the views of respondents is concerned – those of researchers should not be to the fore or influential.

The four obligations are posed as questions for researchers and set out in Table 4.3.

While Guba and Lincoln (1982) argue that all researchers must attend to the questions underpinning trustworthy research, they suggest that the criteria for claiming or judging 'trustworthiness' will depend upon the paradigm informing such judgements. The four criteria traditionally used, reliability, validity, generalizability and objectivity (discussed above) are informed by positivist/rationalist paradigms. Instead, Guba and Lincoln (1982) suggest their own alternatives as relevant to the naturalistic paradigm.

Four criteria for ensuring trustworthy research in the naturalist paradigm

We considered the four traditional, rationalist criteria above – reliability, internal validity, generalizability/external validity and objectivity. The naturalist

Table 4.3   Four obligations for researchers in ensuring trustworthy research (from Guba and Lincoln, 1982: 246)

Obligations for researchers	Questions addressing the obligations
Truth value	How can one establish confidence in the truth of the findings of a particular enquiry for the respondents with which, and the context within which, the enquiry was carried out?
Applicability	How can one determine the degree to which the findings of a particular enquiry may have applicability in other contexts or with other respondents?
Consistency	How can one determine whether or not the findings of an enquiry would be consistently repeated if the enquiry were replicated with the same (or similar) respondents in the same (or similar) contexts?
Neutrality	How can one establish the degree to which the findings of an enquiry are a function solely of respondents and the conditions of the enquiry and not biases, motivations, interests, perspectives and so on of the enquirer?

alternatives that Guba and Lincoln (1982: 246–9) propose are credibility (for internal validity), transferability (for generalizability or external validity), dependability (for reliability) and confirmability (for objectivity).

Credibility

Guba and Lincoln agree that the concept of credibility as an alternative to internal validity must, nevertheless, serve the same function. That is, the researcher must be able to show that the data of enquiry do represent appropriately 'the phenomena those data represent' (Guba and Lincoln, 1982: 246). However, because the naturalist paradigm understands that social reality is only meaningful to the people who participate in that reality, the researcher can ask the informants whether or not 'their realities have been represented appropriately' (Guba and Lincoln, 1982: 246). Is the analysis believable within their understandings and experience of reality? This possibility is not open to researchers in a rational positivist paradigm because this would be seen as being biased or subjective.

Transferability

Researchers positioned within a naturalist perspective would not accept that knowledge generated from research is generalizable beyond the context in which it is meaningful – for example, human behaviour or the meanings that people give to social events. However, within the naturalist paradigm, some form of transferability is possible and even necessary under certain conditions. These conditions exist when the context in which the research is carried out shares sufficient features with another context that may allow some transfer of knowledge gained. Also, the conditions under which particular knowledge claims are made must be acknowledged. For example, if you have conducted research in a child welfare statutory organization, there may be some practice principles that are relevant broadly across the child welfare field, but they would also be limited by the differences between statutory and non-statutory organizations and their effects on social work practice.

Schofield (1993: 208), an educational researcher, asks:

> To what do we [qualitative researchers] want to generalize?
> How can we design qualitative studies in a way that maximizes their generalizability?

She suggests 'three targets for generalization ... *what is*, to *what may be*, and to *what could be*' (Schofield, 1993: 208, 221, original emphasis) and continues:

> Studying *what is* refers to studying the typical, the common, or the ordinary. ... Studying *what may be* refers to designing studies so that their fit with future trends and issues is maximized. ... Studying *what could be* refers to locating situations that we know or expect to be ideal or exceptional on some a priori basis and studying them to see what is actually going on there.

Dependability

Dependability is the alternative concept to reliability associated with replicability of rationalistic research: 'under the same circumstances in another place and time ... Discrepancies or deviations between two repetitions of the same study ... are charged to unreliability (error)' (Guba and Lincoln, 1982: 247).

Within the naturalist paradigm, an expectation of exact replicability is contextually impossible, if not intellectually unsound. Research designs ought not to be repeated automatically in a different context. Most designs emerge consciously to account for contextual differences. The idea of dependability in a naturalist approach relates to stability after taking into account contextual differences.

Confirmability

Within the rational positivist paradigm, the concept of objectivity separates values from facts. Research is seen as a process of neutral enquiry. Naturalist researchers argue that it is impossible to separate values (the researcher's positioning) from how the research question is understood and how the research is conducted. Sometimes the rationalist paradigm relies on findings that show 'quantitative agreement' (Guba and Lincoln, 1982: 247) – for example, the numbers of respondents who ticked this or that category as a response to a structured question. 'What is important is not that there be quantitative agreement but qualitative confirmability' (Guba and Lincoln, 1982: 247). Again, asking the informants by means of a process of consultation is a way of achieving confirmability.

There is also an important political and ethical consideration related to claims of truth associated with views held by a majority, as represented statistically. Just because a large number of people hold a particular view – for example, support the death penalty or mandatory detention of asylum seekers and refugees – does not make that view moral or ethical in human rights terms. Therefore, claims of truth based on a numerical majority to justify particular policies or practices have political and ethical dimensions that ought to inform research directions and debates.

Strategies for achieving trustworthy research within a naturalist approach

Particular strategies are triangulation, transferability and reflexivity. *Triangulation* involves combining 'multiple observers, theoretical perspectives, sources of data, and methodologies' (Denzin, 1970: 310, in Bryman, 1988: 131; Mason, 1994, 1996). For example, triangulation enhances the trustworthiness of the research if there is more than one observer of an interaction or context. It also helps to discuss observations, responses or conclusions with peers who are not directly involved in the research or with other informants. You may find approaching the research from different theoretical perspectives could increase the credibility, although such an approach might complicate the methodology considerably. You may use multiple methods, for example, by not relying solely on interviews, but adding observation, documentary analysis and other media to give alternative or complementary views. You may also combine quantitative and qualitative approaches. It is essential that you document all research processes and keep a diary of your reflections as you proceed as a way of auditing the trustworthiness of the research (Huberman and Miles, 1994: 439; Denzin, 1994: 513).

Transferability (or generalizability in qualitative research) relies on the following strategies, discussed by Schofield (1993: 208–20) in relation to the three domains of generalizability in qualitative research – namely, studying what is, what may be and what could be (see Table 4.4).

Reflexivity is a process by which the researcher continually reflects on his or her participation in the process of knowledge production – that is the research enquiry and the conclusions that are drawn (Fuchs, 1992; Stanley and Wise, 1993). This includes an overt expression of values and assumptions (positioning) informing the choice of question, design, data collection and analysis and conclusions (refer to Chapter 3 where this issue was discussed in relation to the politics and ethics of knowledge).

Reflexivity may be enhanced by the use of a research diary (mentioned above) as it is a way for the researcher to make explicit his or her thoughts and

Table 4.4 Strategies for increasing generalizability (transferability) in qualitative research (Schofield, 1993)

Studying what is	Studying what may be	Studying what could be
Studying the typical	Studying the 'leading edge' of change	Selecting a site that sheds light on what could be
Performing multisite studies	Probing factors likely to differentiate the present from the future	Generalizing from an unusual site to more typical ones
	Considering the lifecycle of a phenomenon	

emerging hypotheses and tentative theories as the research proceeds, making important links between process and outcome (conclusions).

Decolonizing methodologies

Tuhiwai Smith (1999) offers another perspective that enhances the above discussion about criteria for trustworthy research. By means of a discussion of many examples of research conducted in indigenous communities, she shows how research may be both a process of colonization and, more recently, one of indigenous people's resistance to colonization. Resistance in the form of 'decolonizing methodologies' includes challenging the role that research has played in maintaining dominance of colonizers' cultures over indigenous cultures and knowledge:

> Significant spaces have been opened up within the academy and within some disciplines to talk more creatively about research with particular groups and communities – women, the economically oppressed, ethnic minorities and indigenous people. These discussions have been informed as much by the politics of groups outside the academy as by engagement with the problems which research with real, living, breathing, thinking people actually involves. Communities and indigenous activists have openly challenged the research community about such things as racist practices and attitudes, ethnocentric assumptions and exploitative research, sounding warning bells that research can no longer be conducted with indigenous communities as if their views did not count or their lives did not matter. (Tuhiwai Smith, 1999: 9)

Trustworthy research that relies on 'decolonizing methodologies' like this privileges indigenous people's concerns, practices and participation as both researchers and researched (Tuhiwai Smith, 1999: 107). The research approach is overtly political, to achieve decolonization beyond the 'formal handing over of the instruments of government', to a 'long-term process involving the bureaucratic, cultural, linguistic and psychological divesting of colonial power' (Tuhiwai Smith, 1999: 98) and building 'global strategic alliances' and agendas for action (Tuhiwai Smith, 1999: 108).

Trustworthy research from this perspective is set out as a 'series of accounts and guidelines', as a 'map' rather than a practice 'manual' (Tuhiwai Smith, 1999: 9). There are 'critical questions' (Tuhiwai Smith, 1999: 9–10, 173) that represent the political and ethical dimensions of decolonizing methodologies. Listed below are the methodological considerations for trustworthy research with indigenous and colonized peoples.

- Whose research is it?
- Who owns it?
- Whose interests does it serve?
- Who will benefit from it?
- Who has designed the questions and framed its scope?
- Who will carry it out?
- Who will write it up?
- How will its results be disseminated?
- Who defined the research problem?
- For whom is this study worthy and relevant? Who says so?
- What knowledge will the community gain from this study?
- What knowledge will the researcher gain from this study?
- What are some likely positive outcomes from this study?
- What are some possible negative outcomes?
- How can the negative outcomes be eliminated?
- To whom is the researcher accountable?
- What processes are in place to support the research, the researched and the researcher? (Tuhiwai Smith, 1999: 10, 173)

These criteria are also identified as important by non-indigenous researchers who recognize the potential for research to disempower already marginalized groups. For example, feminist researchers offer ways in which research can emancipate oppressed groups or transform structures that entrench inequality (Stanley and Wise, 1993; Olesen, 1994; Everitt et al., 1992; Humphries and Truman, 1994; D. Thomas, 2002). However, decolonizing methodologies goes beyond an intellectual process of linking knowledge and theoretical perspectives to research methods. Instead, the fundamental assumptions of knowledge itself are challenged – how you know and what you know as Western and dominant, taken for granted truths are themselves disputed. An example of a struggle between dominant, Western knowledge and marginalized, indigenous knowledge was included in Chapter 3, about 'the stolen generations' as part of the colonization of Australia.

Tuhiwai Smith (1999) discusses extensively the embeddedness in different worldviews and related epistemologies (how you know what you know) that must be made explicit when decolonizing methodologies. In making her argument for the need to decolonize research and the knowledge that is constructed from it, Tuhiwai Smith uses many challenging examples throughout her book that are too extensive to mention within the scope of this chapter or even this book.

One example that Tuhiwai Smith gives relates to how Maori women have been constructed by non-Maori. In a quote taken from Drake (1989) that Maori 'women suffered a social oppression typical of all societies that reject the fatherhood of God' (Tuhiwai Smith, 1999: 171), Tuhiwai Smith comments that this is an example of an ethnocentric paradigm that uses fundamentalist Christianity as a 'new form of colonialism' (Tuhiwai Smith, 1999: 171). She says that the author does not use any sources to support such a claim, instead presenting what is said as 'common sense' and a universal truth.

A similar example about historical truths has raged in Australia for several years with regard to the stolen generations, where truth is judged solely from the vantage point of white, Western researchers, historians and policymakers (Windschuttle, 2002; Reynolds, 2000a; Manne, 2001a, 2001b; Yallop, 2003). Furthermore, debates about truth and valid knowledge from the perspective of indigenous and colonized peoples are more than intellectual exercises that reside solely in what is considered to be rational – measurable, documented in official Western sources and meeting Western tests of truth and evidence. Instead, they are inextricably linked to ethical and political questions about knowledge and assumptions about truth that are unfortunately excluded from rational debates as extraneous, emotional or subjective.

Furthermore, critical questions about methodology may be extended by more pragmatic questions that are nonetheless significant for indigenous and colonized peoples who live daily with the practical and material consequences of dispossession and colonization. Culturally specific and/or practical questions that are part of decolonizing methodologies include 'Is her spirit clear? Does he have a good heart? What other baggage are they carrying? Are they useful to us? Can they fix up our generator? Can they actually do anything?' (Tuhiwai Smith, 1999: 10). Additionally, indigenous researchers as insiders (Tuhiwai Smith, 1999: 10) are faced with criteria that include their relationships with individuals and groups with whom they wish to work and particular dynamics that may affect their credibility in their own communities.

Tuhiwai Smith (1999: 140) comments that:

> The research community has a number of terms which are used to good effect as exclusionary devices to dismiss the challenges made from outside the fold. Research can be judged as 'not rigorous', 'not robust', 'not real', 'not theorized', 'not valid', 'not reliable'. Sound conceptual understandings can falter when the research design is considered flawed. While researchers are trained to conform to the models provided for them, indigenous researchers have to meet these criteria as well as indigenous criteria which can judge research 'not useful', 'not indigenous', 'not friendly', 'not just'. Reconciling such views can be difficult. The indigenous agenda challenges indigenous researchers to work across these boundaries. It is a challenge which provides a focus and direction which helps in thinking through the complexities of indigenous research. At the same time the process is evolving as researchers working in this field dialogue and collaborate on shared concerns.

Having considered how trustworthy research may be conducted with colonized and indigenous peoples, one could ask whether or not the criteria set out in the list of questions above could be equally applicable in any social work research.

As Humphries (1994) argues, social work research usually aims to achieve social justice on behalf of many marginalized and disempowered groups. Thus, the questions that Tuhiwai Smith (1999) has articulated and we have reproduced above might minimize the chances of social work research being practised in ways that oppress people on whose behalf the research is being conducted.

A methodology for the research-minded practitioner

Finally, after all this 'theoretical stuff', Everitt et al. (1992) make excellent practical connections between political and ethical issues relating to knowledge and its relevance to 'doing social work research'. They discuss how a 'research-minded practitioner' (Everitt et al., 1992: 51–68) might link practical aspects of research to intellectual, ethical and political dimensions. A 'research-minded practitioner' is someone who recognizes as significant, 'the changing character of the situations of practice – the complexity, uncertainty, instability, uniqueness and value conflicts' (Schon, 1983: 14). Everitt et al. (1992: 53) note that:

> Being research-minded would raise these [issues] as central to informed debate, dialogue between all involved in practice, between practitioners, managers, users and workers in other agencies. We use the term dialogue to mean informed reasoned argument and debate between people intent on engaging in relevant and critical discussion in order to genuinely understand. The aim of dialogue is to open up for examination assumptions, theories, observations and judgements.

A research-minded practitioner would work in a participatory way with multiple informants positioned within a range of paradigms. The researcher/practitioner must be aware of, and acknowledge, the different paradigms and the interlinked intellectual, ethical and political assumptions underlying each one. However, this does not mean a blind acceptance of different perspectives, but, rather, an awareness of the political and ethical implications of these differences and their consequences for the research being undertaken:

> Common to all examples [of paradigms] is the responsibility the practitioner has to understand knowledge and its construction and to develop and share this knowledge with those with whom they work. That people have the opportunity to understand the processes of knowledge production, the relationship between knowledge and power, and the skills to understand and have acknowledged their own experiences, perceptions and subjectivities, is fundamental to emancipatory [practice]. (Everitt et al., 1992: 55)

A research-minded practitioner, then, works from a spirit of enquiry, thinking like a researcher in all aspects of social work practice, including how issues and problems are formulated, engagement with informants to generate data, analysis of data and practice evaluation (Everitt et al., 1992: 57–68). For example, a practitioner/researcher may access sources of information (data) to develop case reports, work with clients to make meaning of information about clients and their lives and link their assessments (analyses) of such data to theoretical frameworks, political and ethical issues. Another example is when practitioners engage in participatory ways to develop services such as groups for adolescents, linking their developmental work to theories that they have researched in the literature. Practitioners' evaluation of services they provide would draw on research skills. A third example is when working with communities, where research is used as the approach by which clients/members of a community may generate information about local problems that can be submitted to appropriate authorities to inform and facilitate change. Reflection (Everitt et al., 1992: 53–4; Fook, 1996, 1999) and reflexivity (Taylor and White, 2000) are recommended for good practice, whether one is providing a direct service or conducting research with, or on behalf of, clients. The aim is to foster an ethical relationship with clients that does not objectify them or their experiences and is informed by sound, theoretical analysis (Everitt et al., 1992: 55). As the above examples show, research is as much a part of social work practice as are other more familiar approaches, such as casework and community work, and is an important strategy for achieving social change. Research-minded practitioners are likely to be excellent social workers.

Putting it all together

In this chapter we have extended the theoretical discussion of paradigms we set out in Chapter 3 to include their relevance for research design, data collection and analysis. We have considered that methods by which data may be collected are directly, if not always explicitly, linked to beliefs about the problem being explored and what is valid knowledge about that problem. We have looked at ways of ensuring credible research, exploring the more traditional criteria and also some alternatives within different sets of assumptions. Finally, we have looked at an approach to doing participatory research that connects these theoretical and practical aspects in good social work practice.

In the next chapter, we will look at research design that will discuss different ways of structuring your methodology depending on your research question. Chapters 6 and 7 will explore data generation processes and analyses respectively, again with the central theme of paradigms informing them.

FIVE   Designing research

Introduction

In the previous chapter we looked in some depth at how procedures and techniques (methods) of research are embedded in assumptions and claims regarding how one may legitimately investigate the social world (methodology). In the next chapter, you will be introduced to a number of commonly used methods for collecting and generating data. It is these that are some of the most popularized aspects of social research: the survey, questionnaire, interview and so on. Yet, we need to consider carefully the purpose we may have for using any such procedures in terms of their appropriateness for our research goals and also the ethical and political implications of doing so. This is where research design is important. We concentrate here on the connections between our research question, our approach to different ways of enquiring into social issues and our use of research techniques and procedures.

We begin by reviewing the significance of paradigms and methodology for research design. The main elements of design are set out and we shall look more specifically at frequently used designs in social work, including an examination of sampling procedures. The place of formal ethical procedures in research will be considered next. We will conclude the chapter by exploring further how the concept of design itself may be a little misleading in the uncertain and unpredictable social worlds to which it is applied. There is a vast amount of literature pertaining to the design of social work research. We do not attempt to synthesize this material but, rather, use it largely to signpost the main topics for consideration and suggest lines for further enquiry.

Designing as part of the research process

You have a research question(s), you have reflected on different ways in which to enquire into social issues and how your own social position locates you as a researcher and now some kind of plan is needed to direct how you will go about your research. The details of such planning we shall be considering shortly, but are there any general principles that can guide you in generating an appropriate and workable plan?

**Thinking about general directions for
your research design**

If you still have some interest in the research questions you developed in
Chapter 2, return to them and make a few quick notes on how you
would proceed to enquire into them. (If you have lost a bit of interest in
them now, come up with a couple of new ones!)

Quite often, beginning (and not so beginning) researchers jump ahead to think
of commonly used methods at this point. 'I'll do some interviews' or 'I'll send
around a questionnaire'. The discipline of research design asks us to pause and
clarify: 'What for?', 'What will I be able to do with this information?', 'How
will it assist me in answering my question?' Designing our research involves
clarifying our rationale for adopting certain procedures and techniques, leaving
us better placed to meet the tests for trustworthy research discussed in the
preceding chapter. However, if we are to do this, then we need to design our
research according to methodological considerations.

In broad terms, you will recall that *quantitative* approaches are associated
with research that seeks the confirmation of theory, while *qualitative*
approaches are associated with theory development. Also, that the research
strategy for the former is generally held to be more highly structured than that
for the latter (Kellehear, 1993). These distinctions find their way into discussions of research design, where we commonly find designs classified as either
experimental or *non-experimental*. We shall be examining the features of these
designs shortly. Experimental designs follow the tenets of (positivist) scientific
method and essentially concern designing for the demonstration of correlation
between variables, testing hypotheses about these relationships (hypothetico-
deductive designs). Non-experimental designs are those informed by alternative
methodologies, more concerned with designing for description or exploration.
(The very nomenclature employed in such classifications could be seen as
indicative of the dominance traditionally afforded designs derived from the
natural sciences.)

From this point of view, an 'appropriate' design is thought about in terms of
its suitability for answering the question at hand. That is to say, if we want to explore
a newly identified social issue, then we would employ a non-experimental
design. If we wanted to determine whether or not an intervention leads to
certain outcomes, then we would most likely look to an experimental design. In
this sense, the choice of design is driven by the research question. What we will
then be able to contribute to knowledge about the question is dependent on
what the design (with its strengths and limitations) can deliver and the extent to
which we have been able to implement it in ways consistent with the criteria
that pertain to the methodologies underpinning it.

As Sim and Wright (2000: 18) have suggested, there is a 'complex relationship between theory, a research question, research methodology, research design and research methods'. Figure 5.1 is an adaptation of the way in which they have depicted this relationship.

Elements of research design

A little confusingly, the term 'research design' is used in slightly differing ways. According to Punch (1998: 66), who draws from Denzin and Lincoln (1994):

> At the most general level, it means all the issues involved in planning and executing a research project – from identifying the problem through to reporting and publishing the results ... By contrast, at its most specific level, the design of a study refers to the way a researcher guards against, and tries to rule out, alternative interpretation of results ... Between these two, there is the general idea of design as situating the researcher in the empirical world, and connecting research questions to data.

The idea of 'situating the researcher in the empirical world' illuminates the way in which research design can be thought of as providing a bridge between conceptualizing and operationalizing research. It becomes a means of defining what will be done in order to answer the research question. Expressing it in those terms also helps to underline the significance of considering who is involved in creating the design and the social context(s) in which the research is to take place.

Research design, then, is about making a basic plan for a research project. Sim and Wright (2000: 27) suggest that a 'design specifies the logical structure of a research project and the plan that will be followed in its execution'. They (2000: 27, 38, adapted) propose that the structure (or strategy) for the project would be built by addressing:

- what entities, phenomena or variables to study
- under what conditions to generate data
- what types(s) of data to generate
- from whom (or what) to generate data
- at what time points to generate the data
- what methods to employ for data generation
- what implications ensue for subsequent data analysis.

A research plan would also attend to the practical and administrative arrangements that will need to be put into place for the research to be completed successfully (Alston and Bowles, 1998). These aspects of the plan might refer, for example, to:

- convening an advisory group
- establishing a viable timetable for identifiable stages of the research
- determining procedures for recruiting research participants or gaining access to data sources

Figure 5.1 Locating research design (adapted from Sim and Wright, 2000: 18)

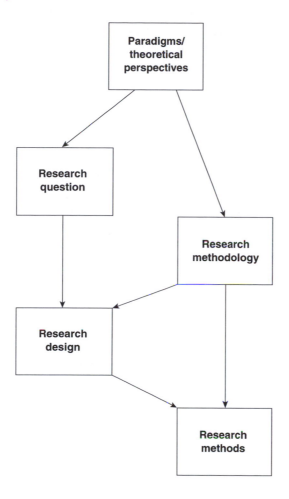

- obtaining necessary ethical approval or agency permissions
- devising means of disseminating results
- costing and budgeting the project.

In clarifying what is actually going to be attempted in the research and putting the plan together, the matter of feasibility again comes to the fore. As Sim and Wright (2000: 28) observe:

> All studies are prone to resource constraints in terms of time, money, availability of suitable equipment or instrumentation, and the number and expertise of available researchers. These all have obvious implications for the design, as do practical factors such as limited access to sources of data or prospective participants.

Faced with such considerations, it is not uncommon for the scope of the project to be reduced and perhaps for the research question itself to be reviewed and amended accordingly. One might conclude, therefore, that the process involves the researcher going back and forth between designing for trustworthy research and planning for its implementation, refining the research question and focus on the way. Again, we are led to ask who is contributing to this process and how decisions are made in these formative stages.

One summary of what makes for a 'good research design' is given by Wadsworth (1997: 27):

> A good research design ensures you will get the best evidence – the most relevant, credible, valid, trustworthy, reliable and authentic possible – and also that you haven't overlooked possible sources of criticism or possible counter-evidence. It matches up the sources available, and the questions needing answers, with the kinds and amounts of evidence needed to develop a case or demonstrate a situation. It allows time for reflection to creatively develop plausible explanations; and, it ensures the purposes of the research are properly met.

The design process provides an important window on to the ways in which research knowledge is constructed. Decisions present themselves in particular ways as a consequence of the methodological principles that stake a claim on their capacities to render 'truths' of some kind. Decision making about designs occurs within these discourses, but is also attending to the social contexts (economic, political, cultural) of their application – that is, the principles have to be made to work in particular circumstances and require continuing reinterpretation to cast a study as good research. At the same time, the design also has to work in terms of furthering the overall purposes of the research. As discussed previously, this may well mean a process by means of which consideration is given as to which design options connect best with the (often diverse) interests and preferences of key stakeholders, including the users and recipients of social work services.

Types of research design

There is no one accepted classification of research designs, of course, and it can become a bewildering exercise to find one's way through the maze of possibilities. Learning to research, therefore, involves learning to identify key decisions that are made in the process of determining a design appropriate to the research question and focus. The list provided by Sim and Wright (2000) given above offers a useful and reasonably straightforward framework.

A starting point here is to consider whether the research strategy is one of exploring, describing or explaining. This will help in establishing the conditions under which data will need to be generated. If the strategy concerns establishing cause–effect relationships, then the conditions will involve a high degree of control by the researcher over the entities being studied. Under these 'experimental' conditions, the researcher will be actively manipulating the situation to accord with the required procedures. On the other hand, if the strategy concerns exploring, then the research will be attempting to create conditions more akin to encounter and dialogue than control.

The matter of what type of data to generate is largely one of determining whether this will be qualitative or quantitative data. In order to answer one's research question, one has to consider here whether or not the data needs to come in the form of numbers that can be used statistically to demonstrate certain patterns or correlations or whether or not the data needs to be such that it can be analysed for meaning, lived experiences, cultural practices and so on. In many instances, particularly in more descriptive research strategies and some evaluative strategies, the research question itself could point both ways.

Decisions concerning from whom (or what) to generate data have to do with the matter of sampling, which will be discussed in more detail later. Suffice to say here that decisions do need to be made as to the size of the sample and the criteria as to who is to be included or excluded from it. The sample size can be from one (single instance) upwards. Where the strategy is to be able to make generalizations from a representative sample based on statistical techniques, then there are certain technical rules that determine requisite size. Hence, the approach to sampling is very much dependent on the underpinning methodology. As qualitative methodologies do not seek to make generalizations, the procedures for composing a sample are quite different.

Decisions regarding the time points for generating data, in basic terms, concern whether this occurs 'at one point in time (*cross-sectionally*) or at several points in time (*longitudinally*)' (Sim and Wright, 2000: 32). The cross-sectional approach generates data pertaining to one specific time. Where trends, patterns or changes over time are sought, then the longitudinal approach requires data to be generated at one or more predetermined or emergent points. Generally, a longitudinal study will be *prospective* – tracing changes into the future. Projects can have a longitudinal character but be *retrospective* – studying back into the past. Life history research might be one example of this.

The final set of decisions to be mentioned here concerns the choice of methods for generating data. These will be considered in detail in the next chapter. Again, they will be chosen according to the research question, methodologies of the project and situation at hand.

The sets of decisions addressed so far represent designs that might be structured as experimental or non-experimental, pursuing strategies of exploration, description or explanation. Where the strategy is one of moving beyond the building of such knowledge to the immediate use of that knowledge-building for achieving beneficial change with and among the research participants, then other sets of decisions also come into play.

Designing for action

It is possible to construe the research process as one of not only generating knowledge but also as a way of achieving social change. Here, research is not supplementary to practice and policy development or simply a source of informed recommendations. Rather, research becomes a vehicle for development, improvement and change to occur. In such approaches, there is a deliberate designing of the research process in order to maximize the possibilities for incorporating research into agendas for change, 'action research' having become perhaps the foremost of these (Reason and Bradbury, 2001). According to Alston and Bowles (1998: 164):

> Essentially, action research is about:
>
> 1 *changing* or *improving* a social situation, and
> 2 *involving* those most affected. (Emphasis in original)

Contemporary action research stems from a number of traditions. In some respects, it is an attempt to challenge dichotomies such as theory–practice, ideas–actions, researcher–researched and so on. These are substituted by concepts of praxis, ideas-in-action, collaborative enquiry and co-researchers – language that constitutes alternative paradigms for the researcher as change agent. Of course, this raises the question as to how change itself is conceived. As Hart and Bond (1995: 14) discuss, there is a continuing debate regarding the work of the commonly accepted founder of action research, Kurt Lewin, and to what extent his approach to the integration of social research and social action was 'democratic or manipulative'. Hence, the term 'participatory action research' is often used by those who wish to associate themselves explicitly with the more democratic and emancipatory versions.

Hart and Bond (1995: 39–43) construct a typology of four types of action research and argue that they emanate from the contrasting 'models of society' they assume. These vary along a spectrum from a model of consensus that is aligned with rational social management to a model of conflict aligned with structural change. Accordingly, the four types of action research – labelled experimental, organizational, professionalizing and empowering – differ as to who defines the problems, how change interventions are pursued, degrees of collaboration and so on. These all represent variations on designing research for action. The variations can be seen to reflect differing power relationships between stakeholders and between researchers and participants.

In their description of participatory, collaborative action research, Kemmis and McTaggart (1988: 9, 10) describe the basic elements of design as involving a thematic concern and four 'moments'. The responsive and evolving character of action research leads them to propose that the research focuses on a 'thematic concern' rather than a research question: 'The thematic concern defines the substantive area in which the group decides to focus its improvement strategies' (1988: 9). Design is then set within a cyclical process of planning, acting, observing, reflecting.

To do action research, a group and its members undertake to:

- develop a plan of critically informed action to improve what is already happening
- act to implement the plan

- observe the effects of the critically informed action in the context in which it occurs
- reflect on these effects as a basis for further planning, subsequently critically informed action and so on by means of a succession of cycles. (1988: 10)

While this cycle provides a conceptual framework for carrying out the research, the participatory dimension inevitably means that this itself will be subject to interpretation and negotiation. Describing their experience of engaging in this kind of research with families of children with disabilities, Bray and Mirfin-Veitch (2003: 80) comment:

> We also had to be wary, as researchers, of being captured by our methodology. While we were concerned with issues of research design and methodology, the parents were focused on the action – what we could do to bring about positive changes for families. Thus conforming to particular requirements of action research models, such as formal action–reflection cycles, was not the concern of the parents, even though it inevitably happened within the range of data gathering, discussion and resultant actions.

The possibility of being 'captured' by one's methodology is highlighted by the tenets of participatory action research. Here, the methodology is not only being appraised for its potential to generate certain ways of knowing but also for its potential to engage with others in a participatory movement towards certain social changes. There is a complicated interplay, then, in the processes of designing for action between constructing trustworthy research and facilitating change. Negotiating this path is a distinctive matter of political and ethical practice and, again, one that requires requisite epistemological grounding (Hammersley, 1995a).

Needs assessment

In order to examine further how research is designed, we shall be taking a look at two areas that have immediate relevance for social work and some of their key features and the issues they raise. The first is needs assessment and the second evaluation. To begin, you may like to think through the following questions about needs assessment.

- Have you ever thought that a particular service was inadequate or lacking in some way?
- What led you to these conclusions?
- What evidence do you have for these conclusions?
- Would other people agree? How would they see the situation?
- What need(s) is this service there to meet?
- Who is defining that need(s)?

'Need' has been a captivating concept in the professionalizing discourses of health and welfare experts. It has also been widely appropriated in discourses of social justice. Viewed from a perspective influenced by positivist ways of thinking, needs take on an objective reality that is open to measurement. Consequently, 'needs assessment is seen as essentially a technical exercise in methodology – measuring something that is already there (Ife, 2002: 62). From a contrasting perspective, one might say that 'it is much more appropriate to think about needs statements rather than about needs per se, as needs only emerge from the act of definition' (Ife, 2002: 258).

Mindful of research as a process of knowledge making, which occurs as a result of certain paradigms and their associated methodologies, the reflexive researcher is much more likely to recognize the defining of need as a political and ideological act. As Ife (2002: 258) puts it:

> When one examines needs statements, it is clear that, while they contain a technical element, they are basically value judgements; they reflect views of rights, social justice and what it means to be truly human. The important question, therefore, is who actually defines need, making the judgement that something is 'needed'.

This is a cautionary note for us when often it appears that a need is almost self-evident and the (moral) imperative for it to be addressed is unequivocal. Even setting a research agenda around needs risks contributing to a politicizing of social issues that accentuate weaknesses rather than strengths. As we approach the assessment of needs (or the construction of need statements), it is important that we maintain an awareness that this is a highly charged exercise and one that accentuates the potential for research to be party to both oppressive and emancipatory practices (Oliver, 1992).

Marlow (2001: 72) (following Royse and Thyer, 1996), outlines five different reasons for conducting needs assessments, which are to:

- determine whether or not services exist in the community
- determine whether or not there are enough clients
- determine who uses existing services
- determine what barriers prevent clients from accessing these services
- document the existence of an ongoing social problem.

This list is useful, but it does concentrate on the role that needs assessment can play in developing services for clients. It is cast very much in service-oriented terms. A broader approach is discernible in the suggestions by Alston and Bowles (1998: 129) as to the importance of needs assessments in planning:

- they assess the needs of the community and, by providing a snapshot of the community's needs, empower the community to seek action
- they allow us to advocate for change and provide information about gaps in services
- they allow an informed allocation of resources, policy formation and planning of services

- they assist us to evaluate whether or not our service is responding effectively to community needs.

Packham (2000) provides examples of a participatory community auditing approach being adopted in the identification of needs of young people in North West England. Listed below is a selection of these (Packham, 2000: 112).

- **Identifying ways of improving a service**   An audit was carried out by New Deal participants to inform a further education college 'of the views and needs of prospective New Deal clients' to enable the college to plan appropriately.
- **Confirming hunches**   Young people dropping in to a city centre project audited the need for, and appropriateness of, counselling services for young homeless people that 'confirmed a need we had previously suspected existed' (project co-ordinator).
- **Identifying needs**   Youth and community workers were employed to carry out an audit with excluded young people in a Single Regeneration Area in Manchester to help set a realistic qualitative baseline from which to target resources and measure change. A total of 500 young people were involved in a range of agency and detached settings, using focus groups, audit teams, drama, art, video and residential methods.

The questions that Marlow (2001: 75–6) poses in order to decide on the type of design suitable for a needs assessment are the following.

- Whose need is being assessed?
- Who will have an input into the design of the needs assessment?
- When will the needs assessment be carried out?
- What type of understanding of need is required?
- What level of description is useful?

These questions align with the key decisions framework of Sim and Wright (2000) discussed above. They again prompt us to think about the research strategy ('level of description') and, generally, that needs assessments will be of an exploratory or descriptive nature. They ask from whom data will be generated, what kind of data ('type of understanding') and at what points in time. Additionally, the questions ask us to consider to what extent participants in the research – those whose needs are to be assessed – will be involved in planning and carrying it out.

   In exploratory needs assessments, the design will want to allow for a depth of understanding to be developed. The purpose is not one of generalizing to a wider population, but, rather, 'to document and interpret as fully as possible the totality of whatever is being studied in particular contexts from the people's viewpoint or frame of reference' (Leininger, 1985: 5, quoted in Sim and

Wright, 2000: 47). As social work is often one of the first on the scene regarding social issues that are arising as a result of changing contexts or being subjugated in existing ones, there is an opportunity for the profession to be active in constructing needs statements about newly emerging or previously hidden topics of concern.

Frequently, this will involve documenting lived experiences and using research to assist in giving voice to the unheard – refugees and people seeking asylum, for example. Almost by definition, this will be research in sensitive and high-risk areas that require careful consideration of the ethical issues involved (Lee, 1993). Enquiring into experiences and meanings, the research would be generating qualitative data. The numbers of participants involved is likely to be small, though, of course, the volume of data generated with them may well be extremely large (the process of sampling is discussed below). In exploratory fashion, the design itself will be non-experimental and loosely structured, enabling the researcher to be responsive to the interests and themes that are encountered along the way.

Descriptive needs assessments can also adopt a qualitative methodology. In this instance, however, there will be prior knowledge that informs a more detailed and structured design than is the case with exploratory studies. Commonly, descriptive studies combine quantitative and qualitative data. Clearly, this will depend on the purpose of the study and the way in which the research question has been developed. While qualitative data can be analysed for an in-depth understanding of the topic, quantitative data might be sought for the breadth it can bring by virtue of its potential to provide generalizations (Sim and Wright, 2000; Oakley, 1999).

Within social work, descriptive studies of needs undertaken using a quantitative methodology have also been aligned with the pursuit of equity and social justice. They usually take the form of social surveys. Demonstration, for example, of unequal patterns of morbidity, incarceration, educational attainment and so on, become the basis for social action, lobbying and advocacy. Social surveys also 'elicit information about demand for, and extent of, services and the level of felt need in the community' (Alston and Bowles, 1998: 137). Descriptions of the incidence and prevalence of social issues are a means of politicizing those issues, though they would do well to be derived from studies deemed to be trustworthy and persuasive if they are to achieve any sustained impact.

The design of social surveys is a specialist field beyond the scope of this book, but some observations can be made (informed by Punch, 1998; Royse, 1999; Sim and Wright, 2000). The research question(s) is developed around identified study variables, such as social or psychological states, behaviour, attitudes and so on. Each variable has to be clearly defined and operationalized – that is, rendered capable of being measured. Suitable measurement tools are chosen or developed. A sample group is constituted, according to procedures that aim to ensure the group is representative of a larger population. As Sim and Wright (2000: 71) explain:

An important characteristic of descriptive studies is that the variables of interest are not manipulated and thus do not represent any deliberate intervention or interference with their natural state. [T]he *setting* for a descriptive study is generally a natural one, but the *conduct* of the study may involve quite a high degree of control. (Emphasis in original)

Descriptive studies that take this quantitative approach do not employ an experimental design as such. They are not testing a theory, nor are they involving the planned introduction of a particular intervention. Nevertheless, they do require that certain conditions and procedures are met in order to achieve the stated criteria of reliability, validity, generalizability and objectivity. This entails the researcher in placing considerable controls over the way the study is conducted. In much evaluation research, tight structuring of design is taken further still.

Evaluations

Evaluation has become a contentious area of social work research and there are clearly several possible reasons for this (Cheetham and Kazi, 1998). In the present discussion, it is the appropriation of experimental designs for use in evaluation studies that is of particular interest, prompting as it does many debates concerning the production of evidence for practice and the significance of different ways of knowledge making. We shall first look at the experimental designs that are informed by traditional scientific method and applied to evaluating social work. Such designs generally concern evaluating for effectiveness (the achievement of outcomes) and so pursue primarily an explanatory research strategy. Then, we shall consider alternative approaches to evaluation that draw from a range of perspectives regarding the processes and purposes of evaluation in social work. Here, we shall draw heavily on the work of Shaw (1996). This review can only be undertaken in summary fashion here, so further study is recommended in order to appreciate the complexities of both the designs themselves and the debates that surround them.

There are some commonly made distinctions about the foci for evaluation in social work. First, evaluation can focus on the activities of practitioners (practice evaluation) or on a particular programme of activity (programme evaluation). Second, evaluation can examine what occurs between practitioners and others (process or formative evaluation) or the consequences of that engagement (outcome or summative evaluation). Combining these, there are four different foci for evaluation, as shown in Table 5.1.

Designs for process evaluation will tend to be exploratory or descriptive and may be informed by either qualitative or quantitative methodologies. These studies might be concerned, for example, with investigating how service users experience a particular piece of practice or therapeutic regime or enquiring into the 'integrity' of a programme (that is, the extent to which what goes on in the programme is consistent with what it claims to be doing). Outcome studies – seeking as they do to evaluate the impact of practice or programme interventions – draw on explanatory designs in order to examine causal links or associations between

Table 5.1 **Four common foci for evaluation**

	Evaluating practice	Evaluating programmes
Process evaluation	Practice process	Programme process
Outcome evaluation	Practice outcome	Programme outcome

actions taken and the effect of those actions. While the importance of evaluating social work outcomes has largely been accepted, the most credible and appropriate ways of going about this has become a contentious issue.

According to Thyer (1989: 320, quoted in Shaw, 1996: 107):

> Our clients deserve the best services our profession can provide, and for the determination of social work effectiveness there is no substitute for controlled experimental research, guided by the philosophy of science known as logical positivism and the tenets of the hypothetico-deductive process.

MacDonald et al. (1992: 618) are equally convinced:

> There is no doubt that randomly allocated equivalent group designs provide the most persuasive and potentially irrefutable evidence of effectiveness (or ineffectiveness) and such studies are essential.

The experimental approach has particular technical features. Sim and Wright (2000: 88) suggest that an experiment 'can be defined as a longitudinal (prospective) design in which an intervention variable is manipulated in order to determine quantitatively its effect on one or more outcome variables, other extraneous variables having been controlled for'. To have internal validity as an experiment, the design has to build in as far as possible, certain key features (Marlow, 2001; Sim and Wright, 2000). These include:

- the use of comparison groups – principally, the experimental group receiving the intervention and the control group not receiving it
- random allocation of participants to groups
- operationalization of variables, whereby 'a concept is translated into its empirical referents' (Sim and Wright, 2000: 92)
- specific inclusion and exclusion criteria in participant selection
- collecting data before the intervention (baseline measures) and at predetermined time point(s) afterwards
- 'blinding', whereby the participant and/or researcher(s) are unaware who is receiving which intervention.

These measures are taken to try to minimize so-called threats to internal validity. Such threats include the possibility that the participants receiving the intervention will differ (in their characteristics or history) from those who do not, changes are a result of factors other than the intervention itself, participants may drop out of the experiment or not comply with it and so on. The more these threats can be countered, the closer this approach is seen to come to establishing causal relationships between the variables under study.

Experimental design is concerned to establish not only strong internal validity but also external validity, which is 'the extent to which the results are generalizable to the wider population' (Marlow, 2001: 98). Generalizability depends very much on the sampling approach. It also depends on the processes by which the comparison groups are composed to ensure that any differences between them are non-systematic and how this equivalence is then maintained in the course of the experiment. For each of the threats to either internal or external validity, further sophistication can be built into a design in an attempt to minimize either their occurrence or impact.

On the other hand, for practical and ethical reasons, an experiment may not be able to contain all the required features. Consequently, there are designs referred to as *pre-experimental* and *quasi-experimental* in which one or more of the features of randomized controlled trials (RCTs – the experimental 'gold standard') are absent. Undertaking an experiment requires a high degree of control and manipulation of variables by the researcher. When this is not feasible or desirable, the research might proceed, for example, without creating a separate control group or randomly assigning participants to it (which is quasi-experimental, as defined by Sim and Wright, 2000: 35) or without the use of any form of control group, which is (pre-experimental). While some of these experimental design weaknesses can be ameliorated by the use of particular statistical techniques that control for external influences (non-parametric ones, for instance), they result in less confidence that the outcome is a consequence of the intervention (MacDonald et al., 1992).

There has been considerable interest in the use of single-case or single-system approximations to experimental design, particularly with regard to the evaluation of practice. As Marlow (2001: 114) explains:

> Rather than depending on control or comparison groups in their search for causality, single-system designs rely on the target behaviour's being measured time and time again. In effect, the client system serves as its own control.

The required elements of such designs, outlined by Marlow (2001: 115) are:

- a clear and measurable definition of 'the target behaviours that are the focus of the intervention'
- a stable baseline measurement – that is, a measure of the target behaviour prior to the intervention
- a clearly defined intervention, which can be introduced at a definite point
- repeated collection of data about target behaviour following the introduction (and withdrawal) of the intervention(s).

Again, there are various different permutations on these designs, depending, for example, on the number of different time points at which data is collected, the number of specific interventions that are included or the extent to which the intervention and design is replicated across 'multiple' clients or systems. As Shaw (1996: 174) explains:

> The more complex [single-system] experimental designs rely on a process of logical inference that Thyer calls 'the principle of unlikely successive coincidence' (1993: 103). If changes occur once in coincidence with the introduction or withdrawal of a specific intervention, then little weight should be attached to that single coincidence but if such changes occur two or more times, then that is probably too much to put down to chance.

While a matter of continuing debate, single-system designs are generally taken to be no more than suggestive of the effectiveness of certain interventions rather than demonstrative of cause and effect mechanisms (MacDonald et al., 1992). Moreover, their perceived benefits have often been associated as much with the explicitness and clarity that they bring to practice, altering the process in distinctive ways as they attempt to evaluate that practice and tentatively to attribute changes to identified interventions (Shaw, 1996).

The use of various kinds of experimental design to evaluate practice has led some to advocate the advancement of empirical research. This has been described by Fischer (1993: 19, quoted in Shaw, 1996: 175) as a:

> Move away from vague, unvalidated and haphazardly derived knowledge traditionally used in social work toward more systematic, rational and empirically oriented development and use of knowledge for practice.

You might like to reflect on this for a few moments. Use the questions listed below to prompt some thoughts about the issues that this raises.

Thinking about issues relating to outcome evaluation design

Try to think of a practice or programme intervention that could be evaluated for its effectiveness.

- How might you set up an experiment to find out whether or not this intervention is effective in achieving particular outcomes?
- Consider how you would need to conduct the experiment to give it validity.
- What possibilities and problems does this pose?

Experimentally based designs – according to the advocates of empirical practice – produce hard evidence and there is an argument that it is hard evidence that the social work profession requires to sustain it amid the challenges of the new millennium (Sheldon, 1998). Yet, there are concerns that designing for experimentation has significant unresolved aspects. Refer to the list of questions below for some of the important issues surrounding empirical practice as discussed by Shaw (1998: 203–4).

- To how much of social work practice can empirical practice methods be applied? (Complicated problems, unpredictability, situations of crisis or infrequently occurring behaviour, single-contact interventions and so on may well pose problems.)
- Is the demand for measurement compatible with the realities and meaning of practice?
- Might experimental designs disrupt the day-to-day delivery of service to such an extent that they are rendered unviable?
- Have ethical issues been given enough attention? (Such issues include, for instance, the risks of regarding research participants as manipulable, the attention, or lack of it, paid to antidiscriminatory practice and the potential to overlook the wider social context.)
- Is empirical practice essentially a non-participatory approach to evaluation?

With the acknowledged possibility of oversimplifying, Shaw (1996: 21) contrasts the *empiricist* methodology for evaluation with the *humanist*: 'Humanist evaluation is likely to adopt qualitative methods of enquiry and stress the importance of discovering the meaning of events to participants'. You will now be familiar with the idea that a broad distinction of this kind is associated with an alignment of methodologies for research and evaluation towards either the natural sciences or humanities. Within his humanist category, Shaw (1996: 23) includes such examples of evaluation as those based on critical theory, feminist methodology, user involvement and participatory action research. He (1996: 115–16) cites these and other influences in developing 'defining elements' for evaluating in practice:

- its *purpose* is evaluating *for* service users
- its process involves

  - participatory evaluating *with* service users
  - reflecting on tacit knowing-in-practice
  - describing practice in ways that render access to its strengths and weaknesses feasible
  - mutual reflexivity of both practitioner and service user
  - legitimation through falsifying and grounded plausibility. (Emphasis in original)

These elements contrast somewhat starkly with the tenets of experimental design. They are more resonant of participatory approaches and qualitative methodologies. Yet, as Shaw (1998: 205) himself notes, 'there are a number of problematic and troublesome issues' with qualitative and humanist methodologies and their use in evaluation. Oakley (1999: 164), a prominent feminist researcher, comments on such issues in this way:

Although the attractions of the qualitative paradigm include a more reflexive and potentially less exploitative attitude to the hierarchy of power between researcher and researched, experience has shown that the early optimism of feminist and other researchers about the democratizing potential of 'qualitative' methods may be less justified than was at first hoped.

Both these commentators arrive at similar conclusions – that designs need to be concerned with the 'appropriateness of the method to the research question' (Oakley, 1999: 156) and the purposes of the research. With regard to the former, Shaw (1998: 207) notes the emergence of a 'disciplined pluralism' and Oakley (1999: 166) echoes our earlier discussion in suggesting that:

> We need to examine all methods from the viewpoint of the same questions about trustworthiness, to consider how best to match methods to research questions, and to find ways of integrating a range of methods in carrying out socially useful inquiries.

This approach derives in part from a view taken by Oakley (1999: 155) about knowledge making that is consistent with a major theme of this book:

> The main point about paradigms is that they are *normative*; they are ways of breaking down the complexity of the real world that tell their adherents what to do. Paradigms are essentially intellectual *cultures*, and as such they are fundamentally embedded in the socialization of their adherents: a way of life rather than simply a set of technical and procedural differences. (Emphasis in original)

As a 'way of life', the practices that constitute the intellectual cultures are political and ethical ones. Hence, the case is once again made for reflexivity – looking at and through the ways of knowing by means of which we 'break down the complexity of the real world', seeing their and our embeddedness.

With regard to the purposes of evaluation, positions taken on the relationship between understanding and action appear crucial. Taking the view that all knowledge claims are without intrinsic authority, Shaw (1996: 110) notes:

> The primary question for any evaluating in practice is no longer whether the social worker or even the service user understands problems more clearly. The purpose of evaluation now becomes whether service users have become *emancipated*. (Emphasis in original)

Of course, the pursuit of 'emancipation' is just as open for scrutiny as that of evaluation (Hammersley, 1995a). However, in this scenario, they are both implicated at one and the same time in the act of researching.

Sampling for experimental and non-experimental designs

As we have suggested, one of the key decisions in research design is from whom (or what) to collect data? Sampling is relevant to all varieties of research design, though, arguably, the more participatory they are the less appropriate the term itself becomes. 'Sampling is necessary because you usually cannot include everyone in the study' (Marlow, 2001: 132). The approach to sampling, however, differs markedly and depends on the aims the research strategy is designed to pursue. The selection of participants (or other forms of data source) needs to be consistent with this strategy.

As we have indicated, within quantitative methodologies, it is largely the ability to make statistically derived generalizations from the group studied to the wider population that governs how participants are selected. Here, the approach taken to sampling is referred to as probability sampling. It is aiming for representativeness in the sample and is crucial to the external validity of the study. This contrasts with the requirements of qualitative methodologies, where the attempt is to obtain what Marlow (2001: 133) refers to as an 'information rich' sample that is sought deliberately with some purpose in mind. The result-ant approach is termed *non-probability* or *purposive* sampling. The features of probability and non-probability sampling, as summarized by Alston and Bowles (1998: 85, 90), are given below.

- **Probability sampling:**

   - each population unit has an equal, or known, chance of selection
   - high degree of representativeness
   - allows researcher to generalize results
   - favoured by quantitative researchers
   - four main types:

      simple random sampling
      systematic random sampling
      stratified random sampling
      cluster random sampling.

- **Non-probability sampling:**

   - each population unit does not have an equal chance of selection
   - no claim to be representative
   - does not necessarily allow the researcher to generalize results
   - favoured by qualitative researchers
   - four examples:

      accidental (or convenience or availability) sampling
      quota sampling
      purposive sampling
      snowball sampling.

Within *probability* sampling, the process of constituting a representative sample by means of random sampling procedures and determining the requisite sample size is very much a technical one. Varieties of random sampling have been developed in order to cater for such factors as the need to build certain 'strata' into the sample (age bands, for example), the absence of an accessible or suitable database from which to draw the sample and the difficulty in identifying the population under study.

What the requisite size is depends on the forms of statistical analysis that are to be employed and the diversity of the population. The greater the diversity, the larger the sample size needed (Alston and Bowles, 1998: 95).

Generalizability of results will be very much affected by the adequacy of the numbers of participants involved in the research. Numbers from 30 upwards are intimated, though the suggestion that 'you should seek technical advice on your sample size before you invest large amounts of time and/or funds in your research' is no doubt a wise one (Alston and Bowles, 1998: 95).

Within *non-probability* sampling, and the methodologies behind it, the aim is not to produce findings that can be generalized via statistical analysis. However, it is just as important that the researcher is clear about what their aims are in sampling and that these are consistent with the focus, purpose and methodology of the research. We may want to ensure, for example, that, within our participant sample, there are quotas of certain characteristics. We may deliberately seek a kind of typicality in a case study or purposely engage people who meet some eligibility criteria in having experienced particular events, for example, or living in a given community or specific set of circumstances. We may be constructing our research about those we readily come across in our work. Our research interests might concern people to whom we have limited access or those who have an identified area of expertise. Broadly, in exploratory and qualitative descriptive studies, we would be concerned with generating new ideas and understandings. The basis of sampling therefore becomes theoretical rather than statistical. Within participatory action research, the basis of sampling would be rather more action-oriented and those engaged in the research identified perhaps by virtue of their shared interests in developing new actions from new theory.

The timing of sample selection, similarly, varies according to the research design. Experimental designs of differing kinds determine the sample structure at the outset. This may be the case, too, for some studies in the ethnographic-inductive traditions (Kellehear, 1993), such as certain descriptive strategies. Designs that aim to develop theory, on the other hand, adopt what Flick (1998: 65) calls a 'gradual definition of sample structure':

> individuals, groups, etc. are selected according to their (expected) level of new insights for the developing theory, in relation to the state of theory elaboration so far. Sampling decisions aim at that material which promises the greatest insights, viewed in the light of the material already used and the knowledge drawn from it.

The approach known as *theoretical sampling* is an example of this. Developed within the work by Glaser (1992: 101) (and colleague Straus) on grounded theory, to which you have already been introduced, theoretical sampling is:

> the process of data collection for generating theory, whereby the analyst jointly collects, codes and analyses his data and decides what data to collect next and where to find them, in order to

develop his theory as it emerges. The process of data collection is controlled by theoretical sampling according to the emerging theory.

Whether one is pursuing a statistically based sampling approach or a theoretically purposive one, the pragmatics of research will be encountered. Flick (1998: 71), in discussing how one balances width and depth in sampling decisions, describes how such decisions can be affected by limited resources of money and time. Negotiating these contingencies and contexts, then, is also a part of research design – one we shall return to at the end of this chapter.

Ethical considerations in research design

In this section we look at some of the ethical protocols for conducting research that pertain especially to design issues. We refer to two examples of prescriptive codes of practice by which researchers are required to abide and one example that is more in the form of a memorandum of good practice. While the codes are those of one country (Australia), their key principles are recognizable elsewhere. We demonstrate how research occurs within a set of institutional arrangements that, in this instance, prescribe or encourage certain research practices deemed ethical. As with all such institutional arrangements, there is a history and context to the fact of their existence and controversy concerning their content and impact (Ife, 2001).

We think it timely to introduce these codes of ethics at this point – in part because they tend to be applied most vigorously at the stage when a research design is being proposed for approval to proceed. Those committees that monitor ethical conduct in research scrutinize the proposed research largely by means of the design submitted to them and determine on the basis of this whether or not to give ethical approval to the project. This procedure tends to suit research designs of the predetermined type more than the emergent type as the policy is largely one of approving (or not) specific steps that the researcher explains they will be taking. According to Kellehear (1993: 13, 14), this bureaucratized committee procedure 'may abrogate the researcher from the responsibility of seeing ethics as part of the ongoing process of research'.

The two formal statements on ethics that perhaps impact most on social work researchers in Australia are the:

- 'National Statement on Ethical Conduct in Research Involving Humans' (NHMRC, 1999)
- Australian Association of Social Workers' 'Code of Ethics' (AASW, 2000).

The 'National Statement on Ethical Conduct in Research Involving Humans' was issued by the National Health and Medical Research Council (NHMRC) in Australia in 1999. The statement sets out principles of ethical conduct and the composition and procedures for Human Research Ethics Committees (HRECs). It includes particular sections on, for example, research involving children, young people, people with intellectual or mental impairment, Aboriginal and Torres Strait Islander peoples and those in dependent or unequal relationships. The statement reaffirms three 'basic ethical principles' (NHMRC, 1999: 11):

- Respect for persons ... expressed as regard for the welfare, rights, beliefs, perceptions, customs and cultural heritage, both individual and collective, of persons involved in research.
- Beneficence ... [the] researcher's responsibility to minimize risks of harm or discomfort to participants in the research process ... Each research protocol must be designed to ensure that respect for the dignity and well-being of the participants takes precedence over the expected benefits to knowledge.
- Justice ... within a population, [a] fair distribution of the benefits and burdens of participation in research and, for any research participant, a balance of burdens and benefits.

Interestingly, the statement acknowledges that there are cultural influences behind many of these principles (1999: 5):

> The basic principles ... reflect the high value that the dominant Western tradition places on individual autonomy. It is important for researchers to recognize that this is not the only way in which human interaction and responsibilities are conceptualized. ... researchers need to be aware of individual's rights within specific local and national socio-cultural contexts.

The statement also broadens the usual definition of research participants to include 'not only those who are the principal focus of the research endeavour but also those upon whom the research impacts, whether concurrently or retrospectively' (NHMRC, 1999: 7).

Since the Nuremburg trials at the end of World War II, which examined the horrific experimentation that had occurred in prisoner of war camps, informed consent has been a core component in codes for ethical research. The statement (1999: 12) adopts the following:

> Before research is undertaken ... the consent of participants must be obtained, except in specific circumstances defined elsewhere ... The ethical and legal requirements of consent have two aspects: the provision of information and the capacity to make a voluntary choice ... obtaining consent should involve (a) provision to participants, at their level of comprehension, information about the purposes, methods, demands, risks, inconveniences, discomforts, and possible outcomes of the research (including the likelihood and form of publication of research results); and (b) the exercise of a voluntary choice to participate.

The statement distinguishes between confidentiality and privacy. On these two matters, it has this to say (1999: 52):

> Confidentiality refers to the ethical and legal obligation that arises from a relationship in which a person receives information from or about another. The recipient has an obligation not to use that information for any purpose other than that for which it was given ... Privacy is a broader concept. A person's interest in keeping personal information private relates to anyone who might have access to that information, whether through a relationship or otherwise.

The professional association for social work in Australia – the Australian Association of Social Workers (AASW) – accepted a revised code of ethics in

November 1999, by which its members are required to abide. The code states that 'in the determination and pursuit of its aims, social work is committed to five basic values: human dignity and worth, social justice, service to humanity, integrity, competence' (AASW, 2000: 4). These values are held to underpin ethical social work practice.

Practice responsibilities are divided into six main categories: general ethical responsibilities, responsibilities to clients, responsibilities to colleagues, responsibilities in the workplace, responsibilities in particular settings, responsibilities to the profession. Special ethical responsibilities of social workers engaged in research are listed within the last but one of these categories, which comprises 14 items (details can be obtained from the website for AASW: www.aasw.asn.au).

The list covers such areas as:

- protecting the privacy and dignity of research participants
- obtaining informed consent to participation
- protecting research participants from unwarranted discomfort, distress, harm, danger or deprivation
- ensuring anonymity and/or confidentiality of research participants and data
- reporting research and evaluation results accurately and objectively
- storing research material securely and for the required period.

From these and the requirements of the statement, you can see how compliance impacts all aspects of research design. The basic ethical principles espoused by the statement align closely with those articulated by the social work profession. The complexity of the social worlds where research is conducted, however, ensures that ethical practice in research is not guaranteed by the enunciation of ethical codes (Humphries and Martin, 2000; Ife, 2002).

As an example of indigenous research ethics, we refer to a memorandum of good practice that was being developed by the Institute of Koorie Education (IKE) at Deakin University, Australia, in the mid-1990s. It is worth quoting at length from the paper, which conveys succinctly much of the thinking that is occurring around indigenous research issues (IKE, 1994: 2):

> the Institute of Koorie Education recognizes that, in addition to ethical matters which apply generally to all researchers in Koorie research, there are specific ethical matters for researchers anticipating involvement in Koorie research projects to consider. These specific matters arise from an appreciation of the history of past research practices into Aboriginal and Torres Strait Islander affairs which have been exploitative and, in so many cases, of little value to the families, clans and communities associated with the research.

The paper states that the Institute is 'committed to research activities which advance the processes of empowerment and self-determination for indigenous people' (1994: 1). In relation to ethical matters, the paper presents a series of guidelines with a primary focus for both Koorie and non-Koorie researchers.

The paper suggests that ethical matters for Koorie researchers 'arise from their difficult position of undertaking a role that has been defined in the past, and still in the present, through forms of institutional life which have served the cultural interests of colonial Australia' (1994: 2). The following understandings, attitudes and practices are among those encouraged (1994: 3):

> Community consultation takes time; sit down and listen rather than take on a controlling role whereby the project is run purely to outsiders' timetables and agenda.
>
> The success or failure of the project will ultimately be decided within the authority structure of the Koorie community; respect the authority of the elders in the community and be prepared to take direction from their advice.
>
> Koorie community members expect to be involved in open and equal (symmetrical) communication about projects that affect their lives; accept and facilitate the need for open and equal interactions with community members, interactions which secure community input into defining the actual work of the research project.

When addressing ethical matters for non-Koorie researchers, the paper (1994: 4) emphasizes how Koorie research:

> must now be inclusive of Koorie community interests ... must be non-invasive of Koorie people's lived experiences and cultural practices ... must be non-exploitative of Koorie knowledge ... must move from the positivistic positioning of Koories as objects of others' enquiries ...

Ethical practice by non-Koorie researchers entails 'cross-cultural sensitivity; that is, researcher preparedness to honour culturally different values, needs, practices and perspectives' (1994: 4). Koorie cultural practices to be respected include, among others (1994: 5):

- Personal, as distinct from professional, relationships in establishing conditions for further interactions.
- The need for extended timeframes in which decisions are made and the collective nature of those decisions.
- The status of individual autonomy within a cultural system of collective responsibility for social action.
- The publication of only appropriate pictorial material and texts.

Additionally, a fundamental challenge for ethical practice by non-Koorie researchers arises from an acknowledgement that in the past 'research has not served the interests of Koorie communities through critical understandings of their socio-political circumstances; it has, however, served to build academic reputations within the research community and universities' (1994: 4).

At the designing research stage and situating ourselves in the empirical world, many ethical matters confront us. Codes of practice can seem tiresome, bureaucratic and socially uncritical – in place to guard against litigation or otherwise protect institutions as much as researchers and participants. Yet, formal ethical procedures can prompt us to consider important ethical issues we may have overlooked in planning our research. They can also act to curb some oppressive practices that might otherwise go unchecked (Ife, 2001). Engagement with the positions of those for whom research practice has proven insensitive or exploitative might also help combat the dangers of ethical complacency.

You might like to try the reflective exercise below. Answering the questions will help you to think through some of the issues that arise when seeking 'informed consent'.

Reflecting on the processes involved in informed consent

Imagine that you have been invited to participate in a research study.

- What would you want to know about the research and the way it is to be conducted before deciding whether or not to participate?
- How would you want this information to be conveyed to you?
- How might the information you require, and the way it needs to be communicated, vary according to your social position and community membership?
- Can you think of any circumstances under which you might find it hard to decline the researcher's invitation to participate?
- What might the researcher do to reduce any sense of coercion or inducement that you might be feeling?

A comment on contingencies and contexts in research design

The term 'design' may conjure up the image of a relatively safe and comfortable process. There is a question to be investigated and the researcher draws on his or her expertise to design a way of doing so, mindful of practical limitations but more or less in charge and uncluttered by extraneous interference. There might be the occasional site visit or consultation meeting, but the information gained is smoothly incorporated into the design process.

If the term does conjure up such an image, then it is arguably somewhat misleading – for research and probably also for many other design processes. Schon (1983), in his seminal book *The Reflective Practitioner*, illustrated how design in architecture required a much more interactive stance between the architect and the local contexts for his or her projects – a continual series of locally created responses to the challenges encountered. As we have seen, Fook (1996) has followed up this theme in portraying examples of 'the reflective researcher'.

One of the contingencies to be negotiated is that of gatekeepers. Even where we attempt to work collaboratively with key players in the research environment, recognizing their place as stakeholders, we might experience difficulties in accessing participants we seek for our sample. Kellehear (1989: 66) describes the experience of the university-based researcher this way:

> From the moment you enter the research setting, be it a village, a hospital or someone's doorstep, you quickly realize you are on someone else's 'territory'. You are no longer in the familiar setting of the university but rather on someone else's 'turf'.

Looking back on his experience of researching advocacy within psychiatric services, Healy (1996: 70) suggests another metaphor to complement that of design. He quotes Taylor (1993: 123): 'the researcher who searches for and discovers a research method is similar to a traveller who sets out on a journey with an anticipated itinerary; sometimes things go to plan and sometimes things change according to contingencies along the way'.

In his account, Healy (1996: 72–3) describes and uses his experiences in this way:

> this chapter tells the story of a research project which at first sight is a sad and sorry tale of frustration, many failures and some successes. The process has been the very antithesis of the idealized model – convoluted, intensely complicated, enmeshed in politics and driven by passion. As well it reveals that these experiences directly mirror the world of its investigations and that in consequence the findings of the project are based as much in the process of attempting to study the world as in the formal, explicit process of research.

Putting it all together

In this chapter, we have begun to explore what is meant by research design, the connection with differing ways of knowing and methodologies and some of the varying types of research design and accompanying ways of selecting a sample. We have shown how ethical and political considerations permeate these matters and have introduced you to some of the more formalized ethical procedures for research. Many of the concepts may not have been easy to grasp, but if you're able to read a piece of research and think through the methodological preferences and ethical issues at play – whether or not the research design appears to make sense in relation to the research question and if the sampling looks appropriate – then you are beginning to appreciate the range of resources that constitute research activity.

We hope that you are also beginning to understand how our approach to research as a political and ethical practice provides an important insight into the decision making involved in research design. The path followed by the researcher isn't one that can be dictated solely by technical considerations. Rather, it is imbued with moral choices, the positioning of the researcher as a knowledgemaker and agent of change, and the requirement to be adept in meeting unexpected contingencies within changing contexts.

SIX   Generating data

Introduction

In Chapters 4 and 5, we looked at the connections between different ways of knowing and their importance in designing a research study and the different ways in which you could organize data generation to achieve the research aims. In this chapter, we look at how to generate data. This chapter will look at different sources, such as people (key informants), organizations and places where people live and work, archives, statistical collections and so on. We will look at how to link the researcher's access to data with the purpose it serves in answering the research questions. However, we will locate data generation in a context in which both ethical and political issues are important considerations. In the section that follows, we will look at the practicalities of how to generate data before we place these processes in a context of participatory research.

Unlike many research texts, we have deliberately not presented quantitative and qualitative methods of data generation as separate sections because we want to demonstrate several things. First, the *method* of data generation – for example, interviews or observation – is often the same for both approaches. However, the methods may differ according to the type of data they generate and the method of analysis that is then applied. Hence, we have presented quantitative and qualitative approaches to data *analysis* as separate sections in Chapter 7. In brief, *quantitative* methods rely on data that can be analysed using statistical techniques. Therefore, the data are usually in a form that is quite structured and easily categorized to allow statistical analysis (as discussed in Chapter 7). So, even if you ask some open-ended questions, if you want to do a quantitative analysis, you must transform the free-flowing responses into categories to which appropriate statistics can be applied (Royse, 1999; Kumar, 1996). On the other hand, *qualitative* data are usually generated to give depth of understanding to people's experiences and feelings. Hence, these data are relatively unstructured in how they are generated and there are various analytical approaches that can make sense of these data, depending on the research aims (Chapter 7). In this chapter, we show how the same methods for data generation may be used, but that the degree of *structure* defines whether or not they are quantitative or qualitative.

In addition to data analysis, the degree of structure in data generation may also depend on other considerations. First, it may depend on whether or not a particular design and methodology that generates particular forms of data will convince all stakeholders. If stakeholders value quantitative over qualitative data, then researchers would be foolish not to take this into account when choosing how to generate their data. Hence, the research methods may rely entirely or partially on relatively structured approaches. Clearly the opposite scenario is also possible and so the researcher may use relatively unstructured approaches. There is clearly a case for mixed methods to account for different stakeholders' positions.

Second, the researcher may consider that some forms of data are more trust-worthy than other forms (Chapter 4) and therefore choose the degree of structure appropriate to generate quantitative or qualitative data. Hence, it is necessary for the researcher to be aware of her or his positioning in relation to the research (as discussed in Chapter 3).

Third, the researcher's understanding of his or her relationship to the informants and their knowledge and power in the process would also be reflected in the degree of structure. Generally, the relative degree of structure is related to the extent to which the researcher has controlled the process and the range of possible responses (Marlow, 2001). Of course it does not necessarily follow that all researchers who choose a relatively structured approach – for example, carrying out a large-scale quantitative study (Truman, 2000; Jayaratne, 1993) – are acting in an oppressive way towards informants. In fact, they may have chosen the approach because it is appropriate to address political and ethical issues. However, it is important to be aware of these potential contradictions when designing research approaches and throughout the research process itself.

The above discussion demonstrates that the researcher must consider carefully the connections between research aims, data generation and analysis. This view is not intended to suggest that the researcher necessarily knows at the outset of the research the precise analytical approach to be taken and certainly our own experience of research indicates that this is the case (D'Cruz, 2001). However, it does help at the outset to at least be aware of the links between aims, methods and analysis, as well as the political and ethical context, so that appropriate data may be generated. The methodology (as opposed to methods) also gives some direction to analytical approaches and, hence, methods. It helps the researcher to think critically and reflexively about why particular methods are selected and be able to justify them not just pragmatically but theoretically, politically and ethically.

Before we move into the main themes of this chapter, we want to point out that we have deliberately avoided using the term 'data collection' and instead have used 'data generation'. This is because we believe that 'data' is not to do with things or objects waiting for us as researchers to go out and collect them, much as one might collect insects or antiques. Instead, we are positioned within the assumptions that data are generated as a result of social processes between the researcher, informants and other data sources, such as policy documents or client files. Therefore, there are no objective facts that become data. Instead, what we generate as data is part of how we have conceptualized the research, the research focus and the content, type and structure of questions by which we explore the topic with informants and engage with documentary sources.

Ways of generating data

There are many ways of generating data. For example, Marlow (2001: 156–79) discusses the following:

- interviews
- questionnaires and scales
- observation
- logs and journals
- stories, oral histories, biographies and autobiographies
- secondary data.

A researcher should select methods for data generation that maintain sufficient intellectual distance so that the research can be conducted in ways that do not set out to prove what the researcher already believes. However, it is important to be able to distinguish between selecting methods that set out 'to prove a particular perspective or manipulate data to arrive at a predisposed truth' (Patton, 1990: 55) and claims of objectivity (this distinction was discussed in Chapter 3).

Linking methods of enquiry with types of data

A useful approach to linking methods of enquiry with types of data is according to the degree of structure in the enquiry process (Marlow, 2001). How you generate data (the method) may be the same for both quantitative and qualitative approaches. However, the degree of structure in the enquiry process is usually linked to the type of data that will be produced – that is, quantitative or qualitative (you will recall that the differences between quantitative and qualitative data were discussed in Chapter 4).

In summary, quantitative data are sought as responses to categories predetermined by the researcher. Thus, the researcher controls the range and content of responses by means of structured questions and fixed categories. Some researchers derive the categories they use in large-scale surveys from qualitative studies or exploratory research. For example, Kumar (1996: 109) discusses this approach as a way of ensuring that the categories used in the survey are reasonably representative of the range of possible responses. Additionally, feminist researchers Martin (1994) and Truman (2000) have demonstrated how they involved 'the researched' in community-based, mixed methods studies and large-scale quantitative studies, respectively. Data derived from structured formats usually lend themselves to quantitative analyses, such as statistics.

Qualitative data are sought as responses to themes or open-ended questions posed by the researcher. The informant primarily controls the range and content of responses because of the scope possible within relatively unstructured methods. This type of data is generally preferred if you want to do non-numerical forms of analysis, such as discourse or narrative analysis. However, qualitative methods per se do not guarantee participatory or emancipatory research. For example, Bryman (2001: 326–7) discusses the:

question of what feminist researchers should do when their own 'understandings and interpretations of women's accounts would either not be shared by some of them [that is, the research participants], and/or represent a form of challenge or threat to their perceptions, choices and coping strategies' (Kelly et al., 1994: 37).

As Millen (1997: abstract) states, 'Doing feminist research on unsympathetic populations can lead to conflicts between the researcher and participants' construction of the meaning of gendered experience.' Bryman (2001: 326–7) cites Millen (1997) and Reinharz (1992: 28–9) as examples of feminist researchers being confronted by such challenges from women as key informants/research participants. These challenges and their responses show the internal contradictions associated with qualitative research as a potentially emancipatory research method.

It is important to be aware of ethical issues relating to methods of data generation. Ethical issues as they apply to social work research were discussed in some detail in Chapter 5, but, in summary, the traditional view of ethical research practice demands that informants are not deceived and can give informed consent, their privacy is protected and they have the right to withdraw their consent and participation at any time (Humphries and Martin, 2000: 72–8). However, in keeping with the main theme of this book that social work research is both an ethical and political practice, we draw on Humphries and Martin's (2000: 78–83) 'feminist and anti-imperialist ethics' to integrally link ethical research practice to methods, discussed below. Their principles to be considered are:

- the principle of partiality
- locating the researcher
- research subjects are active, reflexive beings
- representing others
- encompassing difference
- contextualizing research
- accountability to communities.

While to some extent, our discussion of methods below is presented as a set of neutral techniques, this is mainly for clarity. However, it is intended that a consideration of methods be informed by these ethical principles. It is essential and ethical for the researcher to be aware that all knowledge generated is only a partial view rather than making claims to an absolute truth. The researcher and informants' positionings and subjectivities influence even the most structured methods of data generation and their outcomes. This is because power and knowledge do not solely reside with the researcher who is in a position to control the research process and its outcomes, although formal authority is associated with the researcher's role, position and status. Informants can also influence research processes and outcomes, including their level of cooperation (Smart, 1988) and whether or not they mislead or even lie to (Dean and Whyte, 1978) the researcher. In generating data, the researcher should be aware that she or he has power to represent others as a result of the knowledge that those others as informants give. It is essential for the researcher to be aware of his or her power and assumptions that can create and perpetuate stereotypes that do not validate difference and diversity. The data generation process must be understood in context, both of the overall research and in each interaction between the researcher and informants. Finally, it is important to consider how the methods of data generation and their outcomes take account of communities of interest and potential conflicts and power inequalities between such communities.

Interviews

Social workers are very familiar with interviewing because it is one of the main ways in which we work with people as clients. This familiarity with interviewing as a 'social work skill' shows how social workers already have some connection with a key ability required for social work research. Thus, the discussion below about different types of interviews may provide some insights into social work interviews in service delivery as well as for social work research.

Interviewing may range from being structured to semi-structured and unstructured. Interviews may be conducted with individuals or groups (known as focus groups). The structure of interviews as defined by Patton (1987) differentiates them as qualitative or quantitative. Three approaches to interviewing in qualitative studies are informal conversational, general interview guide and standardized open-ended (Patton, 1987: 109).

The *informal conversational interview* occurs in a spontaneous way. Such interviews are often part of participant observation where the researcher may notice a particular interaction. She or he then clarifies the meaning of the interaction by informally approaching people in the setting being observed and asking them (Pithouse, 1987). This approach is essential to avoid the researcher making assumptions about what is happening and imposing his or her meaning on events that may be understood differently in the context. There are no predetermined questions because they are generated from what is going on immediately in the context and therefore cannot be predicted. This form of interviewing does pose some ethical dilemmas because informants may not realize that they are being interviewed – unlike in more formal interviews where consent is sought and there is a clear start and finish to the interview (Patton, 1987: 110). Do you need to ask people to sign a consent form if you want to chat to them for about ten minutes? When do you need to ask for consent forms to be signed?

An *interview guide* is more structured than an informal conversational interview, because it relies on some general themes to be explored with all informants (Kumar, 1996: 109). These interviews are therefore more formal and participants are usually asked to sign consent forms, agreeing to participate. These interviews also have a clear start and finish time and participants can be given a list of themes to be covered in the interview. However, while there is some structure, the researcher can also ask probing questions and follow up on responses as needed to develop the depth required. The interview still relies on a conversational style because the themes explored operate as a checklist and are not posed as set questions that are asked in exactly the same way for every informant (Patton, 1987: 111).

The *standardized open-ended interview* is more structured still than the interview guide. There is a set of carefully worded questions (Patton, 1987: 112–13) organized in a particular sequence. Each informant is asked the questions in the same order and using the same wording for each question. There is less opportunity for probing and flexibility in the interview process. This form of interview is used when there are many interviewers and the aim is to minimize variations in responses (Patton, 1987: 112–13) that may arise if each interviewer asks the questions in different ways.

Finally, as the name suggests, *closed quantitative interviews* (Patton, 1987: 117) characterize quantitative studies. These interviews are very structured, with 'questions and categories … determined in advance'. The responses are limited to those included in the interview schedule and the informants must choose from these responses (Patton, 1987: 117).

From the descriptions of each type of interview, you may notice that these are ways of naming the different kinds of interview structure. So, the informal conversational interview would be relatively unstructured, while the interview guide would be considered semi-structured and the standardized interview would be structured. The greater extent of structure in closed quantitative interviews limits the spontaneity and flexibility of responses from informants because the researcher has determined the response categories in advance as fixed choices (Patton, 1987: 116–17).

Another approach to understanding interviewing that relates to the degree of structure is how the relationship between the interviewer/researcher and interviewee/informant is understood in relation to knowledge. The most familiar understanding of interviews is that they are processes in which one person asks the questions and the other person answers them. The questions are designed to elicit truth from the informant and it is assumed that there is a neutral relationship between the interviewer and informant. Child protection interviews are an example of such an interview. They are known as *forensic* interviews (Parton et al., 1997: 15, 19) because they seek to uncover facts and truth about what happened to a child and meet legal tests of truth (Parton et al., 1997: 31, 36). Some research writers (such as Holstein and Gubrium, 1995; Humphries and Martin, 2000: 80) would argue that interviews are not one-way transactions in which the researcher asks the questions and the informant answers them. Instead, interviews are interactive processes between researcher and informant(s). Holstein and Gubrium (1995) take the view that data generated in interviews is a negotiated outcome between participants, rather than a fixed 'bit of knowledge' provided by the informant.

Hyden (1994: 37–65) discusses an excellent example of interviewing as an 'act of research' exploring 'woman battering' (violence towards women by their male partners). She shows how the meaning of 'woman battering' is partly a consequence of 'interviewing as a discourse between speakers'. Note that Hyden is not claiming that the women have not suffered some form of violence. Rather, she is claiming that the meaning given to the women's experiences is a consequence of how it is understood within the marital relationship and then within the interviews with her as a researcher.

Thus, it is essential that the researcher is aware of the positioning and sub-jectivities (Riessman, 1994a) of participants in the interview, including him- or herself. The researcher and informants' positioning and subjectivities can significantly influence interview processes and outcomes (Skeggs, 1994; Chandler, 1990; Humphries and Martin, 2000; D'Cruz, 2000).

Questionnaires and scales

Questionnaires and scales are usually structured methods by which numerical data are gathered and are therefore normally associated only with quantitative approaches.

Questionnaires

Marlow (2001: 166), Kumar (1996) and Royse (1999), among others, offer guidance in constructing questionnaire and interview questions to avoid the usual pitfalls, such as asking leading or ambiguous questions. Below are sets of sample questions. Assess the appropriateness of the questions, some of which have actually been used in social research surveys and interviews.

Sample questions taken from Graham (1994: 137–8)

- How healthy are you?
- Are the health practices in your household run on matriarchal or patriarchal lines?
- Has it happened to you that, over a long period of time when you neither practised abstinence nor used birth control, you did not conceive?
- How often do your parents visit the doctor?
- Do you oppose or favour cutting health spending, even if cuts threaten the health of children and pensioners?
- Do you agree or disagree with the following statement? 'Abortions after 28 weeks should not be decriminalized.'
- Do you agree or disagree with the government's policy on the funding of medical training?
- Have you ever murdered your grandmother?

Sample questions taken from Kumar (1996: 119–21)

- Is anyone in your family a *dipsomaniac*?
- Is your work made more difficult because you are expecting a baby?
  Yes ☐   No ☐
- Are you satisfied with your canteen?
- How often and how much time do you spend on each visit to the child care centre?
- Does your department have a special recruitment policy for racial minorities and women?
- Unemployment is increasing, isn't it?
- Smoking is bad, isn't it?
- How many cigarettes do you smoke in a day?
- What contraceptives do you use?

Sample questions taken from Royse (1999: 183–90)

- Have you donated blood or gone to the dentist this month? Yes ☐ No ☐   Don't know ☐
- Don't you agree with the president that the federal government should not overspend? Agree ☐   Disagree ☐   Don't know ☐
- How many hours of television did you watch last year?
- Do you feel that Freud's structural hypothesis is an improvement over his topographic hypothesis?
- How do you black people feel about Jesse Jackson?
- Are you a religious fanatic?
- How many times in the past year have you seen a social worker?
- Are you always in bed by 11.00 p.m.?
- Marijuana should not be decriminalized.

Did you work out that *all* of these questions are other than ideal in one way or another? See the guidelines for constructing good questions taken from Marlow (2001), Royse (1999), Kumar (1996) and Graham (1994) summarized in Table 6.1 and note that, where appropriate, examples have been taken from the listings above to illustrate the points being made.

Questionnaires are often mailed to informants, although sometimes they are given to informants to complete in the presence of the researcher. However, unlike in interviews, the researcher would not directly intervene or engage with the informants as they complete the questionnaire. Researcher intervention would be seen as bias – that is, possibly influencing the responses that the informant may give (Bryman, 2001: 130–1). To facilitate the participants' engagement in the research, there should be a covering letter explaining the research, including addressing ethical issues such as informed consent and anonymity. Mailed questionnaires

Table 6.1   Guidelines for constructing questions (compiled by Marlow, 2001; Graham, 1994; Royse, 1999; and Kumar, 1996)

Guidelines for constructing questionnaires	Guidelines and examples of what not to do
Keep the questions short.	
Keep the questions clear and focused.	Do not use ambiguous questions. 'How healthy are you?' (Graham, 1994: 318) 'Has it happened to you that, over a long period of time when you neither practised abstinence nor used birth control, you did not conceive?' (Graham, 1994: 138) 'How many times in the past year have you seen a social worker?' (Royse, 1999: 189) 'Is your work made difficult because you are expecting a baby?' (Moser and Kalton, 1989: 323) 'Are you satisfied with your canteen?' (Moser and Kalton, 1989: 319) Avoid double-barrelled questions. 'How often and how much time do you spend on each visit?' (Kumar, 1996: 120) 'Does your department have a special recruitment policy for racial minorities and women?' (Bailey, 1978: 97) 'How often do your parents visit the doctor?' (Graham, 1994: 138) 'Have you donated blood or gone to the dentist this month?' (Royse, 1999: 183) 'Do you oppose or favour cutting health spending, even if cuts threaten the health of children and pensioners?' (Graham, 1994: 138)
First ascertain whether or not a respondent is a member of a group in which you are interested.	Do not ask questions that are based on presumptions about informants. 'How many cigarettes do you smoke in a day?' 'What contraceptives do you use?' (Moser and Kalton, 1989: 325)
Use questions that are sensitively phrased and appreciate and validate difference and diversity of experiences.	Avoid asking direct questions on sensitive issues. 'Have you ever murdered your grandmother?' (Graham, 1994: 138) Avoid insensitive, discriminatory or inflammatory language or 'loaded' terms. 'How do you black people feel about Jesse Jackson?' (Jesse Jackson is an African-American politician in the United States.) (Royse, 1999: 187). 'Are you a religious fanatic?' (Royse, 1999: 187)
Ask questions in a way that does not suggest to	Avoid leading questions. 'Do you oppose or favour cutting health spending, even if cuts

(Continued)

Table 6.1 Continued

Guidelines for constructing questionnaires	Guidelines and examples of what not to do
respondents the way in which they are being expected to respond.	threaten the health of children and pensioners?' (Graham, 1994: 138).
	'Don't you agree with the president that the federal government should not overspend?' (Royse, 1999: 184)
	'Unemployment is increasing, isn't it?' (Kumar, 1996: 120)
	'Smoking is bad, isn't it?' (Kumar, 1996: 120)
The respondents are able to answer the questions.	Avoid questions that assume the informants have the necessary background knowledge.
	'Do you agree or disagree with the government's policy on the funding of medical training?' (Graham, 1994: 137)
	'How many hours of television did you watch last year?' (Royse, 1999: 184)
The questions are focused on the present.	Avoid questions where information may be unavailable.
	'How many hours of television did you watch last year?' (Royse, 1999: 184)
Construct questions without the word 'not' in their structure.	Avoid questions with double negatives.
	'Do you agree or disagree with the following statement? "Abortions after 28 weeks should not be decriminalized".' (Graham, 1994: 138)
	'Marijuana should not be decriminalized.' (Royse, 1999: 190)
Use simple language with familiar words from everyday speech.	Avoid jargon or complicated language.
	'Are the health practices in your household run on matriarchal or patriarchal lines?' (Graham, 1994: 138)
	'Is anyone in your family a *dipsomaniac*?' (Kumar, 1996: 119)
	'Do you feel that Freud's structural hypothesis is an improvement over his topographic hypothesis?' (Royse, 1999: 186)

should include a stamped, addressed envelope for the return of the questionnaire. Because mailed questionnaires do not usually have a high return rate (Bryman, 2001: 131–2), the researcher should develop a way of following up with informants. It is usually a case of balancing awareness that some informants may have already returned their questionnaires and may not appreciate receiving reminders with the potential for identifying respondents of returned questionnaires because then assurances about their anonymity are questionable. (Unless you have some way of identifying the respondents to the questionnaires, how will you know who has or has not returned their questionnaires if you say you will send out reminder letters only to those who have not done so?) One way may be to tell informants your process for following up in the covering letter that is sent and repeating this in any follow-up letters (Bryman, 2001: 132–3).

Scales

Scales are ways in which to measure attitudes of informants and usually associated with quantitative approaches.

Likert scales   The most commonly used scale is the Likert scale (Marlow, 2001: 170–1; Royse, 1999; Kumar, 1996). A Likert scale is described as:

> a series of statements [given to a respondent who] is then asked to respond using one of five response alternatives, for example, 'strongly agree', 'agree', 'no opinion', 'disagree', 'strongly disagree', or some variant of these. (Marlow, 2001: 170)

You may well have come across examples of a Likert scale in your everyday experience – questionnaires regarding your satisfaction with a service, for example. For other examples of Likert scales, refer to Marlow (2001: 170–1), Bryman (2001: 134–6) and Royse (1999: 103–24, 236).

Developing your own Likert scale

Using the above examples as a guide, you may like to develop a few questions of your own that use Likert scales, in relation to:

- social work students' level of satisfaction with a research programme
- service users' level of agreement that a family support programme is meeting their needs
- an area of your choice.

What sorts of issues would you need to look at to be able to develop a thorough approach to the questions you ask? You may like to list these issues before you begin designing your questions.

Other scales   Marlow (2001: 170–6) identifies three other scales that are used in social work research, particularly practice evaluations. These are:

- target problem scales
- goal attainment scales
- rapid assessment instrument.

Target problem scales:

> are a means to track changes in a client's target behaviour. This type of scale is particularly useful when actual outcomes are difficult to identify. The scale involves identifying a problem, applying an intervention, and then repeatedly rating the extent to which the target problem has changed. (Marlow, 2001: 170)

Goal attainment scales:

> reflect the achievement of outcomes and are used both to set client goals and to assess whether goals have been met. Goal attainment scaling involves four steps:

1 identifying the problem
2 specifying the areas where change is desired
3 making specific predictions for a series of outcome levels for each area
4 by a set date, scoring the outcomes as they are achieved (five possible outcomes are designated, from least to most favourable). (Marlow, 2001: 173)

Rapid assessment instrument:

is a standardized series of structured questions or statements administered to the client to collect data in practice evaluations. Rapid assessment instruments are short, easy to administer, and easy to complete. The Multi-Problem Screening Inventory (MPSI) (Hudson, 1990) is an example. (Marlow, 2001: 174, 176)

Royse (1999: 175–99) and Kumar (1996: 127–35) give in-depth advice on designing scales. Additionally Royse (1999: 109–30) provides an excellent overview of the variety of scales that have been used in social work research, for example:

- community living skills scale
- children's motivation scale
- quality of life questionnaire
- job satisfaction scale
- rating scale for aggressive behaviour in the elderly
- adult children of alcoholics tool.

He includes an extensive reference list from which the scales have been taken as well as other resources that can assist researchers in developing their own research instruments.

In addition to the examples cited above, Renzetti's (1992) study on partner abuse in lesbian relationships is an excellent example of structured questionnaires and scales being used in an actual research study. She includes the research instruments she used in Appendix A of her book, *Violent Betrayal: Partner Abuse in Lesbian Relationships*. Renzetti's research instruments are a useful way of seeing different types of scales being used in practice. They also help you to see how you can use the same type of scale in one research instrument (questionnaire), but with different categories that name the dimensions of interest to the researcher.

Observation

Like other forms of data generation, observation may also differ in terms of the degree of structure there is and perspectives on the relationships between the researcher/observer and the researched/observed. Very structured forms of observation require the researcher to sit in a location where he or she can record particular items of interest as they occur according to a grid or scale, such as behaviour within a period of time. Examples are child development where children's behaviour and development may be observed according to particular frameworks to ascertain whether or not they are consistent with normal development (Rose, 1989: 132–50) or children's behaviour in a classroom (Marlow, 2001: 165). Bryman (2001: 165–7) cites other examples of structured observation, including 'observing jobs' (Jenkins et al., 1975), 'incidents' (LaPiere, 1934) and 'contrived observations' where researchers set up a scenario and observe what people do in response to it (Webb et al., 1966).

Participant observation is a less structured form of observation, where the 'participant' and the 'observer' roles of the researcher may shift depending on the context being observed and the particular situations and people within that context. The researcher may be a 'participant-as-observer', which may shift to 'observer-as-participant' and back again (Atkinson, 1990; Gold, 1958). The identities of the researcher as 'insider' or 'outsider' (Tuhiwai Smith, 1999: 5, 10, 137–41) become quite explicit and, in indigenous research, are crucial with regard to relationships of power and how this links with knowledge in research (Tuhiwai Smith, 1999). For example, if the researcher also happens to be a member of the indigenous community, there may be complicated expectations regarding what the researcher's role is, especially if there are personal relationships involved. It cannot be assumed that community members will automatically accept someone from their own community as a researcher. In fact, they may sometimes prefer someone who is *not* an indigenous person to be the researcher.

Bogdewic (1999) is an excellent source for explaining the nitty-gritty details of 'doing observation' as a method of enquiry – right down to whether to use paper and pencil, audio taping or other forms of recording. Note that you do not engage as a participant observer without some form of structure and focus, however loose. However, the data you generate as a participant observer may be emergent from the context, rather than fitted into categories that you as researcher have predetermined. We will look at some ways of analysing such data in the next chapter.

An excellent example of participant observation is Pithouse's (1987) study on social work and how it is organized and practised in child welfare offices run by local authorities in Britain. Pithouse (1987) sets out in the appendices of his book a detailed commentary on his methodology including the rationale, ethics and actual methods used (participant observation and interviews with key informants).

Unlike Marlow (2001: 165), we do not consider that observation somehow generates 'objective responses'. Instead, as with interviewing, our position is that observation is an active process where knowledge is negotiated and generated in the interaction between the researcher and the informant (Holstein and Gubrium, 1995; Humphries and Martin, 2000), so it is not a neutral process by which objective truths are discovered. Researchers who engage in participant observation are more likely to appreciate the importance of the relationship between the participant observer and informants and their positioning and subjectivities than those who observe only (Skeggs, 1994; Tuhiwai Smith, 1999). However, Bryman (2001) and Woolgar (1982) claim that some researchers do not make links between different ways of knowing, the status of the data they generate or the claims to truth that they make, such as when ethnographic studies are conducted and the data are treated as objective fact, rather than the outcome of interactions between the researcher as a positioned enquirer and the other informants at the site being observed.

Logs and journals

These forms of data collection can also vary according to the degree of structure that they have (Marlow, 2001: 168–70). Informants may be asked to keep diaries of patterns of behaviour, for example. Elliott (1997) used diaries as a method of enquiry regarding consumers' 'health experience'. The diary:

> offered a means to 'observe' behaviour which is inaccessible to participant observation. …
> Five key advantages [include] the potential of the 'diary-interview' method to accommodate
> different response modes; the extent to which the method captured diarists' own priorities; the
> importance of the research process in illuminating the contexts within which helpseeking took
> place; the role of the diaries as both a record of and reflection on the experience of illness and
> the value of the diary interview method as a means of understanding what is 'taken for granted'
> in accounts of health and illness. (Elliott, 1997: abstract)

Some journals and logs may require a relatively structured form of recording or a combination of levels of structure. For example, Marlow (2001: 168–9) gives an example of a social worker's diary and log that combines an unstructured record of a home visit to see a client and a structured entry that sets out a time-linked record of the client's drinking behaviour.

Stories, oral histories, biographies and autobiographies

Personal life stories are usually written as biographies and autobiographies (stories of people's lives either written by the researcher or the people themselves). Oral histories are another way of telling stories about 'the lives of ordinary people who have not in the past featured in established historical texts' (Clifford, 1994: 105). The importance of stories of various forms for groups who have been oppressed and marginalized is emphasized as a way of reclaiming knowledge about experiences that dominant groups have taken over or interpreted within prevalent ways of knowing. This is particularly important in the process of decolonizing methodologies to restore lost voices and knowledge about colonized societies and peoples (Tuhiwai Smith, 1999; Mies, 1993: 77–9; Jupp and Norris, 1993: 37–8).

Examples of oral histories, personal stories and autobiographies include:

- Rintoul's (1993) *The Wailing: A National Black Oral History* – about indigenous Australians' experiences of colonization
- Brown et al.'s (1994) *Missing Voices: The Experience of Motherhood* – mothers' experiences of pregnancy, birth and motherhood
- Lorde's (1982) *Zami: A New Spelling of my Name* – a political story of identity as an experience of social structure and inequality, including experiences of gender, race and sexuality for a black girl growing up in the United States
- Samuel's (2002) *German Boy: A Child in War* – a German boy's experience as a child living in Germany during World War II
- Verolme's (2000) *The Children's House of Belsen* – about Jewish children who lived in a special house in the concentration camp of Belsen during World War II and the Holocaust.

You may like to read some of these sources or find your own in the history, biography or autobiography sections of libraries and bookshops.

Secondary data

Data that have already been collected, analysed and presented by other people, such as researchers, case workers or policymakers, are known as secondary data. This means that you as researcher have not undertaken the processes of collection and analysis yourself. However, you as researcher can access and make use of such sources in your research. Examples of different secondary sources that are valuable data for social work research include documents such as case files or policy manuals or statistics such as social indicators, agency statistics or census data and even parliamentary debates found in *Hansard* (Marlow, 2001: 176–9; Royse, 1999: 200–25; Cockburn, 2000; Hakim, 1993).

For example, Saunders (2002) did a study that used statistics from the Australian Bureau of Statistics (ABS) and the Organization for Economic Cooperation and Development (OECD) to complement data obtained from his own survey of Australian people's 'attitudes to economic and social change and a range of related welfare issues' (Saunders, 2002: 16). In a chapter that asks, 'Has the economy delivered?' Saunders (2002) sets out comparisons between Australia and other countries on a range of measures and indicators in relation to economic performance drawn from these sources (Saunders, 2002: 26–8, 32–3, 35) and conducts his own analysis in relation to the questions he is addressing in the chapter.

Lupton and Najman (1995: 3–26) provide another example of research that draws on secondary data taken from the Australian Bureau of Statistics, the Commonwealth Department of Health, the Australian Institute of Health and Welfare, as well as other researchers' statistics (Walker, 1991; Steffenson and Coker, 1982). In their chapter analysing 'Sociology, health and health care', Lupton and Najman (1995) use these other data sources as well as data generated by their own research to develop an argument in relation to the sociology of health in Australia.

Similarly, Cockburn (2000) and Hakim (1993) show how agency statistics and documents such as case files and administrative records provide useful sources of data. Reynolds (2000b) has conducted a policy analysis on indigenous social welfare using legislation and organizational documents as secondary sources. We will look at how Reynolds has engaged with (analysed/presented) these documents in the next chapter on data analysis.

Multistrategy or multimethod research: combining data generation methods

Sometimes it is necessary to combine data generation strategies or methods for various reasons. Qualitative and quantitative strategies may be combined for methodological reasons because using only one approach or the other will not allow you to answer the research questions adequately (Mason, 1994, 1996; Bryman, 2001; Marlow, 2001; Kaufman Hall, 2001; Greene, 2002).

Mason (1996: 25) discusses the importance of thinking through the links between data and method at the planning and designing stage:

> you are quite likely to want to build up an analysis using data derived from different sources, and generated using different methods, although your main aim ... is unlikely to augment the reliability of your study. Instead, it may be because your research questions can be approached from a variety of angles or conceptualized in a variety of ways, suggesting a number of possibilities of method and source ... It may be because each research question suggests its own distinctive method and source. Or it may be because you want to use different methods and sources to corroborate each other so that you are using some form of methodological 'triangulation' ... Whatever the reason, you will need to think through the implications of using data from different sources, and integrating different methods, for your overall research design and for the strength, validity, generalizability and reliability of the argument you will wish to construct.

Bryman (2001: 447–54) discusses Hammersley's (1996) classification of approaches to multistrategy research. The first classification is *triangulation*, which is when quantitative research is used to corroborate qualitative research findings and vice versa (Bryman, 2001: 447). The second classification is *facilitation*, which involves one approach being used to aid the other approach. For example, qualitative research may precede a quantitative study by providing hypotheses to be explored further or enhance the design of interview questions (Bryman, 2001: 449–50). Quantitative research may also facilitate qualitative research – by identifying a selection of people to be interviewed in depth following a more structured survey and analysis, for example (Bryman, 2001: 450). The third classification is *complementarity*, which is when two research strategies are used to address different aspects of a study or research question. An example of this might be ethnographers using a structured questionnaire to complement the participant observation method they have used (Bryman, 2001: 450).

Marlow (2001: 180–1) gives an example of research by Dore and Doris (1997), who used 'multiple measures' to 'study a placement prevention programme designed to help substance-abusing mothers who had been reported for child maltreatment get treatment for their addiction'. Dore and Doris (1997) used the Beck Depression Inventory, the Adult–Adolescent Parenting Inventory, the Behaviour Checklist for Infants and Children, and the Denver Developmental Screening Test.

Additionally, it may be politically astute as well as 'democratically engaged' (Greene, 2002) to combine strategies if you know that powerful stakeholders, who need to be convinced about the importance of a social problem or issue, will not give credence to particular approaches. For example, Silverman (1998), Cockburn (2000) and Kaufman Hall (2001) comment that government bureaucrats frequently consider that quantitative data have more validity than qualitative data and therefore will not take as seriously research that is mainly or solely based on qualitative methods. You may recall that an example of this problem in the real world was looked at in Chapter 3 – the stories told by indigenous Australians representing the 'stolen generation' as part of the Human Rights and Equal Opportunity Commission's (1997) report have not been accepted as valid by the Australian government. These stories have been seen as anecdotal, biased and unrepresentative of the true dimensions of the problem and statistics are considered more acceptable.

Another real-world example is the emerging debate among feminist researchers about the value of quantitative studies (Truman, 1994; Jayaratne, 1993; Bryman, 2001). Early feminist researchers rejected quantitative studies as representative of the oppressive power of patriarchy that also was influenced by positivist assumptions. Qualitative research was seen to be a better approach in order to achieve solidarity among women as researchers and informants and as minimizing the worst aspects of power inequalities in research (Chandler, 1990; Oakley, 1981; Reinharz, 1992). However, as Truman (1994) and Jayaratne (1993) have pointed out, there are some aspects of women's lives that can only be researched using large-scale quantitative studies. So, is it possible to do feminist research *and* use quantitative approaches?

Regardless of the reasons for using multistrategy and multimethod approaches, it is important to be aware of the paradigm differences and assumptions informing qualitative and quantitative approaches. For example, Mason (1994) discusses her study involving both quantitative and qualitative approaches, setting out clearly how she has taken into account the paradigm differences and assumptions when conducting her analysis. We will look more closely at this aspect of multistrategy research in Chapter 7 on data analysis.

Having identified a range of possible ways of generating data and whether or not they will be quantitative or qualitative or both, we now turn to the practical and ethical issues surrounding data generation. No researcher can merely decide that he or she intends to generate data in this or that way, from this or that source. There are processes that must be followed. This is called negotiating, maintaining and terminating access.

Negotiating, maintaining and terminating access

All data, whether from primary or secondary sources, are located within particular organizational, legal and ethical contexts. This means that researchers must prove their case for why they want to access particular data and how they will do so. It is especially important that no harm is done to people who are key informants or archival, historical or private materials that have public or private significance. Therefore, researchers are usually required to submit proposals to ethics committees outlining their plans for accessing data and how they will protect their sources, people in particular. The processes for negotiating, maintaining and terminating access are both courteous and proper ways of establishing your research credibility.

Bell (1993: 58–9) gives an excellent overview for novice researchers as to why it is important to negotiate access and some very practical tips such as:

Clear official channels by formally requesting permission to carry out your investigation as soon as you have an agreed project outline.

> Speak to the people who will be asked to cooperate. ...

> Remember that people who agree to help are doing you a favour. ...

She (1993: 58–9) also mentions some possible pitfalls, such as:

> Getting the management's permission is one thing, but you need to have the support of the people who will be asked to give interviews or complete questionnaires. ...

> Even if you explain the purpose of the study and the conditions/guarantees verbally, participants may forget.

> If you say an interview will last ten minutes, you will break faith if it lasts an hour. If you are conducting the investigations as part of a degree or diploma course, say so. ...

While Bell focuses especially on insider research – that is, research done by someone who works for an organization – her guidelines are also useful for researchers whose research focus is outside their employing organization because issues of knowledge and positioning related to insider and outsider status need to be considered. Bell's (1993) guidelines are also useful for researchers who may work in one section of an organization – say, policy – but want to access informants who work in another section – as practitioners, for example.

Punch (1986) and Humphries and Martin (2000: 74–8) discuss research that avoided negotiating access that is normally associated with issues of informed consent, privacy and deception. The best-known examples are Milgram's (1963) 'study of obedience' (Humphries and Martin, 2000: 75) and Humphreys' (1970) 'study of men's sexual behaviour' (Humphries and Martin, 2000: 76). These researchers argued that it was necessary to deceive their informants in order to discover important knowledge that would otherwise be unknown. However, Punch (1986) and Humphries and Martin (2000) show how it is quite a complicated argument that can disguise and entrench the researcher's power in relation to informants.

Tuhiwai Smith (1999: 137–41) and Boulton (2000) add a political dimension to the issue of negotiating, maintaining and terminating access that is associated with the identities of researchers and informants. In particular the researcher's possible positioning as insider, outsider and sometimes both identities at different times in the process is not clear-cut. For example, Tuhiwai Smith (1999: 137–8) gives an excellent example of her shifting identities between insider and outsider in a 'language revitalization movement' in her local community that involved other Maori mothers like herself. The shifts in her own identity positions from insider to outsider and back again had consequences for her access to, and relationships with, the other women and their interactions with her. It is also interesting to note the mundane markers – for example, cars, the presentation of the home and children – that come to signify and distinguish identity in different ways.

> Through my different tribal relationships I had close links to some of the mothers and to the woman who was the main organizer. With other women I shared a background in another way as I had taught some of their older children at the local school. To my academic supervisor I

was well and truly an insider in this project. When I began the discussions and negotiations over my research, however, I became much more aware of the things that made me an outsider. I was attending university as a graduate student; I had worked for several years as a teacher and had a professional income; I had a husband; and we owned a car which was second-hand but actually registered. ... What really struck me when I visited the women in their homes as a researcher, having done so on previous occasions as a mother, were the formal cultural practices which the women observed. An interview with a researcher is formal. I could see immediately that homes were extra spotless and I knew from my own background that when visitors are expected considerable energy goes into cleaning and dusting the house. There was also food which I knew had been prepared for my visit. The children were in their pyjamas (the top matching the bottom) all bathed and ready for bed at 7.30 p.m. ... on the night of the interview everything was in the kind of order which is organized solely for the benefit of the outsider. ... After the project was completed and I had reported back to them on the finished piece of work, our former relations were restored and have continued ... (Tuhiwai Smith, 1999: 138)

Boulton (2000: 89–91) discusses the idea of the 'insider–outsider continuum' as an example of access to knowledge that may shift and that the outsider has to learn and negotiate with insiders:

> The mutual recognition of the researcher's outsider status by both researcher and respondent can be seen to mark a boundary between their worlds. The extent to which such boundaries become barriers to understanding must be considered.

For researchers who are already insiders, 'there is no boundary to cross' (Boulton, 2000: 90). Citing research about a pool hall by Sanders (1973), who participated as an insider and became part of everyday interactions, Boulton (2000: 90–1) notes that there are few distinctions between interviewing and normal conversations: 'The danger here was that those ordinary, routine, everyday things which are essential to an understanding of the world being researched would remain unnoticed.' That is, if you as a researcher are an insider, you need to be able to treat what you take for granted as normal in your everyday interactions as data in research. Thus, you may become an outsider to some extent by asking critical questions about what you know or think you know and why and how you know these things in that context.

The next section extends this discussion of the relationship between insiders and outsiders and access to information, sources and knowledge by looking at how data generation processes are relationships of power rather than techniques that you use to collect data and find truth.

Data generation processes as relationships of power

A participatory approach by the 'research-minded practitioner' (Everitt et al., 1992) makes explicit that power is fundamental in the research relationship. An anti-oppressive value base recognizes the potentially unequal relationship associated with the formal authority of the researcher in relation to informants. Additionally, we have discussed above the potential for research as a process and its outcomes to subjugate and oppress less powerful peoples, most explicitly seen in places where colonization has disadvantaged indigenous peoples and the experiences of groups usually disadvantaged or marginalized in a society.

Social workers who value participatory and emancipatory research for its value in addressing injustice and inequality would work from an ethical position of 'rights, reciprocity, empowerment and anti-oppression' (Everitt et al., 1992: 85). Some ethical considerations intersect with methodological questions. For example, Everitt et al. (1992: 86) ask:

> How far will revealing the research approach to practice affect that practice (Shipman, 1988)? Will other participants in the process respond to the increased attention, thus creating a 'Hawthorne effect'? …
>
> Do all participants have equal rights to be informed about the research-minded process? … participation has to be understood in the context of power relations. … there may well be situations in which research-minded practitioners wish to reflect critically on the practices of those more powerful than themselves. … Research-minded practitioners, critically reflecting on the practice of social welfare, may well be less powerful, both in themselves and in their emancipatory ideas, in organizations and contexts which are fundamentally sexist, heterosexist and racist. …

Additionally, power and ethics are interconnected in the data generation process. Ethics are situated in the context of the research and include considerations as to the appropriateness and practicality of 'taking account of all perspectives' (Everitt et al., 1992: 87). Dialogue between stakeholders/research participants is essential to discuss differences and shared perspectives (Greene, 2002; Everitt et al., 1992: 87):

> If a 'community of inquirers' exists, differences in perspectives can be discussed and understood. Differences may be ironed out. They may be reflected upon and new understandings reached. The texture of the account will be all the richer if different perspectives are included and theorized. (Everitt et al., 1992: 87–8)

Greene (2002) comments that:

> Respecting diverse standpoints requires dialogue with other people, listening to their stories, and relating to their uniqueness without collapsing these divergent views into a generalized amalgam (Coulter and Wiens 2002, p. 8) without essentializing them, and without losing your own unique standpoint:
>
>> Visiting is therefore not to see through the eyes of someone else, but to see with your own eyes from a position that is not your own … in story very different from [your] own. (Biesta 2001, p. 398)

An awareness of the 'partiality' of knowledge (Humphries and Martin, 2000: 79; Everitt et al., 1992: 88) and reciprocity creates a collaborative and power-sharing relationship in knowledge generation between the researcher and informants (Everitt et al., 1992: 88).

However, there are alternative views about what is considered to be a simplistic understanding of the relationship between the apparently more powerful researcher and the less powerful researched and the encouragement to use collaborative approaches to share and equalize power. Writers who acknowledge that researchers can and do exercise power in relation to research questions, processes of enquiry and outcomes for informants, also argue that informants and gatekeepers exercise their own versions of power (Delaney, 1988; Van Maanen, 1988; Skeggs, 1994; Barn, 1994; Scanlon, 1993; Byrne-Armstrong, 2001; D'Cruz, 2000). Informants and gatekeepers may exercise power in a variety of ways, including limiting access to key people, documents or places, refusing to participate or withholding information that is sought by the researcher. Equally, in some cases, it may not be possible to negotiate, maintain and terminate access in a formal way that implies there are clearly identifiable informants all the time who can give consent to the research and the researcher's access to the information about the informants' contexts. Punch (1986), for example, discusses the politics and ethics of fieldwork in relation to criminal justice systems, drawing on his extensive research experience, primarily as a participant observer. (The word 'fieldwork' in Punch's vocabulary and also more generally in research texts refers to participant observation for ethnographic and anthropological studies. It does not refer to fieldwork as social workers in some contexts use it to mean working with clients.) As an example of the problem of access, Punch asks when and how a researcher in a fieldwork situation should signal her or his intention to document an incident involving many people who are often unidentifiable, say, when observing police conduct in relation to a crowd at a large public protest. The normal expectations that individuals involved in research should give informed consent are not particularly meaningful in such research.

Categorizing people – identity, diversity and positioning

It is usual in most research for informants to be asked to indicate details about themselves by means of tick boxes, scales or one-word answers. The form of such questions that occur at the start or end of the interview or questionnaire cover aspects such as sex (female or male), gender (man or woman), age (group or specified), ethnicity, religion, disability, marital status and so on. Such questions about each informant's identity may then appear later as descriptions of the research participants, separated from what are set out as the main questions about the research topic. In other words, informants are not asked how their experiences of being whatever they are relates to the topic under consideration – for example, poverty or being put in jail.

Truman and Humphries (1994: 3) use the example of racism and cite Graham (1993: 32) who says:

most typologies do not invite people to record their experiences of racism, but to define themselves in terms of physical and cultural attributes … 'race' typologies typically combine a complex of dimensions [political boundaries, geographical definitions and colour] into a single scale.

In general, research approaches that use the 'categorizing people' method tend to silence rather than facilitate the voices of those who are marginalized or disadvantaged. The categories are fixed and usually derived for bureaucratic purposes rather than necessarily representing the *meaning* of identity for individuals and groups and their lived experiences in relation to identity. The categories treat all individuals categorized in particular ways as exactly the same, stereotyping them. For example, if it is assumed that all 'Indian' people in hospital would like particular food rather than them being asked about how their religious and regional backgrounds may influence food habits (Ahmad and Sheldon, 1993). The categories do not necessarily allow people to belong to multiple identity categories, which is the case with the example given above regarding 'race'. Furthermore, the categories that claim to represent particular groups may be used to treat those groups as problems or deviant in some way and the research that is undertaken may reinforce these perceptions – using ethnicity or race profiling to identify criminals, for example. Perhaps most disturbing is the potential for categories that are used thoughtlessly in social research to be taken over by people with more repressive agendas, such as racist or anti-women groups.

Awareness by social workers as researchers of the politics and ethics of categorizing people is essential when framing research questions to ensure that they are participatory and can achieve emancipatory objectives. Notice the differences between the questions in the two columns in Table 6.2.

The next section looks at how a theory of power can help in formulating research that is emancipatory in practice as well as intent.

A participatory approach to generating data: research and empowerment

Humphries (1994: 185–204) discusses 'elements for an analytic framework' by means of an 'empowerment' approach to social research. She points out that a claiming that research is emancipatory does not necessarily mean that it is and, instead, may be used as a way of subverting empowerment and emancipatory objectives.

Humphries (1994) develops her empowerment approach to research by synthesizing structural and postmodern and poststructural theories of power – for example, Foucault (1978, 1980) and Sawicki (1991). This integrated approach to power in research is summarized in Table 6.3.

Humphries (1994: 187) sees the two apparently opposed perspectives of power as complementary and providing a more complicated understanding of

Table 6.2 **Categorizing people and research perspectives**

Categorizing people	Critique-based alternatives – using categories in a non-discriminatory way
As deviant	
'Why do battered women stay with partners who abuse them?' (Renzetti and Lee, 1993: 28)	'What factors make battering possible or even permissible?' (Renzetti and Lee, 1993: 28)
By excluding or misrepresenting groups	
The General Household Survey in the UK that asks informants to classify their personal relationships in the context of the household in which they live using categories that refer to legal definitions of marriage: 'married', 'cohabiting', 'single', 'widowed', 'divorced' or 'separated' (Truman and Humphries, 1994: 5–6)	'How useful is the legal definition of marriage in understanding personal relationships?' (Truman and Humphries, 1994)
By keeping invisible what is considered to be the normal identity category, such as looking at lesbianism	Explicitly conceptualize and explore heterosexuality (Truman and Humphries, 1994: 10)
'What is lesbianism and why is it so common? How does lesbianism affect the whole of a woman's life?' (Truman and Humphries, 1994: 10, based on Kitzinger and Wilkinson, 1993)	'What is heterosexuality and why is it so common? How does heterosexuality affect the whole of a woman's life?' (Kitzinger and Wilkinson, 1993)
As a problem group	
'Why are there so many black children [in Britain] in foster care?' (Barn, 1994)	'What are the processes that involved the entry of black children into care?' (Barn, 1994)
Stereotyping	
'Why are black people more vulnerable to schizophrenia than white people?' (Truman and Humphries, 1994: 16)	'What are the social processes which lead to a disproportionate number of black people being diagnosed as schizophrenic?' (Truman and Humphries, 1994: 16)

power as both macro-level domination and existing in everyday micro-level relationships between people:

> In terms of empowerment we have presented to us dimensions of power which (i) allow that, potentially, dominated groups may have access to power, (ii) emphasize its productive rather than negative potential and (iii) demand that resistance is carried out in local struggles against the many forms of power exercised at the everyday level of social relations.
>
> This view of power can result in a clearer understanding of for example power relations inherent in the researcher–researched relationship, and reveals not a simple hierarchical loading based on socially ascribed characteristics, but complex multifaceted power relations that have both structural dominance and structural subordination play *on both sides*. (Original emphasis)

Table 6.3   An empowerment approach to research (Humphries, 1994: 186)

Postmodern and poststructural approaches to power	Structural approaches to power
Power is exercised rather than possessed	Power is only possessed or owned by certain individuals or groups
Power is not primarily repressive, but productive	Power is oppressive and repressive
Power is analysed as coming from the bottom up	Power is imposed from above by more powerful onto less powerful individuals and groups

Humphries' (1994: 190–1) 'framework for empowering research methodologies' draws on Said's (1978) work on colonialism and knowledge. She shows how research approaches that claim to be empowering may, in fact, be the opposite. The three concepts taken from Said (1978) are 'accommodation, accumulation and appropriation' (Humphries, 1994: 191).

Accommodation refers to research practices that conform with, and do not challenge, ideas that represent dominant ways of knowing that may be experienced by marginal groups as oppressive. The researcher then engages in 'reconstruction' or 'repetition' (Said, 1978, in Humphries, 1994: 191) of structures that maintain the dominant perspective and that claim to understand and explain all experiences within that perspective (Humphries, 1994: 191).

Accumulation – a concept also borrowed from Said (1978) – refers to a form of colonialism and imperialism in which materials from 'the Orient' or 'the East' (read as marginal or disadvantaged groups) are acquired, organized and disseminated as specialized knowledge by researchers external to those cultures or groups: 'It is a way of controlling what seems to be a threat to some established view of things' (Said, 1978: 59). The communication about the lives of oppressed groups in specialized language 'results in surveillance and regulation rather than "empowerment"' (Humphries, 1994: 198).

Appropriation of power is 'the purpose and effect of ... *accommodation* and *accumulation* ...' (Humphries, 1994: 200, original emphasis). Appropriation means that there is the potential for researchers to act as colonizers and oppressors. This is particularly the case if researchers from dominant groups conduct research on or about marginalized groups, such as indigenous peoples, poor people, women. There is significant potential for marginalized groups' experiences to be conceptualized, analysed and explained using the dominant groups' theoretical and value frameworks (Tuhiwai Smith, 1999). Hence, marginal groups' experiences, knowledge and voices become contained and codified as scholarship and knowledge and are then the property of the dominant group. Marginal groups become objectified as 'the Other', as objects of research and part of a particular ideological position and relationship to dominant groups.

It cannot be emphasized enough that social workers need to develop a theory of power because, without such an understanding, all social work approaches to social problems, including those made via research, become part of the problem rather than contributing to solutions. As Humphries (1994: 203) comments:

> Where discussions of empowerment are not grounded in a theory of power and in the wider nexus of political, economic and social power relationships, too easily concerns about social justice can be incorporated into existing beliefs and ideologies. The beneficiaries are more likely to be the research professionals than the research subjects.

Putting it all together

In this chapter we have looked at how to generate data (as methods). We have also looked at how researchers can use the same methods, but that the level of structure designed into the enquiry process influences whether the data produced will be quantitative, qualitative or both. We have also looked at both primary and secondary data sources.

However, we have also extended the understanding of data generation beyond methods to a focus on the politics and ethics of knowledge. We have looked at the importance of negotiating, maintaining and terminating access to data sources. We have explored the necessity for researchers to be aware of their duty of care to informants, to protect their rights to privacy and safety. We have extended this ethical requirement for research to an understanding that the research relationship is also a political one. Regardless of how a researcher may seek to conduct proper, ethical research, the process of enquiry and its outcome as knowledge is always embedded in power relationships between the researcher and the researched.

SEVEN   Making sense of data: analysis

Introduction

After data have been generated using one or more of the methods discussed in Chapter 6, you must analyse them. This means that data must be organized so that you can make sense of the information because, whatever methods you have used to generate them, the data will not be in a form that readily answers your research question.

For example, you may have decided to send questionnaires to 100 individuals and read (review) 20 case files as your primary methods of enquiry. Each respondent, or source – for example, a single person from a sample of 100, a single case file from a sample of 20 – will give you data from one case (source). This means that the single case will cover all the questions or themes you have sought to explore in your questionnaire or documentary review. However, it is only when you have received responses from every one of the people selected for your sample or collated the material from every file chosen that you have a full data set, which must then be analysed.

What is data analysis? Why is it necessary?

After you have completed the data generation process, the data you will have are still only a collection of information about single cases, whether it is each of the 100 individuals who has completed your questionnaire or each of the 20 case files you have read. To be able to answer your research question, you first must be able to find the *patterns* connecting cases – similarities, differences, negative cases – in the total sample. You should then be able to draw appropriate conclusions related to the literature and how your research has contributed to knowledge about the topic that you explored in your literature review. Your analysis must consider how the patterns in the data relate to the literature. In other words, what contribution to existing knowledge has your research made? Does it replicate and support the literature? Does it extend the literature? Does it identify gaps and/or challenge claims in the literature? During the process of analysis, the researcher should become familiar with the data, yet also behave as if she or he were a stranger viewing it (Everitt et al., 1992: 105). This process of 'making the familiar strange' (Everitt et al., 1992: 105) is essential in challenging what might otherwise be taken for granted, thus missing opportunities for new insights and social change.

The main forms of data that you will have are numbers (quantitative), text (words or images, which are qualitative) as transcripts, case files, field notes or diaries, or a combination of the two. There are different ways of making sense of the data you have generated depending on their form (numbers or words/ images) and how they help answer the research question.

Before looking at different methods of analysis, we will briefly consider triangulation as data complementarity, not data consistency or replication. You may recall that triangulation was discussed in Chapters 4 and 6 as a way of addressing trustworthiness, especially in naturalistic research (Guba and Lincoln, 1982; Bryman, 2001; Mason, 1996), and as ways of encouraging different ways of knowing and enhancing the political influence of the research (Greene, 2002).

Triangulation as complementary data sets

If you used more than one method of data collection, usually recommended as a triangulation strategy, you will have different data sets. Each data set will correspond with its particular method of enquiry. For example, if you were to research a question about patterns of juvenile offending and the social work response, these are some of the data collection methods you might use. Table 7.1 links the methods with their data sets.

The different data sets are not meant as a cross-check for the consistency across data sets because each set has been derived from a different source, using a different method. Therefore, each set has to be judged for trustworthiness within its own assumptions, including the different criteria for trustworthiness that we looked at in Chapter 4.

Next, try the following exercise about problem solving in research.

Table 7.1 Linking data generation methods and data sets

Data generation methods	Data sets
Agency statistics on juvenile offending patterns over six months (secondary data)	Statistics
Files of a sample of cases selected from those recorded statistically	Selected text about the cases as recorded by the agency workers
Semi-structured interviews with social work practitioners about the cases	Transcripts and/or handwritten notes that correspond to the questions asked in the interviews

---

Problem solving in research – linking paradigms, methods and criteria for trustworthiness

Now that we have come this far in this book, use a problem-solving approach to consider what it means to judge each data set within its own assumptions and criteria for trustworthiness (refer to Chapters 3 and 4 to help you with this exercise). What are different assumptions that apply to statistical collections, semi-structured interviews and case files in terms of how reality is understood and explained?

Have you concluded that you cannot use the different data sets as checks on each other because:

- a statistical collection relies on an understanding of a reality that is measurable and objective
- case files only record what is relevant for an organization and it is usually someone's recorded version of events within organizational requirements
- interviews about files and practices are another version/ reinterpretation of what is on file?

The second and third points are more likely to be based on an interpretive paradigm. Can you see how this might be so? How might these three data sets complement each other in answering the research question?

The main point of the above discussion and exercise is to emphasize that you can strengthen your research methodology by using triangulation strategies. Each data set can be used to complement the others and uncover new or different information (Marlow, 2001: 221–2; Mason, 1994, 1996; Bryman, 1988: 131–3; 2001). For example, Bryman (1988: 131–3) cites several studies (Lacey, 1970, 1976; Cook, 1984) where triangulation of methods allowed the researcher to confirm the patterns in the research. In another example (Galton and Delamont, 1985), ethnographic data enhanced that generated by a quantitative method. Finally, Shapiro (1973), Huberman and Crandall (1982) and Trend (1978) found that data generated by different methods were contradictory and prompted them to explore these patterns, thus making new discoveries and directions for research.

However, in analysing data generated by triangulation, you cannot and must not use one set of data to validate (as a check on) the other sets. For example, you cannot decide that the statistics are true because somehow they are more objective and use them to judge the truth of the information you get from the case files and what the workers tell you. Neither should you decide that what the workers tell you is somehow better than the statistical information. The fundamental issue here is that it is not appropriate to select one data set as the correct version and standard by which to judge other data sets because, to use a familiar cliché, it would be like comparing apples with oranges. It would be quite silly to decide that oranges are not good-quality fruit because they don't have shiny red skins and a crunchy texture! However, you can compare the quality of different oranges using appropriate criteria that are applicable to oranges. In the same way, you can judge the validity of each data set according to relevant criteria that apply separately to statistics, documents and interviews.

Mason (1994: 89–110) draws on an example of her own research on family obligations and responsibilities between adult kin to discuss how multiple data sets were linked in analysis taking into account the paradigm differences associated with each set. Mason (1994: 90–1) says that:

> The first stage was a large-scale interview survey (978 respondents), using a statistically representative sample of the population of Greater Manchester [UK], achieved through random cluster sampling. In the survey, respondents were asked questions about what they thought people should do for their relatives in a variety of hypothetical circumstances. We used the vignette technique, where respondents are given imaginary people in imaginary situations and asked to decide what those people should do …
>
> Our aim in this part of the study was to discover whether, and to what extent, there was a consensus in the general population about 'the proper thing to do' for relatives in a variety of given circumstances. Our focus was on public statements and general levels of agreement. We did not try to get at what people actually did for their own relatives nor how they felt about them in this part of the study.
>
> The second stage of the project involved a more qualitative study, where we conducted 120 in-depth, semi-structured, tape-recorded interviews with 88 people. … In this part of the study we *were* trying to discover what people actually did in practice for their own relatives, and also the processes by which they came to do it and make sense of it: did a sense of obligation or responsibility have a role in the process? How did people in practice work out what to do for their kin, or ask of their kin? …
>
> From the beginning, then, we were using the two parts of our study to ask distinct sets of questions about family obligations. Not only were we employing different methods to generate different types of data, but we anticipated that these would tell us about different aspects of family obligations. … Our view was that an understanding of kin obligatedness *in practice* would require an analysis of the relationship between the two data sets and the social processes they expressed. (Original emphasis)

Mason (1994: 99–107) discusses how different data sources may be linked to be able to conduct a sound analysis and enhance the validity of the study, but *not* as a triangulation (validity checking) strategy. She (1994: 99) suggests three sets of questions that the researcher should consider in undertaking this process:

1 Data on what? *What* do these data tell me about and, crucially, what can they *not* tell me about?
2 Strength of claim. *How well* do these data tell me this? How convincing are claims I want to make on the basis of the data? How can I make the strongest claims possible, without pushing the data 'too far' by making claims which are beyond their capacity?

3   Integration of data. How best can I integrate and make sense of different forms of qualitative data? How can I integrate quantitative and qualitative material? The answer to this must take full account of, and be consistent with, the researcher's answers to (1) and (2). (Original emphasis)

Data analysis: patterns and meanings in data

Data analysis is a process of making sense of the responses you have received as a result of using various methods of data generation. By means of analysis, researchers aim to generate patterns and processes, develop meanings and try to understand and explain contradictions and multiple versions of meaning generated by participants (Everitt et al., 1992: 105). However, depending on the paradigm, you may see the analysis as generating truth or as a partial version – that is, yours as the researcher – or as a tentative approximation (Glaser and Straus, 1967, in Everitt et al., 1992: 105).

Although we are presenting data analysis as if it comes after data generation in a sort of linear progression, we recommend that, in practice, data generation and analysis are developed together in the design/methodology that is informed by the research question(s). Therefore, the following questions that Everitt et al. (1992: 102) pose with regard to data analysis are equally relevant when you are planning your research.

- Is it the most meaningful way to understand or present issues? Does this way of understanding and presenting data shed light on its meaning?
- Whose interests are served by the research approach?

During the data analysis process, the ethical and political considerations relating to different ways of knowing become apparent as you seek to make sense of the data. In particular, there is the issue of different perspectives given by different informants – for example, service users compared with service providers, funding bodies, policymakers or politicians. If you are working in the recommended participatory or emancipatory way (Everitt et al., 1992), this should not be confined to how you involve different informants in the data generation process. It is an equally important consideration during data analysis because this is when your own research has to meet criteria for trustworthiness. These criteria include methodological rigour and ethical and political considerations, which are interlinked. Methodological rigour and ethical and political issues in relation to how you have generated data have been discussed in Chapter 6.

With data analysis, you need to make sure that you approach the process of understanding emerging patterns in the data in a technically sound way. In keeping with a participatory approach to research, it is also recommended that informants are involved in data analysis rather than it being solely the role of the researcher (Everitt et al., 1992; Humphries, 1994). However, you also need to be aware of the consequences of how different stakeholders may interpret the patterns and conclusions that are drawn and the actions that may flow from different people's interpretations of the conclusions. This is especially important if you consider that different interpretations of research related to stakeholders' positioning and subjectivity may be linked to differences in power between stakeholders. Therefore, even one stakeholder may have a significant influence on how research is interpreted if there is considerable power related to that one position. In Chapter 3, we looked at some examples of such differences between stakeholders in relation to some publicly controversial issues that included research and social work practice.

Working with people – negotiating knowledge and meaning

It is an excellent ideal that social work researchers involve key informants, especially people who are normally silenced in relation to the development and effects of social policies, such as service users and sometimes even service providers. However, the real world is not that simple. You are more likely to find that there are different meanings and versions of truth within groups (for example, service users) and between groups (for example, between service users and policymakers; Everitt et al., 1992: 106–7).

Some researchers who advocate a participatory approach to research suggest that the meaning of the data should be negotiated (Everitt et al., 1992: 106–7). However, the difficult question is whose view is closest to reality (Everitt et al., 1992: 107)?

One approach that is offered is for the researcher to acknowledge that there is no one truth, that there are different sides and we cannot avoid taking sides, so must say whose side we are on (Becker, 1970, cited in Everitt et al., 1992: 107). This approach allows the researcher to make his or her positioning and subjectivity explicit as an ethical practice so that there can be no pretence that there is neutrality and value-free research (and knowledge). Of course, it is probably most beneficial to be aware of one's positioning at the start of the research and keep engaging in a reflective (Fook, 1996) and reflexive (Riessman, 1994a) way throughout the research process. (You may recall that use of a journal or diary to record such thoughts was recommended in Chapter 4 in relation to doing trustworthy research.)

A common strategy that is used by stakeholders who disagree with research conclusions is to accuse the researcher of bias. This is most usual when the research conclusions support the view of marginalized people (Becker, 1970). As a result of a 'hierarchy of credibility' (Becker, 1970), those at the top of an organization or other social structure are seen to have the full truth, while others lower down have only a partial appreciation of truth or none at all (Everitt et al., 1992: 107–8). Thus, the researcher is accused of bias when she or he challenges the hierarchy of credibility, but this rarely occurs the other way round. Telling the truth, as it is understood by marginalized and less powerful groups, challenges vested interests, especially when public officials try to maintain a belief that things are as they are represented to be (Everitt et al., 1992: 108).

However, it is simplistic to take the view that the only truth lies with subordinate groups because such a position denies the possibility of multiple truths and meanings. Hence, while it might be ethical for social workers to represent the position of client groups to redress imbalances of power relating to being heard, this does not mean that people in more powerful positions do not have valid views or are not entitled to them. Instead, the test for social work research is how to design, analyse and present conclusions from research that can address ethical commitments to disadvantaged groups while also addressing the political dimension (the ability to convince powerful stakeholders). A political approach may include judicious selection of data generation strategies as well as ways of getting the message across in the analysis and report. However, there is no guarantee that even these strategies will influence powerful interests and, therefore, additional strategies may include community work, advocacy and lobbying for change based on the research. Examples include the social capital projects by the Community Service and Research Centre University of Queensland (Australia), Kaufman Hall (2001) and Griggs v Duke Power Co. (1971).

In the next section, we explore the importance of organizing data as a step before analysis.

Data organization

There are differences in how quantitative and qualitative data are organized before you can conduct the analysis. While there are procedural differences, the most obvious difference is in the relationship between data organization and data generation. Quantitative data are usually generated first, followed by organization and then analysis – often by computer because of the large amount of data. Qualitative data generation, organization and analysis, however, are usually interlinked. For example, a researcher who is conducting a semi-structured, in-depth interview may ask additional questions that emerge due to the researcher's positioning in relation to the study. These additional questions are a form of immediate analysis in the context of the active interview (Holstein and Gubrium, 1995), so data generation and data analysis are closely linked. Furthermore, when the researcher engages with qualitative data following the data generation process, there is another layer in which how the researcher engages with the data becomes part of the analysis and must be made explicit.

This overview of the differences in the research process between quantitative and qualitative data will be explored in more detail below.

Organizing quantitative data

Usually quantitative studies involve responses from a large number of informants, which is necessary if valid statistical analyses are to be conducted. The data may be of different types on the same questionnaire or survey, but they must be organized to make them ready for statistical analysis, usually by computer.

Quantitative data are generated in formats that allow different types of statistical analysis. These different formats are known as *levels of measurement*, indicating how often something occurs and/or the strength and direction of change and/or the relative differences between events or people. These different levels of measurement generate different kinds of data – nominal or categorical, ordinal, interval and ratio. There are excellent definitions and examples in various research texts of these different data types, such as Bryman (2001: 217–22), Marlow (2001: 57–9), Kumar (1996: 58–62), Royse (1999) and Babbie (1999).

The different levels of measurement have a particular relationship to the statistical analysis that can be done. *Categorical/nominal variables* can be summarized using frequency counts, which means how often (frequently) the category appears. Bryman (2001: 218–22) differentiates between *dichotomous variables* and *categorical/nominal variables*. Dichotomous variables have only two responses to choose from. Here are some examples of categorical/nominal and dichotomous variables.

- **Categorical/nominal variables**

  Sample question (Bryman, 2001: 218):

  Which of the following best describes your *main* reason for going to the gym? (Please tick one only.)
  Relaxation ☐ 1
  Maintain or improve fitness ☐ 2
  Lose weight ☐ 3
  Meet others ☐ 4
  Build strength ☐ 5
  Other (please specify) ☐ 6

- **Dichotomous variables**

  Sample question (Bryman, 2001: 218):

  Do you have sources of regular exercise other than the gym?
  Yes ☐ No ☐

  Additional examples:

  Gender: (woman, man)
  Sex: (female, male)

Summarizing categorical data using frequency counts produces a description according to the selected variables and how these variables are distributed numerically as absolute frequencies (actual numbers) and relative frequencies (percentages, as a proportion of the total). However, the categories have no mathematical significance or relationship to each other. They are socially derived descriptions only that, as Marlow (2001: 58) points out, can only indicate yes or no responses. So, for example, the sex or ethnicity of respondents are nominal variables. You would only be able to represent them numerically as a frequency count of how many of your respondents were male or female and their ethnicity. You may recall that in Chapter 6 we discussed Truman and Humphries' (1994) criticism that the above approach to descriptive data is too restrictive of people's actual identities and experiences. Truman and Humphries (1994) gave the example of how categories of ethnicity may be too limiting. Also, consider how transgendered or transexual people would be represented with only a choice of woman or man, male or female. Instead of the simple statistical description that is usually produced, Truman and Humphries (1994) recommend that direct links should be made between the descriptive categories and respondents' experiences that are being explored in the research.

As you proceed through the levels of measurement, they become increasingly associated with mathematical relationships and can be analysed using more sophisticated statistics. Therefore, items of *ordinal data* have a relationship to each other as a logical sequence in how they are rank ordered. Categories may range from low to high or vice versa. However, the distances or differences between each category are arbitrary as there is no mathematical relationship between them. Below are some examples of ordinal variables.

- **Ordinal variables**

  Sample question (Bryman, 2001: 218):

  How frequently do you usually go to the gym? (Please tick.)
Every day	☐	1
4–6 days a week	☐	2
2 or 3 days a week	☐	3
Once a week	☐	4
2 or 3 times a month	☐	5
Once a month	☐	6
Less than once a month	☐	7

Additional examples include attitude or opinion surveys using Likert scales, asking, for example, if you strongly agree, agree, disagree, strongly disagree (Kumar, 1996: 61).

Items of interval data have a relationship to each other and must be set in rank order for logical reasons. They have regular (or equal) intervals or differences between one point and the next, so it is possible to generate mathematical relationships between categories. Some examples are given below.

- **Interval data**

  Sample question (Bryman, 2001: 219):

  During your last visit to the gym, how many minutes did you spend on the weights machines (including free weights)?

_____ minutes [the possible difference between the number of minutes indicated by one respondent and another is one minute].

Additional examples include: IQ, temperature and attitudinal scales, such as the Thurstone scale (Kumar, 1996: 61).

Finally there are items of *ratio data*. These are in rank order, have a fixed zero starting point, a relationship with each other as regular intervals between points and there is an actual meaning given to the value of the data. Ratio variables are sometimes seen as being similar to interval variables (Bryman, 2001: 219, 222; Royse, 1999: 235) because the differences between responses are equal. However, other writers see ratio variables as different because of the fixed zero point (Kumar, 1996: 62). Here are some examples of ratio variables.

- **Ratio data**

  Sample question (Bryman, 2001: 218):

  How old are you?
  _____ years [the possible difference between each respondent's age is one year].

Additional examples include age in years/months, income, number of children, height and grades.

Data organization procedures for quantitative data

Coding is an important procedure. When organizing quantitative data, this means that data taken from a survey or questionnaire must be in a form that allows for mathematical calculations to be done. Usually data from large quantitative studies are entered into computer databases so that it is easier and quicker to generate simple descriptive patterns, such as frequencies, and more complicated patterns that require statistical analyses as tests of significance.

Thus, all data that require statistical analysis must be reduced to a simple code. Researchers who have asked semi-structured questions to enhance structured questions and wish to conduct statistical tests of significance must translate the open-ended responses into categories or themes that can then be coded. This is because you cannot enter the full text from open-ended responses and then conduct statistical analysis as it is not in the right form to do so.

Royse (1999: 229) gives an example of coding responses to the open-ended question 'Why did you quit school?' The various responses were grouped into categories or themes that the researcher derived, such as 'financial reasons' or 'uninterest' that were then given number codes of 1 and 2 respectively. Often, the codes are numbers that represent different responses that have been selected by respondents – as with the numbers alongside the tick boxes in the sample questions earlier in the chapter. The respondent circles the response and its corresponding code number is later entered into the computer by the researcher. This can make data organization and entry quite easy. Sometimes, codes can be letters (known as 'string' variables) that represent a particular response. Thus, for example, you may use 'M' and 'F' to represent the sex of respondents, but it is simpler to use numerical codes. Kumar (1996: 199–224) and Bryman (2001: 239–59) give excellent introductions to data coding and entry into computers so that statistical software may be applied in the analysis. For example, SPSS for Windows, available in Mac and PC versions, is one of the many statistical packages designed to analyse quantitative data in the social sciences (Bryman, 2001: 239–59). Other popular software for quantitative analysis in social science research is MINITAB (Marlow, 2001: 199–200) and SAS (Sarantakos, 1998: 335–41).

In the next two sections, we will look at two main ways of analysing and presenting quantitative data statistically. The first is to use statistics to describe informants and their responses and the second is to use statistics to draw inferences about the significance of relationships between variables and the extent to which the hypothesis is validated or not. Remember that quantitative studies – especially if influenced by positivist paradigms and using experimental designs – investigate research questions as hypotheses to be tested (proved or disproved). Quantitative data analysis may look at whether or not the patterns sought relate to only one variable (*univariate analysis*), two variables (*bivariate analysis*) or more than two variables (*multivariate analysis*) (Bryman, 2001: 222–32). Table 7.2 shows the link between these analytical dimensions.

We will not be doing any more than identifying key concepts and processes – there are many other research and statistics texts that deal extensively with quantitative data analyses (Bryman, 2001; Kumar, 1996; Sarantakos, 1998; Babbie, 1999; Royse, 1999). As there is quite specialized knowledge required to undertake sound quantitative analyses and understand texts that explain these processes, if you are uncertain about basic statistical concepts, you may like to read the following books that we have found helpful:

- A. Graham (1994), *Teach Yourself Statistics*, Hodder Headline Arnold, Teach Yourself Books (especially Chapter 5, Summarizing Data)
- D. Rowntree (1981), *Statistics without Tears*, Pelican.

Additionally, we strongly recommend that you consult a statistician or someone with proven experience in undertaking quantitative research when undertaking such studies, unless you have a thorough understanding of the complexities of statistical logic that inform data collection and analysis. For example, statisticians were part of the research team in Mason (1994: 107–8) and D'Cruz et al. (2002). It is essential to get the design technically correct from the start or your study will be seriously flawed and criticized for methodological errors. However, if you involve a statistician, you as a social work researcher must know what kinds of questions you want answered and how to interpret the statistics that are produced so that they make sense from a social work research perspective. How do the data and the statistical patterns relate to literature and theory? How does it help answer the research question? Do not trawl through the raw data just to see what emerges ('trawling' means running every possible form of analysis with selected tests of significance). This is

Table 7.2   Quantitative data analysis – linking the purpose of the analysis, methods and complexity in relation to the number of variables (Bryman, 2001: 222–32; Marlow, 2001; Kumar, 1996; Babbie, 1999)

Purpose of the analysis	Type of analysis	Number of variables involved
How many? What is the proportional distribution?	Frequency (absolute and relative)	Univariate
How many? Where do the main clusters appear?	Measures of central tendency – mean, mode, median, normal distribution	Univariate
How many? What is the distribution and its variation?	Measures of dispersion or variability – normal distribution, range, standard deviation	Univariate
How many? How does one variable relate to other variables? Relationships, not causality (cause and effect)	Contingency tables, Pearson's coefficient (strength and direction of the relationship); Spearman's rho	Bivariate
Is the relationship between two variables spurious? Is there an intervening variable in the apparent relationship between two variables? Is a third variable moderating the relationship between two variables?	Refer to texts on advanced statistical techniques (see, for example, Bryman and Cramer, 2001) or a statistician	Multivariate

costly as well as bad research. It is costly because of the time it takes to produce and print every possible statistical test on large quantities of data. It is bad research because it suggests that you are unclear about your research question and how the data you have generated relates to answering it. It also suggests that you are trying to find significance in your data to prove the relationships in the data rather than knowing what relationships you require and doing appropriate tests to explore the significance of these relationships.

Quantitative data analysis – descriptive statistics

Descriptive statistical analyses ask the question 'How many?' in relation to the actual and proportional distribution in the sample, the clustering, distribution and variation in the emerging patterns and relationships between variables. The sections below give a brief overview of these types of descriptive analyses.

How many? What is the proportional distribution?

Frequency counts tell you how many informants there are in the sample, particular descriptive characteristics, such as gender and age, and simple patterns in different responses, such as how many people responded in particular ways. A simple head count is known as *absolute frequency*. Getting the *proportion* or *percentage* of different responses in relation to the total is known as *relative frequency*. The absolute frequency alone is helpful, but the percentage gives a greater understanding of the patterns of representation. It is also important to present the absolute frequency with the relative frequency because the actual numbers give some context for understanding the percentages.

To understand how this works, let us look at an example. You have interviewed ten people about their experiences with a family support service. Six people (60 per cent) tell you that they found it helpful, two (20 per cent) say it made no difference and two (20 per cent) say it made things worse. Presenting the absolute numbers is fine, but they are enhanced by the percentages. However, it is not appropriate to present only the percentages as it gives a misleading impression of the actual numbers they represent.

How many? Where do the main clusters appear?

In addition to simple statistical counts, researchers also need to know where the data clusters. What is the central or most frequently occurring response? Is there just one such cluster or more? These questions relate to *measures of central tendency* – the mean, mode and median (Babbie, 1999: 350–3), which are also three ways of measuring the average (Babbie, 1999: 352).

The *mean* is the arithmetical average (Babbie, 1999: 352). The *mode* is the most frequently occurring response. It is possible to have more than one mode in a distribution – it just means that there is not only one popular response pattern. The *median* is the middle response if you think of it as (hypothetically) setting out every single response you have received in a row. (You can do this yourself with very small samples but, normally, a computer can work it out for you.) You then take the middle response or score.

The mean, mode and median often occur at the same point in a distribution of responses, but this is not always the case. Hence, the shape or pattern of the distribution of responses will not conform to the *normal distribution* (Bryman, 2001: 94; Arber, 1993b: 77–8; Marlow, 2001: 234–5). The distribution is then described as skewed (Marlow, 2001: 235).

How many? What is the distribution and its variation?

Measures of dispersion or *variability* are related to the measures of central tendency described above. They refer to the *range* and *standard deviation* and use the normal distribution as a way to understand the patterns in the data.

The *normal distribution* assumes that there is a standard way in which responses ought to be arranged that produce a symmetrical pattern. This pattern, when associated with the sample of respondents, is assumed to replicate the patterns in the main population and, thus, conclusions drawn from the study may be generalized to the whole population (Bryman, 2001: 94). In the normal distribution, the mean (the average), the mode (most frequently occurring) and median (central point) all occur in the same place in the pattern, this being the midpoint. Then, all other responses are distributed within the range of the available responses (the lowest to highest points) with a pattern of variation between the responses known as the standard deviation. When the measures for a study are combined in relation to different variables, a pattern that is specific to that study/variable is generated that has its own 'height' (mode, median and mean) and 'width' (range), although the overall shape may conform to the bell-shaped curve of the normal distribution (refer to Marlow, 2001: 235, for examples of different normal distributions).

The normal distribution is used as a way of predicting where most of the scores or responses ought to occur if the sample were to consist of the whole population from which it is drawn (this is what makes it reasonable to make generalizations from such results). It is usually proposed that approximately 68 per cent of all scores/responses lie within one standard error on either side of the mean (or average) with a further (approximately) 28 per cent within two standard errors on either side of the mean. (Three standard errors on both sides of the mean account for around 95 per cent of the sample; Babbie, 1999: 186–7; Bryman, 2001: 94). Another way of explaining it is that about 50 per cent of responses ought to be below the mean and the other 50 per cent above it. Of the 50 per cent on each side of the mean, 34 per cent would be one standard error below and above (that is, the majority of responses).

The normal distribution is regarded in statistical analysis as a useful device for understanding the patterns in data as a representation of distribution and comparison of individuals or events in relation to a group. However, Hacking (1990) and Rose (1998: 109–10, 120; 1999) discuss the political and ethical aspects of the normal distribution as being fundamental to social control of populations and individual 'normalization', especially with the increasing reliance on risk assessment in many aspects of social life. Certainly there is increasing reliance in policy making that looks at where the greatest demand seems to exist based on the clusters around the mean or average as being the real extent of a problem (the mainstream or the norm). People who do not fit the majority sit on the 'outliers' (Bryman, 2001: 225) – in policy terms, at the margins – and, because of small numbers, are seen to not represent the norm or general experience or view of a problem or issue. The danger of ignoring people who do not represent a numerical majority is that they may be denied services because the extent of the problem is defined solely according to sheer numbers (as demand) and not according to needs that may be relevant to those small numbers of people. For example, it is argued that elderly men are increasingly forgotten in service provision among the elderly because more women survive into old age than men (Thompson, 1994; Arber and Ginn, 1991).

How many? How does one variable relate to other variables?

Relationships between variables are *measures of association*. The main relationships of interest are *causality* and *correlation*. This is when bivariate analyses are conducted and, if these relationships need to be tested to establish their validity, it may be necessary to conduct multivariate analyses, which are rather more complicated and beyond the scope of this book. However, if you are looking at statistical relationships between variables, then you need to understand the following concepts, which are relevant within experimental or explanatory designs that rely on statistical analyses:

- dependent and independent variables
- cross-tabulations or contingency tables.

In an experimental study, the researcher aims to find out whether or not a particular factor (the independent variable) causes, or has an association with, another factor (the dependent variable). In an experimental design and working to falsify or disprove (Abercrombie et al., 1988) the experimental hypothesis, which is that there is a relationship between the independent and dependent variables, the researcher performs whatever the interventions are (independent variable) on the dependent variable to observe and record what happens. The researcher would then use inferential statistics to ascertain if there is any relationship between the variables and the significance of the observed relationships. Have they occurred by chance or is there a causal or correlational relationship between them that suggests the experimental hypothesis has been proven? The researcher uses cross-tabulations or contingency tables to set out the statistical relationship as absolute and relative frequencies between the independent and dependent variables and tests of significance. These tests of significance are known as inferential statistics.

Quantitative analysis – inferential statistics

Here are two definitions of inferential statistics:

> Inferential statistics allow us to determine whether an observed relationship is due to chance or whether it reflects a relationship between factors, and they allow us to generalize the findings to the wider population. (Marlow, 2001: 250)

> Inferential statistics are used to test hypotheses about differences between groups and to aid us in understanding the probabilities of obtaining our results by chance. (Royse, 1999: 36)

Because quantitative analyses rely entirely on statistical calculations to generate patterns and indicate the strength of the claims that can be made with regard to the wider population, it is essential that the researcher using such approaches is cognizant of the rules by which trustworthy analysis can be conducted.

One important rule is to identify and minimize sources of error that will otherwise affect the quality of the statistical analysis and the conclusions that can be drawn (Marlow, 2001: 250–1). Sources of error include measurement and the reliability and validity of the research instrument, so-called 'extraneous variables' that are seen as unrelated to, but interfering with, variables of interest to the research, and chance (Marlow, 2001: 251–2). The idea of sources of error in quantitative analysis and how to correct for them assumes that there are ways of ensuring accuracy and truth. (We looked at concepts of reliability and validity in Chapter 4, control groups and sampling in Chapter 5. We also discussed how the assumptions of what 'error' is and how to correct it are informed by a particular perspective on reality, but that they are also necessary to meet the requirements of sound statistical analysis.)

Testing hypotheses

Inferential statistics are essential when testing a hypothesis, which is a central consideration in most quantitative studies. Marlow (2001: 251–2) identifies three types of hypotheses.

- **Two-tailed or non-directional**   States only that there is a relationship between variables. An example is that 'gender *is likely to have* a relationship to hospitalization for depression' (Marlow, 2001: 252, emphasis added).
- **One-tailed or directional**   States that there is a relationship between variables and the 'direction' of the relationship – whether it is positive or negative. An example is a statement that 'women are *more likely than men* to be hospitalized for depression' (Marlow, 2001: 252, emphasis added).
- **Null hypothesis**   This is a statement that there is no association between variables. While some sources (see, for example, Marlow, 2001: 252; Bryman, 2001: 233) state that a null hypothesis is necessary in experimental designs, others (such as Royse, 1999: 15–16) say that it is optional. Examples of null hypotheses are '*there is no relationship* between gender and visiting the gym' (Bryman, 2001: 233, emphasis added) and 'female adolescents who participate in organized sports *are no more likely* to report eating disorders than female adolescents who are not involved in athletics' (Royse, 1999: 16, emphasis added).

Hypotheses are developed and justified through connecting both professional and personal experiences and professional literature, rather than relying uncritically on personal impressions or whims. Hypothesis testing relies on tests of significance.

Tests of statistical significance

Tests of statistical significance are important in quantitative studies that aim to generalize the conclusions about the research sample to the wider population. They are a way of testing hypotheses. If statistical significance is demonstrated, the researcher can reject the null hypothesis – that there is no relationship between the variables. The researcher needs to be confident about the strength of the conclusions as being indicative of an actual relationship between variables that has not occurred by chance or error (Bryman, 2001: 232–6; Marlow, 2001: 252–3; Royse, 1999: 239–42; Babbie, 1999; Kumar, 1996).

Bryman (2001: 233) gives a definition of a test of statistical significance:

> A test of statistical significance allows the analyst to estimate how confident he or she can be that the results deriving from a study based on a randomly selected sample are generalizable to the population from which the sample was drawn. When examining statistical significance in relation to the relationship between two variables, it also tells us about the risk of concluding that there is in fact a relationship in the population when there is no such relationship in the population. If an analysis reveals a statistically significant finding, this does not mean that finding is intrinsically significant or important. The word 'significant' seems to imply importance. However, statistical significance is solely concerned with the confidence researchers can have in their findings. It does not mean that a statistically significant finding is substantively significant.

Basically, this definition tells us that even if a statistical test shows that there is a high degree of confidence (probability) that a relationship between variables has not occurred by chance (is significant), it may not have any meaning and relevance in terms of knowledge or theory. It is the researcher's role to draw meaningful conclusions about the contribution made by the apparent relationship between variables. It is a case of asking 'So what?'

It is possible for a researcher to falsely conclude that there is a relationship between variables by rejecting the null hypothesis – known as a Type I error. It is also possible to falsely conclude that there is no relationship between variables, instead accepting the null hypothesis – known as a Type II error. Ways of avoiding such errors include larger samples and levels of measurement – for example, ratio variables that allow for stronger statistical tests to be used (Marlow, 2001: 253).

Statistical tests

For a detailed discussion of types of statistical tests and their applications, refer to Royse (1999: 239–51), Bryman (2001: 232–4) and Marlow (2001: 253–9). The following are ones you are likely to come across:

- chi-squared (χ^2) analysis
- *t*-test
- analysis of variance (ANOVA)
- correlation coefficient.

Here is a summary table by Marlow (2001: 254), reproduced here as Table 7.3, showing the types of statistical tests for bivariate analysis (relationships between two variables) and when you would use them.

Hacking (1999) argues that statistical tests may be used to generate theories of causality that are applied unquestioningly (as representing objective truths) and in discriminatory ways in social life. He gives the example of various

Table 7.3 Types of statistical tests and some conditions for use of correlational analysis (Marlow, 2001: 254, Table 13.1)

	t-test	ANOVA	Correlation coefficient	Chi-squared analysis
Comparing means of two populations	Yes	No	No	No
Comparing means of more than two populations	No	Yes	No	No
All variables at interval/ratio level of measurement	No	No	Yes	No
One variable only at interval/ratio level of measurement	Yes	Yes	No	No
All variables at ordinal/nominal level of measurement	No	No	No	Yes

statistical studies in the UK (MacKenzie, 1981; Herrnstein and Murray, 1994) and their abuse in meeting particular ideological agendas, such as race stereotypes (Hacking, 1999: 57).

However, and as discussed in earlier chapters and in line with Everitt et al. (1992), Truman (2000) and Jayaratne (1993), quantitative research can meet pragmatic and strategic objectives. It is also possible for a researcher undertaking quantitative research to work in an anti-discriminatory way, making explicit the value base and personal positioning and relevance of method for the question to avoid the positivist approach that claims to separate values from the research process.

Quantitative analysis – displaying data

After you have completed your analysis, you will want to display your data in ways that capture and communicate the main patterns and relationships as they relate to your research question. Some ways of displaying quantitative data include tables and graphs (Marlow, 2001, Chapters 12 and 13; Kumar, 1996, Chapter 16).

Tables may present information about one variable (univariate). These are called frequency tables and normally include absolute numbers and percentages. Tables with information about two variables (bivariate) are called crosstabulations. Tables with information about more than two variables (polyvariate or multivariate) are quite complicated (see Kumar, 1996: 226–9, for examples of tables and advice on effective presentation).

Graphs are pictorial displays of numerical data, that may enhance data presented in tabular form (tables). Examples of graphs are histogram, bar chart, stacked bar chart, 100 per cent bar chart, frequency polygon, cumulative frequency polygon, stem and leaf display, pie chart, line diagram or trend curve, area chart and scattergram (see Kumar, 1996: 230–40, for when and how to use different types of graphs).

Rose (1998: 102–3) describes graphs and tables as 'moral topographies', by means of which the problematic aspects of populations may be mapped and made governable.

Organizing qualitative data

In the section above we showed the processes and procedures associated with data organization and analysis for quantitative data. *Qualitative* data analysis is less clear cut. Indeed, it has been described as 'messy' because, unlike in quantitative studies, the stages are dynamic and closely interrelated (Bryman and Burgess, 1994a: 2).

Qualitative research relies on relatively semi-structured or unstructured data generation approaches that include observation/participant observation, interviews and official and private documents, such as case files, policy documents and diaries (Huberman and Miles, 1994: 430). Qualitative data are usually in the form of text – notes taken of observations, interviews, transcriptions of audio-taped interviews and, indeed, official documents; for example:

> Essentially, a raw experience is converted into words, typically compiled into extended text. A portion of the raw experience may also be captured as still or moving images; these images can be used in a variety of ways, most of them also involving conversion or linkage to words. (Huberman and Miles, 1994: 429–30)

However, these raw data are not in a form that can be easily analysed. Therefore, the researcher needs to develop a data management approach that includes processing a large volume of data to ensure that they are not 'miscoded, mislabeled, mislinked and mislaid' (Wolfe, 1992: 293).

Huberman and Miles (1994) recommend a good storage and retrieval system that can allow for 'easy, flexible and reliable use of data', whether the researcher is working alone or in a team. Furthermore, being aware that qualitative data analysis is a dynamic process, such a system of data management will allow documentation of the analysis over the life of the research as a way of ensuring its trustworthiness. It is a form of auditing or confirming the analysis as it proceeds (Guba and Lincoln, 1982).

Qualitative data analysis is not a separate stage that comes after the data generation process. Instead, it is an ongoing process that ought to be a feature of data generation as well as a stage that follows it. Bogdan and Biklen (1982) distinguish these interrelated aspects of qualitative data analysis as 'analysis in the field' and 'analysis after the field'. The word 'field' suggests that the research approach is likely to involve participant observation and ethnography. However, the ideas are associated with any qualitative research that is influenced by naturalistic paradigms (Guba and Lincoln, 1982), although researchers who undertake quantitative research to meet political and ethical commitments could also find these ideas helpful.

Basically, 'analysis in the field' means that the researcher ought to be 'constantly engaged in preliminary analytic strategies' (Bryman and Burgess, 1994a: 7). This means that there is openness and critical awareness of the research as it is in process and a willingness to modify aspects in response to contextual issues. For example, the research focus may need revision or the data might suggest new lines of enquiry. The researcher's journal, in which reflections about the research process and any analytical insights that require further exploration are documented, integrates analysis with data generation and therefore broadens the meaning of both processes.

The second aspect of analysis that approximates what is usually understood as data analysis is 'analysis after the field'. This process involves coding and other ways of pattern-making from data, once the data generation process has been completed. These analytical methods and techniques are discussed below.

Interactive processes between data generation and data analysis may be managed by means of the following storage and retrieval functions, as proposed by Levine (1985):

> ... formatting (how materials are laid out, physically embodied, and structured into types of file(s)), cross-referral (linkage across different files), indexing (defining codes, organizing them into a structure, and pairing codes with specific parts of the database), abstracting (condensed summaries of longer material, such as documents or extended field notes), and pagination (numbers and letters locating specific material in field notes – for example, B J K 1 22 locates for Brookside Hospital the first interview with Dr Jameson by researcher Kennedy, page 22).
>
> These functions, historically accomplished with notebooks, index cards, file folders, and edge-punch cards, can be carried out far more easily and quickly with computer software ... Even so, a physical filing system is also needed for raw field notes, hard copies of transcriptions, audio tapes, memos, and the like.

Huberman and Miles (1994: 431, Table 27.1) provide an excellent summary of qualitative data management and its links to analysis in 'What to store, retrieve from and retain', reproduced below:

1 **Raw material:** field notes, tapes, site documents.
2 **Partially processed data:** write-ups, transcriptions. Ideally, these should appear in their initial version, and in subsequent corrected, 'cleaned', 'commented-on' versions. Write-ups may profitably include marginal or reflective remarks made by the researcher during or after data collection.
3 **Coded data:** write-ups with specific codes attached.
4 **The coding scheme or thesaurus,** in its successive iterations.
5 **Memos or other analytic material:** the researcher's reflections on the conceptual meaning of the data.
6 **Search and retrieval records:** information showing which coded chunks or data segments the researcher looked for during analysis, and the retrieved material, records of links made among segments.
7 **Data displays:** matrices, charts, or networks used to display retrieved information in a more compressed, organized form, along with the associated analytic text. Typically, there are several revised versions of these.
8 **Analysis episodes:** documentation of what you did, step by step, to assemble the displays and write the analytic text.
9 **Report text:** successive drafts of what is written on the design, methods, and findings of the study.

10   **General chronological log or documentation** of data collection and analysis work.
11   **Index** of all the above material.

As discussed above, qualitative data may be described as being primarily in the form of texts or documents because all data generated, regardless of method, are transformed into documents of some type. These may be transcripts or notes from semi-structured or unstructured interviews, formal records, such as case files, or journals and field diaries that record observations. From this perspective, qualitative data analysis may be equated with documentary analysis.

Qualitative data as documents

Jupp and Norris (1993) discuss 'traditions in documentary analysis' whereby they trace the trajectories by which documentary analysis has emerged with different approaches associated with particular paradigms. They specifically discuss 'positivism and documents', 'the interpretive tradition and documents' and 'the critical tradition' and 'discourse analysis'. Jupp and Norris' discussion illustrates how qualitative data in the form of documents does not of itself represent an interpretivist or feminist paradigm. The paradigm within which the researcher is positioned is represented by the stance in relation to documents as data, the research focus and how the data are analysed. For example, in a positivist paradigm represented by *content analysis*, the text is seen as an objective and unambiguous representation of 'attributes, attitudes and values relating to individuals' (Jupp and Norris, 1993: 41). The values and power differences between authors of texts and those who read the texts or in relation to wider social and cultural relationships are not considered. Alternatively, an *interpretivist* approach to the text, from perspectives of ethnomethodology, social interactionism and labelling theory, considers the place of the individual in generating meaning via texts and that readers may read these texts differently. This approach looks at how meaning is constructed in people's social lives, such as juvenile delinquency (Cicourel, 1964, 1968), and how individuals experience their lives, for instance in prisons (Cohen and Taylor, 1972). However, such approaches may be criticized for separating the individual from a structural analysis including the influence of power, ideology and conflict.

The *critical* tradition, informed by Marxism (and class analysis) and Foucault (and discourses), centralizes structural arrangements and, in particular, the place of power, so is overtly political (Jupp and Norris, 1993: 45).

Documentary analysis may also be informed by feminist paradigms (Stanley, 1992; Stanley and Wise, 1993; Olesen, 1994) and indigenous or post-colonial paradigms (Stanfield, 1994; Tuhiwai Smith, 1999) as emancipatory approaches to social research.

Qualitative data analysis – looking for patterns and meanings

Qualitative data analysis, like quantitative analysis, also involves looking for patterns and meanings. However, as you will recall from the sections above, the patterns in quantitative analysis are in the statistics that are generated. You as the researcher need to interpret the meanings of the statistical descriptions and tests that you conduct. With qualitative analysis, however, the researcher is more involved in generating the patterns and interpretation of meaning.

Some argue that the researcher is an 'instrument' (Punch, 1993: 185–6) in the process. Stakeholders positioned within different paradigms or who disagree with the research outcomes can make accusations of bias and subjectivity as ways of attacking the credibility of the research. Therefore, the personal, intellectual and value positionings of the researcher ought to be made explicit and justified ethically and politically, acknowledging that there are likely to be opposing views and what these might be. It also means that, in practice, it is more difficult for qualitative data to be presented as findings separately from the discussion, which is usually the format for quantitative studies. This is because the findings and the discussion are closely intertwined in a qualitative study.

Qualitative data analysis – methods and techniques

There are many methods and techniques for analysing qualitative data. Some of these may be linked to particular theoretical approaches (paradigms), while others have developed purely as techniques for making patterns from documentary sources.

In this section, we give an overview of some of the most well-known methods and techniques. These are briefly defined with an explanation of the key theoretical influences. Examples of 'how to do' the actual method are also set out. Additional readings are cited as examples of the method in practice. We also encourage you to seek your own examples of the analytical methods and techniques in practice. You can do this by carrying out literature searches of databases using keywords. Another approach is to locate examples cited as references in research texts.

Content analysis

Content analysis involves the development of codes and categories by the researcher based on theory and literature and their application to documents, which are data sources. A special example of content analysis is the collation of data according to themes that you as the researcher have developed. This may be apparent in standardized open-ended interviews (Patton, 1987: 112–14) where you have asked specific questions of all respondents. Informants' responses may then be grouped under the specific questions or themes and re-presented in the research report.

Content analysis relies on 'researcher-constructed categories' (Marlow, 2001: 214) rather than those generated by the informants – known as 'indigenous categories' using an 'emic' approach (Marlow, 2001: 212–14). Some social work-related studies that have relied on content analysis are Petr and Barney (1993), Allen-Meares (1984) and Ryan and Martyn (1996, 1997).

Marlow (2001: 214) justifies the inclusion of content analysis as a qualitative approach by stating that:

> Studies using researcher-constructed categories can be considered interpretive or qualitative as long as the study follows the major principle of interpretive research – namely, the data are considered in context rather than through rigidly imposed categories.

Content analysis – which paradigm(s)?

Bearing in mind what you have read in Chapters 3 and 4 and Jupp and Norris' (1993) commentary on content analysis discussed above, how would you respond to Marlow's statement in line with the following questions. Is content analysis qualitative and interpretive, quantitative and positivist or can it be both? How do you justify your conclusions?

The following are the steps involved when carrying out content analysis (Alter and Evens, 1990).

1 Select the constructs of interest and define them clearly.
2 Select a unit of analysis (word, sentence, phrase, theme, and so on) to be coded.
3 Define the categories. They should be mutually exclusive and should be fairly narrow.
4 Test this classification scheme on a document/recording.
5 Revise if reliability is low and test again until an acceptance level of reliability is achieved.
6 Code the text of interest and do a category count.

Analytical induction

Analytical induction is particular to qualitative studies. It challenges the assumptions in quantitative, experimental studies influenced by positivism that aim to prove or test theories using the hypothetico-deductive method (Sarantakos, 1998: 10). Using this method, hypotheses considered to represent theory are arranged from the most general to the most specific. Research is planned to test the validity of the theory by proving or disproving hypotheses. Analytical induction, on the other hand, argues that theory about the social world should emerge from that world, referred to as 'indigenous categories' (Marlow, 2001: 214) rather than theories developed external to the context being imposed by the researcher.

Bryman and Burgess (1994a: 4) provide a brief description of the analytical induction process:

> The researcher begins with a rough definition of a problem or issue (e.g. drug addiction). Appropriate cases are examined and a possible explanation of the problem is formulated and

the investigator then examines further appropriate cases to establish how well the data collected fit the hypothetical explanation. If there is a lack of fit, the hypothesis is likely to need reformulation and further research is conducted. There then follows an iterative interplay between data collection and revision of the hypothesis as research reveals cases that do not fit with each reformulated hypothesis. Indeed the original problem may be redefined in the process. The sequence continues until cases that are inconsistent with what ends up as the last reformulated hypothesis do not appear.

A special example of analytical induction is grounded theory. The development of this approach is attributed to Glaser and Strauss (1967). It was later set out as a set of 'procedures and techniques' by Strauss and Corbin (1990). The main feature is 'the meshing of theorizing and data collection' (Bryman and Burgess, 1994a: 4). The grounded theory approach is comprised of a series of main steps, 'which collectively are concerned with "the discovery of theory from data"' (Glaser and Straus, 1967: 1; Bryman and Burgess, 1994a: 4). Coding of different types – 'open coding' (Strauss, 1987) or 'initial coding' (Charmaz, 1983; Glaser, 1978) and 'axial coding' (Strauss and Corbin, 1990) – are key features in generating theory from the data.

Marlow (2001: 217–19) uses an analytical technique that she calls 'proposing hypotheses', whereby hypotheses are generated from data rather than tested, as in the hypothetico-deductive method. The generation of hypotheses from data is associated with interpretive studies. Marlow (2001: 217–19) describes the process of representing 'causality and linkages' by means of flow-charts that may 'reveal contextual interrelationships among factors and their circular and interdependent natures'.

The generation of hypotheses from data may offer ways of validating qualitative data via 'rival or alternative hypotheses, negative cases, triangulation, and preservation of the context of the data' (Marlow, 2001: 220).

Rival or alternative hypotheses may be compared with the proposed hypotheses that have also been generated from the data. The researcher can then consider 'which hypothesis appears to most closely reflect the data. In some cases, both hypotheses appear to be supported' (Marlow, 2001: 220).

Negative cases are exceptions in data that challenge the overall pattern suggesting a particular hypothesis or conclusion. Negative cases must be actively sought to avoid drawing erroneous conclusions and to strengthen researcher credibility by demonstrating a commitment to refute and amend, as well as confirm, emergent conclusions or claims (Olesen, 1994; Morse, 1994; Miles and Huberman, 1994: 271; Huberman and Miles, 1994).

When you encounter a case that does not fit your theory, ask yourself whether it is the result of (1) normal social variation, (2) your lack of knowledge about the range of appropriate behaviour, or (3) a genuinely unusual case. (Marlow, 2001: 220–1)

Qualitative researchers have developed software to help with analytical induction approaches, such as grounded theory (Richards and Richards, 1994). Miles and Huberman (1994: 312) describe these programs as 'code-and-retrieve' (such as NUDIST, The Ethnograph, ATLAS/ti) or 'theory builders' (NUDIST, ATLAS/ti) and CAQDAS (computer-assisted qualitative data analysis sofware) (Bryman, 2001: 406–7). There are debates about the usefulness of CAQDAS (Bryman, 2001: 407–9), which include the potential for decontextualizing the data, code-and-retrieve functions are given greater emphasis so may fragment the flow of the text and they may favour particular analytical approaches, such as grounded theory, over others. However, many qualitative researchers who have used computers for organizing and coding their data still return to the transcripts to conduct the interpretive aspects of analysis that computers cannot do and get a contextual sense of their data (Okely, 1994; Mason, 1994; Bryman and Burgess, 1994b: 221). For more information about computers for qualitative research, access the CAQDAS site at the University of Surrey, UK (e-mail: a.lewins@soc.surrey.ac.uk; website: www.soc.surrey.ac.uk/caqdas).

Discourse analysis – conversations, interviews and official documents

Discourse analysis is an analysis of language as a social structure that connects knowledge and power. This approach looks at how language is used to produce versions of knowledge that then gain legitimacy in a political, social, cultural and professional sense. Words represent versions of knowledge and also operate as devices of power: '… words which are used and their meanings depend on where they were used, by whom and to whom' (McDonnell, 1986, in Jupp and Norris, 1993: 47). We would add that when (in time) particular words have particular meanings is also important because place (the 'where' of things) does not remain fixed in time. Thus, there are no universal or fundamental truths that are meaningful to everyone, everywhere, every time.

There are major implications that follow from the assumption that discourses can differ. These include the overt recognition of differences in knowledge related to values and beliefs and that it is not a case of agreeing to disagree, but participants actively engaging in relationships of power to give legitimacy to their version of knowledge and discredit others. These relationships of knowledge and power are expressed in language, as a way of representing knowledge and a device of power that represents what is legitimate and marginalizes other versions (Potter, 1996).

Thus, social workers can contribute to knowledge and social change by exploring what Smith (1990) calls 'the relations of ruling'. What is considered to be legitimate knowledge at a particular time and place? How does it come to be legitimate? How is legitimate knowledge expressed? What are other versions and what happens if there is disagreement about what may be accepted as the legitimate version? Whose voices and knowledge is silenced, by whom and why? These are some of the questions that are explored in discourse analysis and can contribute much to exploring and expressing 'subjugated knowledge' (Hartman, 1992) about social problems and how they may be understood by participants with an interest. These participants include the people who experience a particular problem, such as racism or domestic violence, policymakers, service providers, funding bodies, media and politicians, to name a few. Examples of discourse analysis include Frankenberg (1993), Mickler (1998), Morgan (2000) and D'Cruz (2002).

Below are two examples of discourse analysis, shown by means of brief extracts. The first example, taken from Probyn (1977: 129–30) is a discourse analysis of a 'criminal/prison autobiography that describes a first appearance … before a juvenile court in London'. The line numbers in the first extract are shown to indicate where each line starts in the original text. The second extract is Morgan's (2000: 124–5) analysis of Probyn's text.

> *2 Hard, cold official eyes focused upon me as I came to a halt in front of the bench. There were tables to the left and right of me and seemingly hosts of people, all staring at me*
> *4 with unnerving intensity. I felt an oppressive guilt, as though I had committed some outrageous and disgusting crime from which I could never be redeemed. The whole*
> *6 attitude and atmosphere of that court seemed to me, from the very moment I entered it, to be one of absolute and unrelenting condemnation.* (Probyn, 1977)

The quality of force in a text (Fairclough 1992) describes the way in which its social purpose is realised through language and structure. Here the delinquent as unknowing object is powerfully portrayed in the first paragraph by an assertive persuasive modality. This is combined with ambivalence created by the use of a series of dualities which construct the thematic meaning: guilt/innocence, knowledge/ignorance, power/vulnerability, childhood/adulthood, justice/discrimination. Strong nouns and adjectives – hard, cold, absolute, unrelenting, outrageous, disgusting (1–7) – re-create the power of the remembered experience in an emotional sense. (Morgan, 2000: 124–5)

A second example of a discourse analysis is given below (D'Cruz, 2002). This example shows the text being analysed woven into the researcher's theoretical positioning. It is taken from an article that discusses three case studies of how responsibility for child maltreatment is socially constructed in particular cases and how gender is an important consideration (D'Cruz, 2002). The article is discussing how mothers 'become responsible' in child protection cases, even when they are not actually culpable, whereas the men who are culpable 'become invisible' (Milner, 1993). The extract here is a small segment of the analysis of one of the cases. The numbers at the start of each paragraph are there because this was the format used by the journal in which this article appeared. The paragraph numbers are used instead of page numbers if extracts are cited because online journals do not have page numbers as printed journals do. The superscript number refers to the endnote (included at the end of the extract) that is part of the researcher's reflexive engagement with the data and analysis.

Case B 'substantiated physical abuse – risk acceptable' '(excess corporal punishment)'; Person believed responsible: 'parent' '(female)', Ethnicity: not stated

3.20

Case context: A teenage girl reported to a child protection worker that her parents had hit her. The worker contacted the girl's mother that day. The investigation was conducted and concluded the same day, with the substantiation of physical abuse and the mother categorized as person believed responsible. This case shows how patriarchal mothering as a daily practice and a public expectation positions women/mothers as sites of surveillance and normalization and influences child protection practical constructions of the identities, 'responsible mothers, invisible men'. …

'Responsible mothers, invisible men' in practice

3.25

I was curious to understand why only the mother was the focus of the investigation. Positioned as I was within the literature, this seemed to be a practical construction of 'responsible mothers, invisible men'.

HD: *the girl … identified three separate incidents where she was hit by both her parents.* … So is it the most recent incident that you would investigate in terms of person responsible?[18]

Worker: … in terms of dad, *I don't remember* [1] what I did with dad. I suppose I focused primarily on … the incidents with mum … *When I phoned, mum was home* [2a]. … *Mum answered the phone* [2b] and she agreed to come in. … I suppose I could have got side tracked in that the focus of [the girl's] *concerns* [3a] were mum. This *stuff* [4a] to do with dad was not the primary thing she talked about … and there was an *incident … that day* [5a] … mum had been *cross* [3b] with her … the *stuff* [4b] to do with dad got lost in the *conflict* [3c] with mum. … the conflict between the two children, the pressure that puts on mum and how she responds [6]. … The *issue* [4c] with dad was *not a current concern* [5b] and it got lost.

HD: … *maybe mum was the person … primarily responsible for the daily care of the children?*

Worker: certainly … I suppose my assessment was that the [family] conflict [was] … parent teen stuff … the primary issue … *that was the thrust of the intervention with mother and child* [7]. (Emphasis added)

3.26

This extract shows how patriarchal mothering assumptions played out in mundane detail, intersected with the basic expectation that a 'type of maltreatment' and a 'person believed responsible' are identified (the mother confirmed hitting her daughter) constructing identities of 'responsible mothers, invisible men' (Stark and Flitcraft, 1988; Milner, 1993). The father's disconnection from childcare maintained his invisibility from public surveillance, suggested by his apparent disappearance from the worker's consciousness [1], colloquially, 'out of sight, out of mind'. The mother's 'place' at home [2a] and as gatekeeper [2b], and assumptions that she was primarily responsible for the daily childcare and responding to family conflicts [6, 7], also increased her visibility to public examination as 'person believed responsible' for 'hitting' her daughter. The immediacy of the incident with the mother [5a], unsurprising as she had most responsibility for the children (Carlson, 1992), contrasted (Potter, 1996) with the father's 'issue' [4c] as 'not current' [5b]. The more generalized descriptions (Potter, 1996) of the father's actions, as 'stuff' [4a, 4b] and 'issue' [4c], contrasts with specific vocabulary (Potter, 1996) for the mother's actions [3a–c]: 'concerns', 'cross', 'conflict'. …

Endnote for the above extract

[18]Note that the worker's response to this question took 305 lines which I interpreted as her extreme discomfort with the question about an aspect of her practice which she had taken for granted. However, here I have only included the 'relevant' lines, not the 'digressions'.

Related to discourse analysis is *semiotic analysis* – how words and material culture are representations or images of a particular social and cultural reality – and *conversation analysis*. This latter approach may be applied to interview transcripts and conversations between observed participants. Some examples of this approach are in Wooffitt (1993), Holstein (1988) and Silverman and Perakyla (1990).

Policy analysis

One form of documentary analysis is policy research. Formal documents, such as archival materials, existing laws, policies, even *Hansard* (the verbatim printed and public record of debates by politicians in Parliament), may be analysed. These documents offer a particular perspective on social and political agendas and their consequences at a particular time and in a particular place.

Two examples of policy analysis that draw on a variety of official documents from various periods of time in Australian governance are by Reynolds (2000b) in relation to indigenous Australians, and Edwards (2001) 'from problem to practice'.

The official documents used in Reynolds' analysis, such as legislation, resolutions of conferences, parliamentary debates, petitions and major reports, were referred to as secondary data sources in Chapter 6. These 18 separate documents are set out as an appendix to Reynolds' chapter and he refers to them as he discusses his analysis, as set out below in a brief extract from it.

In a section on land rights for indigenous Australians, Reynolds (2000b: 106–7) discusses the brief history of the landmark Mabo decision in 1992 by the Australian High Court. Document 3.11 [The Mabo Case 1992: High Court of Australia 175 CLR 1 F.C. 92/014] and Document 3.12 [Native Title Act 1993 Acts of the Commonwealth of Australia, No. 110 of 1993, pp. 2129–31] are relevant to the extract that follows.

Eddie Mabo, a Murray Islander living in Townsville [Queensland, Australia], decided to use the courts in an attempt to achieve recognition of his traditional title to his family's land which was, in a legal sense, Crown land. The prognosis for his case was not promising. The Australian Courts had, since the first half of the nineteenth century, determined that Australia was *terra nullius* when the British first arrived. The indigenous people, it was argued, had not effectively used or owned the land. When the British Crown claimed sovereignty, all the land became the property of the Crown and Aborigines and [Torres Strait] Islanders were afforded the status of permissive occupiers of Crown land with no legal right of possession at all. This view of Australian law was reaffirmed by Mr Justice Blackburn in the … case, *Milurrpum v Nabalco* in 1971.

After an arduous and difficult path through the courts, the High Court's decision in the case of *Mabo v Queensland*, No. 2, was handed down in June 1992 [Document 3.11]. It rejected *terra nullius* and gave a ringing endorsement to the concept of native title. Justice Brennan declared that:

the Meriams (of Murray Island) are entitled as against the whole world to possession, occupation, use and enjoyment of the island (*Mabo v Queensland*, No. 2 175 CLR, 1991–92, p. 76).

The Federal government decided to legislate to give statutory protection to native title while validating all existing titles. The Native Title Act consumed many hours of passionate debate in both the House of Representatives and the Senate [Document 3.12]. Lobbyists of all persuasions crowded the corridors of Parliament House trying to affect the final outcome of the legislation. When the bill finally passed the Senate, after the longest debate in its history, the crowded galleries broke into applause. (Original emphasis)

Edwards (2001) takes a slightly different approach. She draws on case studies of different policy initiatives – income support for young people, child maintenance and child support, university education and fees and unemployment policy. Each case study is treated as a 'public policy "laboratory"' (Edwards, 2001: 10) demonstrating distinct policy processes in which Edwards herself was a participant and that she documented in a journal. The analysis relies on links between actual policy changes over time, as defined by formal legislation, and a discussion of the context, players, processes, power relationships and outcomes, in part as documented in Edwards' journal.

In a chapter discussing 'income support for young people: the search for a single allowance', Edwards (2001: 12–55) begins by setting out a 'chronology of events March 1983 to January 1987' (Edwards, 2001: 12). Below is an extract from Edwards' (2001: 28–9) analysis of the policy-making process, from a section on 'developing objectives and options'. The section interjected under the heading 'A wording exercise' and indented is an extract from the author's journal.

> ... In January 1984, a few months after the DEYA [Department of Education and Youth Affairs] background paper had been released, a discussion paper, *Income Support for Young People*, was produced jointly by OYA [Office of Youth Affairs] and the SWPS [Social Welfare Policy Secretariat]. Its origins can be traced to a meeting of the State Youth Ministers Council in November 1983. Its purpose was 'to expand on [the background paper] and to indicate some of the major options to address' (OYA/SWPS 1984: 4). The paper was mainly the work of five people from the two organizations concerned: Alan Abrahart and Meredith Edwards [the author] from the OYA and Vic Rogers, Jim Cox and Marion Dunlop from the SWPS.
>
> **A wording exercise**
>
> *1 February 1984* Spent three hours arguing with SWPS (mainly Vic Rogers) over final wording for income support paper. Alan Abrahart also there.
> *3 February 1984* Meeting for two hours fighting over words and phrases with Vic Rogers of DSS [Department of Social Security] and again from 3.30 p.m. to 5.30 p.m. Today was the day for getting paper together to deliver to Ministers ... Had until 11 a.m. to make final amendments. Mad rush. A.A. just moved on to the next rushed job – consultation process once the paper is printed.
>
> The paper put forward four principles for an improved system of youth income support: it should be simple; it should provide 'adequate' financial support for 'all young people in need'; it should be consistent with the broader aims of programmes for young people, including participation in further education and training and attention to the needs of disadvantaged groups; and it should provide levels of income support sufficient to recognize aspirations for 'independence and self-determination' among young people (p. 13). ...

Narrative analysis

Riessman (1994b) writes that narrative is assumed to be a recent discovery in social research, but has, in fact, been known for some time in other fields of writing and research as biographies, autobiographies and so on. A fundamental feature of narrative is that people tell their stories from their own points of view. Therefore, the interpretive and constructed nature of truth underpins narrative approaches. Hence, notions of absolute and objective fact are quite meaningless because people tell their own stories about what is important for them. However, personal and private narratives usually articulate within 'a community of stories' (Riessman, 1994b: 67–9), allowing the expression of culture and history, as well as giving power to individuals to tell their lives in their own words. Furthermore, personal stories that mesh with a community of stories (Riessman, 1994b) give insights into everyday experiences of inequality, oppression and other ways in which power is used and abused that may never be known if research approaches that are considered to be more objective are used.

Life stories, oral histories, biographies and autobiographies are different forms of narrative. In Chapter 6, several examples of such texts were cited as approaches to generating data. Here, below, are extracts from three texts that show how data generation and data analysis are almost inseparable processes in this form of research. The first extract is from a chapter entitled 'Reconciling our mothers' lives', written by three indigenous Australian women (Huggins et al., 2000) in *Race, Colour and Identity in Australia and New Zealand* (Docker and Fischer, 2000). The extract is part of a story by Jackie Huggins about her mother's experiences during the 1930s and 1940s with regard to 'the work of class and race' and what it means for her own identity as an indigenous Australian woman (Huggins et al., 2000: 52):

> …Aboriginal women were sent to work as domestic servants and nursemaids on station [large pastoral and grazing properties] homesteads and, in some cases, as stock-workers at the station. This began when they were 13 and 14 years of age, and in some cases younger. Domestic service was a cruel time for my mother, as it was for so many women of her generation. The working relationship was of the master–slave order: the men were addressed as 'boss', the women as 'mistress'. Many women endured appalling treatment, including beatings, being locked up in cells, subjection to sexual abuse. It was an experience that stood in gruesome contrast to the loving companionship they had known among their own people.
>
> Mother was very reluctant to talk about the regular beatings she received from one white mistress. I stumbled on this fact accidentally when my aunty told of my grandparents' attempts to get Rita out of the way of this mistress before she killed her. Of course, there were the rare exceptions when the white employers treated their workers with respect. Despite what my mother had to endure, she still had time to speak generously of those families who were kind to her, displaying a graciousness and lack of bitterness I, growing up as a young Murri woman, could never understand. I see her forgiveness of those actions now as a pillar of strength, not weakness – because they broke the mould when they made our grandmothers and mothers.

The next extract is from Lorde's (1982: 45, 155) autobiography in *Zami* as 'a young black girl growing up in thirties Harlem [USA], a teenager lives through Pearl Harbor, a young woman [who] experiences McCarthyism in fifties Greenwich Village' (back cover).

One day (I remember I was still in the second grade) my mother was out marketing, and my sisters were talking about someone being *Coloured*. In my six-year-old way, I jumped at this chance to find out what it was all about.

'What does *Coloured* mean?' I asked. To my amazement, neither one of my sisters was quite sure.
'Well,' Phyllis said. 'The nuns are white, and the Short-Neck Store-Man is white, and Father Mulvoy is white and we're Coloured.'
'And what's Mommy? Is she white or Coloured?'
'I don't know,' answered Phyllis impatiently.
'Well,' I said, 'if anybody asks me what I am, I'm going to tell them I'm white same as Mommy.'
'Ohhhhhhhhh, girl, you better not do that,' they both chorused in horror.
'Why not?' I asked, more confused than ever. But neither of them could tell me why.

That was the first and only time my sisters and I discussed race as a reality in my house, or at any rate as it applied to ourselves. (Original emphasis)

(My straight Black girlfriends … either ignored my love for women, considered it increasingly avant-garde or tolerated it as just another example of my craziness. It was allowable as long as it wasn't too obvious and didn't reflect upon them in any way. At least my being gay kept me from being a competitor for whatever men happened to be upon their horizons. It also made me much more reliable as a confidante. I never asked for anything more.)

The third extract is from 'a black oral history' (Rintoul, 1993: 179–80) of Australian indigenous people's memories of the colonization of Australia. The section in italics is Rintoul's introduction to the particular individual's story.

Cadley Sambo

Cadley Sambo was born in Coolgardie, Western Australia, in the 1930s. His sister was five or six years old when the Native Welfare sent her to Mogumber settlement. He doesn't remember the day it happened. His family stories included the branding of people to identify them with their station [cattle property]. 'There was a station ... where they branded the Aboriginal bloke there. They branded my uncle and a lot more. They branded them so they knew they belonged to there. They couldn't leave there, see.' He is from the Guberin tribe.

Coolgardie was all right, but I went away as a little boy. I went to Southern Cross [a town west of Coolgardie] because my family shifted. They were running from the Welfare – Neville [Mr Neville was the Chief Protector of Aborigines during the 1920s and 1930s]. He was the Welfare and he collected all the little half-caste kids; anybody a little bit white, he collected them all and sent them to Mogumber. He had a tracker with him, but they couldn't catch us because at the same time we were running bush. They had mounted police then, on horses, and they'd come into the camp and they'd dance their horses all over our camp, all over the food. Terrible. My mother used to paint me with burnt quandong [a tree] to make my skin darker so the police thought I was a full-blood. Once in Merredin [town] I was put in a chaff bag so the police wouldn't see me. My parents jumped on an old goods train and when they got off they put me in a bag and carried me up the bush. I was only small, but I remember that. I was big enough to know that the police were coming for us and they didn't want us to be caught. You've gotta be quiet, so they'd think they were carrying a swag [bag, backpack].

Notice that this third extract is a little different in structure to the other two. In it as an oral history, the author/researcher has compiled other people's stories into a 'national black oral history' (Rintoul, 1993), whereas the extract from

Huggins is a connection between a personal story and that of another (her mother) and Lorde's story is autobiographical.

They all show, by means of narrative, the practices of oppression and inequality associated with race, ethnicity, gender and class. If you read Lorde's entire book, she shows the complicated ways in which her sexuality – lesbian – and her race – black – contributed to her marginality and oppression within the wider society and within groups of women, white and black. Huggins et al. (2000), Rintoul (1993) and Lorde (1982) also show how in narrative findings and analysis are inseparable, especially when the researcher reflects on his or her life as a political analysis (Lorde, 1982) or makes links between autobiography and biography, as in Huggins et al. (2000), or oral history (Rintoul, 1993).

The truth of narratives, especially when they relate to public policy evaluations and commentaries, is a controversial issue. A good example of this is the Human Rights and Equal Opportunity Commission's (1997) report, *Bringing Them Home*. From a research point of view, 'Our analytic interpretations are partial, alternative truths that aim for "believability, not certitude, for enlargement of understanding rather than control" (Stivers, 1993, p. 424)' (Riessman, 1993: 22–3). This is where our understandings of paradigms as theoretical and value perspectives of truth and valid knowledge help us to work out the positionings of different stakeholders, including ourselves as social workers and the people whose experiences may be subjected to disputes about truth and lies.

Narratives – truth or lies?

Here's another exercise to get you thinking about what is truth and what are lies.

What paradigm do you think informs the Australian government's position discussed in Chapter 3 that the stolen generations of indigenous Australians comprise 'less than 10 per cent' and therefore do not constitute a 'generation'? How might you respond to this claim as a researcher positioned within the values and ethics of social work? Think of other examples from your experience of current affairs or social issues – how stories of people's lived experiences are dealt with by people who occupy different positions, such as policymakers or service providers.

Ethnography

Ethnography is:

a term coined in the context of anthropology to denote 'literally, an anthropologist's "picture" of the way of life of some interacting human group'. (Wolcott, 1975, p. 113).

It 'always involves the study of behaviour in "natural settings", as opposed to the experimental settings of psychology' (Fielding, 1993: 157). The researcher must gain an understanding of the symbolic world. This includes how people in the setting give meaning to their experiences.

An ethnographic study is usually produced after a researcher has spent considerable time in a setting, learning the language and patterns and rules of behaviour within that setting.

An ethnographic study involves a '"curious blending of methodological techniques"' (Denzin, 1970). This means that the methods of enquiry may include participant observation, conversation-style interviews involving key informants, and documentary review. Data are collected primarily in the form of field notes and diaries (Bogdewic, 1999), although in-depth interviews (Patton, 1987) may be audio-taped, with the permission of the informants. These audio-tapes are later transcribed (typed up) as text.

Important issues to consider in analysing data/preparing an ethnography include your status as potentially insider/outsider in various combinations at different times in the process. Some examples of ethnographic studies include classics such as Goffman (1961), Griffin (1961), Becker (1963) and Cicourel (1968), as well as more recent studies by de Hoog (1972), Pithouse (1987) and Rojiani (1994).

When you analyse/write up your ethnography, you may choose to describe, explain and/or hypothesize from your data. Two inductive approaches to structuring ethnographic data are set out in Table 7.4.

Another approach is the use of metaphor as the organizing concept in analysing your data and writing your ethnography. Miles and Huberman (1994: 250) say that:

> The notion that research should focus only on matter-of-fact, literal – even actuarial – description, with cautious, later ventures into interpretation and meaning, is responsible for much intellectual poverty and misery. … Metaphors, seen as one major type of … literary device, involve comparing two things via their similarities and ignoring their differences. … People can only grasp abstract ideas by mapping them onto more concrete ones.

An example of a familiar metaphor is 'the empty nest' (Miles and Huberman, 1994: 250). In analysing and representing different 'images of organization', Morgan (1986) uses metaphors, such as 'Organizations as machines', as 'organisms', 'brains', 'cultures', 'political systems', 'psychic prisons' and 'instruments of domination'.

Qualitative data analysis – presentation as representation

Qualitative studies usually present findings as being integral to the analysis. In fact, apart from the content analysis discussed above, all other approaches tend to present data within some frame, which has been constructed by the researcher

Table 7.4   Two inductive approaches to ethnographic analysis

Inductive analysis: Lofland (1971)	Inductive analysis: Bogdan and Biklen (1992)
1 *Acts:* action in a situation that is temporally brief, consuming only a few seconds, minutes or hours	1 *Setting/context:* general information on surroundings that allow you to put the study in a larger context
2 *Activities:* actions in a setting of more major duration – days, weeks, months – constituting significant elements of people's involvements	2 *Definition of the situation:* how people understand, define or perceive the setting or the topics on which the study bears
3 *Meanings:* the verbal productions of participants that define and direct action	3 *Perspectives:* ways of thinking about their setting shared by information ('how things are done around here')
4 *Participation:* people's holistic involvement in, or adaptation to, a situation or setting under study	4 *Ways of thinking about people and objects:* understandings of each other, outsiders, objects in their world (more detailed than above)
5 *Relationships:* interrelationships among several persons considered simultaneously	5 *Process:* sequence of events, flow, transitions and turning points, changes over time
6 *Settings:* the entire setting under study conceived as the unit of analysis (Lofland, 1971)	6 *Activities:* regularly occurring kinds of behaviour
	7 *Events:* specific activities, especially ones occurring infrequently
	8 *Strategies:* ways of accomplishing things; people's tactics, methods, techniques for meeting their needs
	9 *Relationships and social structure:* unofficially defined patterns, such as cliques, coalitions, romances, friendships, enemies
	10 *Methods:* problems, joys, dilemmas of the research process – often in relation to comments by observers (Bogdan and Biklen, 1992)

as the discussion above has shown. The degree of researcher intervention in relation to the voices of the informants may vary considerably, with narrative approaches being most likely to represent the informants' stories as fully as possible and the researcher offering minimal commentary. Other approaches can and do involve the researcher's interpretations and these must be explicitly stated as the positioning of the researcher. The researcher usually also acknowledges the partiality of the claims being made because no individual or piece of research can ever claim to present the complete truth. The word 'representation' used in the heading above indicates that, within a qualitative approach, all a researcher can do in the presentation of the study is to represent what has constituted its data. It is not presented as absolute truth, but as a partial version. It is also a re-presentation (retelling in a reconstituted way) of the truths of the informants using the researcher's voice.

Putting it all together

We have finally come to the end of this rather long chapter. In it we have tried to show you the complexity of data analysis. This is important because there are so many ways in which data can be 'made sense of' in relation to the research question. However, it is also important to understand that the analytical approach isn't just a case of quantitative *or* qualitative. You also need to know what sorts of messages you want to convey from your research and how best to describe, understand, explain and theorize about social problems and issues that are of interest to social workers and the people who experience these problems. You also need to take into account in your analysis how to work in a participatory and emancipatory way, using research as another social work strategy. This chapter has sought to do all these things, as well as introduce you to the rich world of analytical resources for social work researchers. In the final chapter of this book, we will look at reporting research.

EIGHT Reporting and disseminating research

Introduction

After all the struggles, satisfactions, exasperations and expended energy, you have made it to the final chapter. You might be thinking that it's almost time to gather up your things and look ahead to the next venture, that you can probably move through this bit pretty quickly and it may not add that much more anyway. If any of these sentiments hold true for you, which would be entirely understandable, you may well be mirroring a process that so frequently occurs in research. Little time and attention is left for the final and crucial phases, ensuring that the outcomes of research reach a wider audience.

We shall be using this chapter to put it all together as, in some senses, research does come together in the reporting and disseminating phase. Indeed, to construct such reports, the various components that have comprised the research from beginning to end are described. The chapter will therefore consider what happens following the analysis of data. It will also use that process to review the research journey represented by the places shown you in this book and revisit some of the major themes that we have been discussing.

Ambivalences

As Cheetham and her colleagues (1992: 120) have argued:

> Research in the social work field will almost always be in some sense 'applied'; which is to say that, if sensibly conceived and successfully carried out, it will contain some truths which have a purchase at some level on policy, management or practice. There is therefore a need to feed conclusions of studies into debates, in the various locations at which they take place, about policy and practice. More than this, there may be lessons to be learnt, and an opportunity afforded by research findings specifically to educate, persuade or otherwise influence policymakers, managers and practitioners towards more effective organization and practice.

Because of the potential for improving policy, management or practice, those who facilitate your research, by providing funds (for example, an external funding body), time (such as the agency that employs you) or access to participants or other sources of data (gatekeepers), may make such resources possible on the condition that you report your findings to them. In fact, writers such as Kellehear (1993) would argue that there is an ethical imperative to disseminate one's research findings. There is a responsibility to give something back to those who have participated in the research and committed their time and attention to it. Also, a common condition of formal ethics approval for research is that participants will receive some form of feedback. Yet, as Fuller and Petch (1995: 87) observe:

> Researchers have not always given [dissemination] the priority it deserves. There are several reasons for this, ranging from lack of time or energy once the study is completed, through diffidence about the importance of the findings, to (even) a misguidedly high-minded reluctance to communicate the rich subtleties of one's conclusions to audiences sometimes impatient for simple messages.

Reluctance may derive also from a concern felt by many social researchers that, no matter how interesting they may believe their results to be, their audience may not be interested at all. This may well be a consideration if there have been long delays between collecting the data and reporting the findings. The poignancy of divergent time frames is captured by Cheetham et al. (1992: 121):

> given the tendency of research questions to be formulated in terms of today's issues and the equal tendency of research to reach fruition tomorrow, researchers will sometimes find they have an interesting story to tell to an audience which has long since departed.

In the end, however, should we allow ourselves these excuses? Rabbitts and Fook (1996: 169) think not:

> How much work remains in draft form in the heads and filing cabinets of countless social workers? There are the standard excuses: 'not enough time'; 'it's easier said than done'; 'most of what is published is not useful to practitioners anyway'. These may all be true, but are not really excuses. We don't have much time, but why have we prioritized other activities over writing? Writing for publication can be excruciatingly difficult, but which social worker has not had to engage in painful activity? And if most of what is published is not useful to practitioners, isn't it up to us to begin to change that?

Dissemination: communication and change

You might like to pause at this point and consider the questions below.

Thinking about dissemination

Think back to some of the ideas you have had for research studies.

- Why, if at all, would you want to disseminate the messages from your research?
- Who would you want to reach? How might you go about this?
- Would different approaches to disseminating be required for different audiences? How might they differ?

Four straightforward reasons for dissemination are given by Fuller and Petch (1995: 88):

- inform others
- ensure that research is used
- meet obligations to participants
- clarify interpretations and recommendations.

Of course, these are not necessarily so straightforward in practice. It is possible that our research findings are controversial and sensitive. The perception of speaking the truth to power may evoke a range of responses in us – withdrawal, heroism or martyrdom, for example. Assessing the likely impact on a range of involved parties may be highly complicated. Similarly, the process of feeding back to participants holds both benefits and risks that can be time-consuming and demanding to manage.

For such reasons, thinking about dissemination is a front-end activity, not something we hope to achieve simply by writing up our findings. Anticipating the readership of our research, we would want to conduct the research in such a way that we create interested audiences as we go. Moreover, we will have been making judgements as to the kinds of research that our audience(s) will find persuasive and credible. This will have played its part in determining our methodologies and designs for the study. Then, we would want to draw on our understandings of communication so that we can be as effective as possible in ensuring our messages are not only sent but also received.

Theoretical developments in this field offer us more sophisticated ways of conceptualizing both the form (or media) of communication and process – appreciating, for instance, the diversity in people's identities and positions as readers and the significance of this for our dissemination strategies. The limitations of regarding dissemination as an instrumental and somewhat technical process are exposed by such understandings, which, again, situate the activity as a social practice to be accomplished rather than a task to be performed.

The aim of informing others relates to one particular view about the role of the researcher. As intimated, our aim might not only be to inform but also to increase the possibilities that this information will be acted on for the improvement of practice and policy and, in some sense, move in emancipatory directions for service users and communities. Reporting and dissemination, therefore, are part of a broader consideration regarding the connections we draw between research and social and/or personal transformation. This brings into relief the ways in which we conceptualize processes of change and transformation and the purposes we construe for research in this regard. The position of this book has been that social work research is a political and ethical practice and that it has a special place within wider transformative practices.

As regards different channels and media for dissemination, Fuller and Petch (1995: 96) offer the following list:

- research reports
- summary reports
- pamphlets
- items in newsletters
- articles in the social work press or professional journals
- local/national press
- academic journals
- oral presentations – meetings in your own agency, conferences, seminars, workshops and so on
- poster displays.

Adding other media (for example, making a video or audio tape) and, increasingly, online capabilities, even this simple list becomes quite formidable. The conclusion reached by Fuller and Petch (1995: 96) is that:

> Researchers therefore need to plan a dissemination strategy, take account of resources and time that can be made available, and decide on priorities. This really involves thinking clearly, once any advance undertakings have been met, about where the main interest of the research lies.

In this respect, Patton – a researcher with a long-standing interest in evaluation and the utilization of research findings – offers an observation from his own studies into this topic that underline the importance of understanding processes of communication and change. He (1997: 44) notes:

> Two factors emerged as consistently important in explaining utilization: (a) political considerations … and (b) a factor we called the *personal factor* … The personal factor is the presence of an identifiable individual or group of people who personally care about the evaluation and the findings it generates. Where such a person or group was present, evaluations were used; where the personal factor was absent, there was a corresponding marked absence of evaluation impact. (Emphasis in original)

From our point of view, this 'personal factor' will not come down to the personalities of individuals, but, rather, will relate to their social positioning towards the research and what it represents for them and the craft with which the researchers have engaged others in the transformative processes of research.

This discussion has focused on dissemination from the vantage point of the researchers themselves. Dissemination is, of course, a matter of concern at other levels and in other forums. There are various agendas involved. Professional associations may be active in promoting research activity and research findings among their members to increase the reputation and status of the profession. Grant-making organizations may be committed to ensuring that their funded projects promote effectively the outcomes of their research. Government policies – particularly those concerned with modernizing welfare and enhancing performance – may well establish infrastructure to support the wider dissemination of research findings among human services practitioners and managers. Information gateways on the Internet are being put in place and maintained, providing new forms of access to current research. Thus, the environment may well be changing towards a scenario of too much rather than too little information. It would not be surprising, therefore, if salient areas of debate turned to policies and processes being put in place for managing rather than making knowledge.

Reporting – representation, persuasion and analytical work

The research report is customarily the foundation written document, yet here, as Punch (1998: 266) comments, 'the rethinking of research which has accompanied both the paradigm debates and the emergence of new perspectives has included research writing: how the research is to be put into written form, and communicated'.

There remains a relatively conventional format for reporting studies that derives largely from quantitative methodologies. It reflects underlying assumptions about ways of making knowledge. The bulk of the writing is done once the research has been completed and that work is presented under a series of more or less prestructured headings. Marlow (2001: 273) offers a typical list of such headings for a research report:

- statement of the research topic
- literature review
- research questions and hypotheses
- research design
- sampling strategy
- data collection method(s)
- results
- discussion
- limitations
- recommendations for future research
- implications for practice.

Marlow suggests that this basic format can be applied to a range of different kinds of research study and believes it holds good whether or not the methodological approach has been primarily quantitative or qualitative, allowing for some latitude under the 'results' or 'findings' section when it comes to qualitative data.

In terms of presentation, Sarantakos (1998) advises that the writing should be done with clarity, precision, objectivity, fairness, impersonality and so on. In other words, the main criteria for the report are that it should be accurate and complete. It then becomes, as far as possible, a neutral medium that conveys to the reader a true representation of the research processes and outcomes.

There is a different approach to writing, however, that attends to the rhetorical and persuasive devices that render it legitimate and plausible to the reader. Gilbert (1993b) suggests that all forms of report writing involve social acts of communication and persuasion. The writer deploys linguistic devices and these work, or don't, according to the distinctive beliefs and customs at play in constructing truth value within different knowledge communities. Denzin (1994) follows a similar approach in discussing the 'art and politics of interpretation'. Here, the relationships between truth, reality and text are presented as highly complicated. The writer is seen to be engaged in a practice that is at once expressive and productive, involved in a complicated interchange between meaning, interpretation and representation. The act of writing becomes a political act in the sense that the researcher/writer has a positioned sense of self in order to connect with his or her text and reader and make knowledge claims that carry legitimacy and authority in relation to members of diverse interpretive communities.

Others observe how such perspectives are leading to rather more in the way of experimentation with newer forms of writing than happened in the past. Punch (1998: 266) refers to a 'proliferation of forms of writing in qualitative research', and cites Miles and Huberman (1994: 299), who forecast that 'the reporting of qualitative data may be one of the most fertile fields going; there are no fixed formats, and the ways data are being analysed and interpreted are getting more and more various'.

The issues concern written form but go beyond that. There is a different view of the performance of writing – that it is not so much representational as 'a way of learning, a way of knowing, a form of analysis and enquiry' (Punch, 1998: 279). Punch (1998: 280) quotes Coffey and Atkinson (1996: 109):

> The net effect of recent developments is that we cannot approach the task of 'writing up' our research as a straightforward (if demanding) task. We have to approach it as an analytical task, in which the form of our reports and representations is as powerful and significant as their content.

These considerations have moved us into what might be termed the politics of writing, which combines with the politics of knowledge to produce a heady atmosphere of alternative practices in reporting. Choices emerge as conventional ways of approaching and thinking about the writing task are seen as historic and fulfilling certain customs and traditions, ones that need to be critically evaluated and appropriated or not according to the purpose and obligations of the research. Richardson (1994) argues that writing – particularly reporting on qualitative research – can become a creative exercise when the traditional dualisms of fact and fiction, literature and science no longer hold. At the same time, she advocates the importance of maintaining reflexivity on the part of the writer and, especially, a continuing engagement with the political aspects of knowledge making.

As noted previously, we need to remain cognizant of the complementary politics of reading. The interpretation of reports in both their content and form is within, but also outside, the influence of the author, as is control over their exposure and use. Institutions of publishing, in many respects, act as gatekeepers in the promotion of research. Within many organizations, the suppression, burying or reframing of reports that are politically unfavourable remains a stark possibility. At the extreme, too, it is not unknown for legal injunctions to be sought to prevent researchers from speaking out. Reporting, as we saw with dissemination, is more than a technical exercise – it occurs in socio-political contexts, with ethical implications.

Having an impact – communities of practice

The expectation that research be disseminated is associated with an agenda for research that it has an impact and assumes a social significance beyond research communities themselves, that it exerts some agency in social change and development. Indeed, the relationship between social research and social change has long been debated and the interest in dissemination strategies is perhaps the most recent manifestation of this.

Meanwhile, indigenous perspectives in Australia have emphasized how research has been exercised largely within colonizing practices that have opposed the interests of their communities. This has been occurring while Western researchers have been formulating various models regarding the potential for research to have some effect on social issues. The three most notable of these models have been referred to as the engineering, enlightenment and critical models (Hammersley, 1995a).

The *engineering* model sees researchers intervening directly in social matters on the basis of their expert knowledge and with institutionalized authority. In the *enlightenment* model, the researcher seeks a much less direct role by taking responsibility to 'impact on the policy climate through processes of intellectual association and influence' (Bloor, 1997: 222). The *critical* model argues for action-oriented research for progressive change, 'achieved through emancipation rather than policy influence' (Bloor, 1997: 222).

Bloor (1997: 236) – himself a qualitative researcher rather than a practitioner – concludes that what he terms 'practitioner-oriented research' offers a promising model for effecting meaningful social change as a result of research practices:

> The qualitative researcher may become part of his or her local practitioner collectivity and trades on that position as a collectivity member to disseminate research findings ... There is therefore the opportunity for practitioners to make evaluative judgments about their own practices and experiment with the adoption of new approaches described in the research findings.

You will have noticed that the possibilities for linking research and change by making connections between researcher and participant or stakeholder communities is a recurrent theme in the literature. Theoretically, this theme might be traced to the idea of there being networks of communities of practice with their distinctive cultures and discourses and research activity constituting a particular network(s) of such communities. From this perspective, then, having an impact involves making connections between communities of practice. This might be sought, for example, by means of the intended merger of researcher and participant, as in some applications of participatory action research, or a sense of shared membership, as in Bloor's example above, or it might be related more to the positioning of respective members and their reflexive appropriation of certain linguistic or change strategies.

A common observation is that, whatever variation is pursued, the matter of achieving impact requires its own analysis and action and needs early consideration and planning. Wadsworth (1997: 87–8) offers a framework for developing a plan for action to be taken once the key messages from the research have been determined. In summary, these are as follows.

- Work out what you want to achieve.

  - What do you want to happen?
  - What action do you want taken?

- Who would need to know, understand and accept your key messages in order to make these things happen?
- What do you want each of these people to do?
- What would be the best ways to present your key messages to these people for these purposes?

  - What do you want to get over to them?
  - How, where and when is this best done?

Knowledge making in a world of knowledge management

We have argued for social work research that is inclusive of different ways of knowing and different ways of knowledge making, reflexive in its relationships with others, critical within its embeddedness in networks of power and ethical in its pursuit of anti-oppressive and transformative practices. We have emphasized the importance of contextualizing our understandings and actions. We need to ask, what are the prospects for approaching social work research in this way? Is this viable within current and future contexts of practice?

In some respects, one could say that the approach to social work research we are advocating has emerged out of just such considerations. It positions the researcher in the specifics of their local contexts and presents existing knowledge on the concepts and techniques of research as a resource that is there to be drawn on in systematic and purposeful ways according to the situation in hand. Yet, there are questions here about the places occupied by social work researchers and the features of their everyday communities of practice. To what extent do they allow for the approach we are supporting?

Systems of governance within human service organizations have been subject to continuing change in recent decades and this has altered substantially the roles and relationships of the professionals working within them (Scarborough, 1996). Waves of new public management ideologies have re-cast work cultures and practices and, in broad terms, have established that the professional is there to serve the organization's goals and not vice versa (Jones, 1999). The management of performance occurs via an array of mechanisms and processes, including the increasing use of instructional computer software within the workplace (Hough, 2003). Knowledge, including research-based knowledge, is becoming institutionalized as a result of the production of best-practice standards and accompanying compliance procedures. Such developments would seem to threaten both the scope for knowledge making by social work researchers and its alignment with participatory, transformative processes.

Within these developments, there has been some call for the promotion of cultures of learning and research in human services. This would certainly appear consistent with strategic objectives to deliver effective services of high quality, responsive to consumers and communities. As Gregory (1997: 202) says, human service organizations:

> probably require greater capacity for learning and adaptation … otherwise they may continue to categorize and act on people in the light of inadequately examined, self-validating, organizational (and professional) beliefs.

Yet, as he describes, the working environment 'leaves little time and energy for critical reflection on the assumptions that underpin their work' and 'there may tend to be an inverse correlation between the certainty of task technology and the political sensitivity of that task' (1997: 202).

What would seem to be required is an analysis of the spaces and places created for social work research within the contemporary contexts of its practice. Addressing the policy domain, for example, Muetzelfeldt and Briskman (2000) observe the fragmentation of services that has accompanied the use of (competitively based) contracts and now the consequences of partnership approaches from centre-left politics still searching for effective forms of collaborative management. They suggest that different channels of connectedness and communication have arisen, formal and informal, to counter fragmentation. This then generates new sets of conflicts and contradictions and alternative possibilities for the exercise of discretion and interorganizational learning processes. Such an analysis points to emergent professional roles that might well hold opportunities for creative research processes.

Addressing the practice domain, Fook (2002: 161–5) offers some helpful suggestions (summarized below) for seizing opportunities for critical practice in hostile environments.

- **Reframing our practice as contextual**   This involves breaking the opposition between 'practice' and 'environment' by 'working with the context no matter what that context might be' and 'creating different microclimates within broader contexts'.

- **Expropriating and translating the discourse**   This involves 'identifying aspects of the dominant discourse that may be turned to other ends' while 'emphasizing the organizational benefits'. The translation, for example, of 'evaluation', 'quality' and 'community consultation' in this way could create possibilities for critical research practices.
- **Identifying contradictions, complexities and points of alliance**   The assumption here is that contexts are complicated and so there will always be aspects that are 'ambiguous or in conflict', creating the potential for alliances on specific projects or initiatives.
- **Contributing to change while being part of the problem?**   'If we understand that each specific context in which we work, and even each specific act within it, has the potential to function in a number of ways simultaneously, then this indicates that we need to engage with people or situations in ways which minimize the harmful functions and maximize the empowering ones.'

What is research? Revisited

In the very first exercise, you were invited to 'exorcise the demons' associated with research. Below, you are invited to consider what, if anything, has changed in your view of research now that you have reached the end of this book.

Exorcising your demons once more

- Recall your responses the first time you completed this exercise.
- How different, if at all, does research look to you now?
- What has changed? Try to be as specific as possible.
- Now what, if anything, do you see as the contribution of research to you, your practice and social work?
- What does this tell you about your own ways of knowing, practising and researching?

Conclusion

In this book, we have attempted to cover material that is theoretical, analytical and also technical. The issues are complicated ones. Moreover, the political and ethical aspects we have raised throughout do pose both intellectual and personal challenges. As we noted at the outset, the subject of research often seems far removed from the reasons people choose to become social workers. We hope we have been able argue persuasively enough that research be understood as an integral part of the practice and policy of social work. We take it to be so because we see research as crucial to the mission of social work. At the same time, we are aware that both research and social work have not always behaved well towards the people and communities whose interests they claim to serve. We would like to think that this book makes some contribution to minimizing these aspects and furthering the positive impact that both research and social work can achieve. Research is a demanding but rewarding activity and we hope you decide that it is one worth pursuing.

References

AASW (2000) 'Code of ethics'. Canberra: Australian Association of Social Workers.

Abercrombie, N., Hill, S. and Turner, B. (1988) *The Penguin Dictionary of Sociology* (2nd edition). Harmondsworth: Penguin.

Aboriginal Health Council of South Australia (1995) 'Reclaiming our stories, reclaiming our lives Part 1', *Dulwich Centre Newsletter*, 1: 1–22.

Ahmad, W.I.U. and Sheldon, T. (1993) '"Race" and statistics', in M. Hammersley (ed.), *Social Research: Philosophy, Politics and Practice*. London: Sage. pp. 124–30.

Allen-Meares, P. (1984) 'Content analysis: it does have a place in social work research', *Journal of Social Science Research*, 7: 51–68.

Alston, M. and Bowles, W. (1998) *Research for Social Workers*. St Leonards, New South Wales, Australia: Allen & Unwin.

Alter, C. and Evens, W. (1990) *Evaluating Your Own Practice: A Guide to Self-Assessment*. New York: Springer.

Altheide, D.L. and Johnson, J.M. (1994) 'Criteria for assessing interpretive validity in qualitative research', in N. Denzin and Y. Lincoln (eds), *Handbook of Qualitative Research*. London: Sage. pp. 138–57.

Angen, M.J. (2000) 'Evaluating interpretive inquiry: reviewing the validity debate and opening the dialogue', *Qualitative Health Research*, May, 10 (3): 378–95.

Arber, S. (1993a) 'The research process', in N. Gilbert (ed.), *Researching Social Life*. London: Sage. pp. 32–50.

Arber, S. (1993b) 'Designing samples', in N. Gilbert (ed.), *Researching Social Life*. London: Sage. pp. 68–93.

Arber, S. and Ginn, J. (1991) *Gender and Later Life: A Sociological Analysis of Resources and Constraints*. London: Sage.

Atkinson, P. (1990) *The Ethnographic Imagination: Textual Constructions of Reality*. London: Routledge.

Babbie, E. (1999) *The Basics of Social Research*. Belmont, California: Brooks/Cole.

Bailey, K.D. (1978) *Methods for Social Research* (3rd edition). New York: The Free Press.

Barn, R. (1994) 'Race and ethnicity in social work: some issues for anti-discriminatory research', in B. Humphries and C. Truman (eds), *Re-thinking Social Research*. Aldershot: Avebury. pp. 37–58.

Becker, H. (1963) *Outsiders: Studies in the Sociology of Deviance*. Glencoe, Illinois: The Free Press.

Becker, H.S. (1970) 'Whose side are we on?', in J.D. Douglas (ed.), *The Relevance of Sociology*. New York: Appleton-Century-Crofts.

Bell, J. (1993) *Doing your Research Project: A Guide for First-time Researchers in Education and Social Science* (2nd edition). Buckingham: Open University Press.

Beresford, P. and Evans, C. (1999) 'Research note: research and empowerment', *British Journal of Social Work*, 29: 671–6.

Biesta, G.J. (2001) 'How difficult should education be?', *Educational Theory*, 51 (4): 385–400.

Blaikie, N. (1993) *Approaches to Social Enquiry*. Cambridge: Polity Press.

Blainey, G. (2000) 'Positives outweigh negatives in the past 100 years', speech given to the Samuel Griffith Society, November 2000, published in *The Australian* newspaper and reprinted with permission (http://www.mrcltd.org.au/uploaded_documents/MRC_News3_Pt6_Positives_Outweigh_Negatives.htm).

Bloor, M. (1997) 'Addressing social problems through qualitative research', in D. Silverman (ed.), *Qualitative Research: Theory, Method and Practice*. London: Sage.

Bogdan, R.C. and Biklen, S.K. (1982) *Qualitative Research for Education*. Boston, Massachusetts: Allyn & Bacon.

Bogdan, R. and Biklen, S.K. (1992) *Qualitative Research for Education: An Introduction to Theory and Methods* (2nd edition). Boston, Massachusetts: Allyn & Bacon.

Bogdewic, S. (1999) 'Participant observation', in B.F. Crabtree and W.L. Miller (eds), *Doing Qualitative Research*. Thousand Oaks, California: Sage. pp. 47–69.

Boulton, D. (2000) 'Unusual terms: what do you mean by …?' in B. Humphries (ed.), *Research in Social Care and Social Welfare: Issues and Debates for Practice*. London: Jessica Kingsley. pp. 86–91.

Bouma, G. (1993) *The Research Process*. Melbourne: Oxford University Press.

Bray, A. and Mirfin-Veitch, B. (2003) 'Disabled people and research: putting families first', in R. Munford and J. Sanders (eds), *Making a Difference in Families: Research That Creates Change*. Crows Nest, New South Wales, Australia: Allen & Unwin.

Brookfield, S.D. (1987) *Developing Critical Thinkers: Challenging Adults to Explore Alternative Ways of Thinking and Acting*. Buckingham: Open University Press.

Brown, S., Lumley, J., Small, R. and Astbury, J. (1994) *Missing Voices: The Experience of Motherhood*. Melbourne: Oxford University Press.

Bruyere, G. (1998) 'Living in another man's house: supporting Aboriginal learners in social work education', *Canadian Social Work Review*, 15 (2): 169–76.

Bryman, A. (1988) *Quantity and Quality in Social Research*. London: Routledge.

Bryman, A. (2001) *Social Research Methods*. Oxford: Oxford University Press.

Bryman, A. and Burgess, R. (1994a) 'Developments in qualitative data analysis: an introduction', in A. Bryman and R. Burgess (eds), *Analysing Qualitative Data*. London: Routledge. pp. 1–17.

Bryman, A. and Burgess, R. (1994b) 'Reflections on qualitative data analysis', in A. Bryman and R. Burgess (eds), *Analysing Qualitative Data*. London: Routledge. pp. 216–26.

Bryman, A. and Cramer, D. (2001) *Quantitative Data Analysis with SPSS Release 10 for Windows: A Guide for Social Scientists*. London: Routledge.

Burgess, R. (1984) *In the Field: An Introduction to Field Research*. London: Routledge.

Byrne-Armstrong, H. (2001) 'Whose show is it? The contradictions of collaboration', in H. Byrne-Armstrong, J. Higgs and D. Horsfall (eds), *Critical Moments in Qualitative Research*. Oxford: Butterworth-Heinemann. pp. 106–14.

Campbell, B. (1988) *Unofficial Secrets: Child Sexual Abuse, the Cleveland Case*. London: Virago.

Carlson, B. (1992) 'Questioning the party line on violence', *Affilia*, 7 (2): 94–111.

Chandler, J. (1990) 'Researching and the Relevance of Gender', in R. Burgess (ed.), *Studies in Qualitative Methodology: Reflections of Field Experience*. Greenwich, Connecticut: JAI Press. pp. 119–40.

Charmaz, K. (1983) 'The grounded theory method: an explication and interpretation' in R.M. Emmerson (ed.), *Contemporary Field Research*. Boston, Massachusetts: Little, Brown & Co.

Cheetham, J. and Kazi, M.A.F. (eds.) (1998) *The Working of Social Work*. London: Jessica Kingsley.

Cheetham, J., Fuller, R., McIvor, G. and Petch, A. (1992) *Evaluating Social Work Effectiveness*. Buckingham: Open University Press.

Cicourel, A.V. (1964) *Method and Measurement in Sociology*. New York: The Free Press.

Cicourel, A.V. (1968) *The Social Organization of Juvenile Justice*. New York: Wiley.

Cicourel, A.V. (1974) 'Police practices and official records', in R. Turner (ed.), *Ethnomethodology*. Harmondsworth: Penguin. pp. 85–95.

Clifford, D. (1994) 'Critical life histories: key anti-oppressive research methods and processes', in C. Truman and B. Humphries (eds), *Re-thinking Social Research: Anti-discriminatory Approaches in Research Methodology*. Aldershot: Avebury. pp. 102–22.

Cockburn, T. (2000) 'Case studying organizations: the use of quantitative approaches', in B. Humphries (ed.), *Research in Social Care and Social Welfare: Issues and Debates for Practice*. London: Jessica Kingsley. pp. 59–68.

Coffey, A. and Atkinson, P. (1996) *Making Sense of Qualitative Data: Complementary Research Strategies*. Thousand Oaks, California: Sage.

Cohen, S. and Taylor, L. (1972) *Psychological Survival: The Experience of Long-term Imprisonment*. Harmondsworth: Penguin.

Commonwealth of Australia (1999) *National Statement on Ethical Conduct in Research Involving Humans*. Canberra: AusInfo.

Community Service and Research Centre, University of Queensland, Ipswich, Australia (www.uq.edu.au/ csrc/socialcapitalprojects.php).

Connell, R.W. et al. (1975) *How to do Small Surveys – A Guide for Students in Sociology, Kindred Industries and Allied Trades*. Adelaide: Flinders University.

Cook, J.A. (1984) 'Influence of gender on the problems of parents of fatally ill children', *Journal of Psychological Oncology*, 2 (1): 71–91.

Coulter, D. and Wiens, J.R. (2002) 'Educational judgment: linking the actor and the spectator', *Educational Researcher*, 31 (4): 15–25.

D'Cruz, H. (1998) '"Taking responsibility" for "physical abuse": gender and disability', in *Australian Women's Studies Association Conference Proceedings*, Adelaide, South Australia, pp. 18–27.

D'Cruz, H. (1999) 'Constructing meanings and identities in practice: child protection in Western Australia'. PhD thesis, Department of Applied Social Science, Lancaster University, Lancaster.

D'Cruz, H. (2000) 'Social work research as knowledge/power in practice', *Sociological Research Online*, 5 (1). (www.socresonline.org.uk/5/1/dcruz.html).

D'Cruz, H. (2001) 'The fractured lens: methodology in perspective', in H. Byrne-Armstrong, J. Higgs and D. Horsfall (eds), *Critical Moments in Qualitative Research*. Oxford: Butterworth-Heinemann. pp. 17–29.

D'Cruz, H. (2002) 'Constructing the identities of "responsible mothers, invisible men" in child protection practice', *Sociological Research Online*, 7 (1). (www.socresonline.org.uk/7/1/d'cruz.html).

D'Cruz, H., Soothill, K., Francis, B. and Christie, A. (2002) 'Gender, ethics and social work: an international study of students' perceptions at entry into social work education', *International Social Work*, 45 (2): 149–66.

de Hoog, J. (1972) *Skid Row Dossier*. Melbourne: Sun Books.

Dean, J. and Whyte, W. (1978) 'How do you know if the informant is telling the truth?', in J. Bynner and K. Stribley (eds), *Social Research: Principles and Procedures*. London: Longman. pp. 179–88.

Delaney, C. (1988) 'Participation–observation: the razor's edge', *Dialectical Anthropology* (vol. 13). The Netherlands: Kluwer Academic Publishers. pp. 291–300.

Denzin, N.K. (1970) *The Research Act in Sociology*. Chicago, Illinois: Aldine.

Denzin, N.K. (1989) *The Research Act in Sociology*. Chicago, Illinois: Aldine.

Denzin, N.K. (1994) 'The art and politics of interpretation', in N.K. Denzin, and Y.S. Lincoln, (eds), *Handbook of Qualitative Research* (2nd edition). Newbury Park, California: Sage. pp. 500–15.

Denzin, N.K. and Lincoln, Y.S. (eds) (1994) *Handbook of Qualitative Research* (2nd edition). Newbury Park, California: Sage.

Dominelli, L. (1997) *Sociology for Social Work*. London: Macmillan.

Dore, M.M. and Doris, J.M. (1997) 'Preventing child placement in substance-abusing families: research informed practice', *Child Welfare*, 77 (4): 407–26.

Drake, M. (1989) *The New Maori Myth*. Auckland: Wycliffe Christian Schools. p. 20.

Edwards, M. with Howard, C. and Miller, R. (2001) *Social Policy, Public Policy: From Problem to Practice*. St Leonards, New South Wales, Australia: Allen & Unwin.

Elliott, H. (1997) 'The use of diaries in sociological research on health experience', *Sociological Research Online*, 2 (2) (www.socresonline.org.uk/2/2/7.html).

Ellis, C. and Flaherty, M.G. (eds) (1992) *Investigating Subjectivity: Research on Lived Experience*. Newbury Park, California: Sage.

England, S.E. (1994) 'Modelling theory from fiction and autobiography', in C.K. Riessman (ed.), *Qualitative Studies in Social Work Research*. Thousands Oaks, California: Sage. pp. 190–213.

Epstein, I. (1987) 'Pedagogy of the perturbed: teaching research to reluctants', *Journal of Teaching in Social Work*, 1: 71–89.

Everitt, A., Hardiker, P., Littlewood, J. and Mullender, A. (1992) *Applied Research for Better Practice*. London: Macmillan with British Association of Social Workers.

Fairclough, N. (1992) *Discourse and Social Change*. London: Polity Press.

Fanon, F. (1992) 'The fact of blackness', in J. Donald and A. Rattansi (eds), *'Race', Culture and Difference*. London: Sage with Open University Press. pp. 220–40.

Featherstone, B. (1996) 'Victims or villains? Women who physically abuse their children', in B. Fawcett, B. Featherstone, J. Hearn and C. Toft (eds), *Violence and Gender Relations*. London: Sage. pp. 178–89.

Featherstone, B. (1997) 'What has gender got to do with it? Exploring physically abusive behaviour towards children', *British Journal of Social Work*, 27: 419–33.

Feyerabend, P. (1975) *Against Method*. London: New Left Books.

Fielding, N. (1993) 'Ethnography', in N. Gilbert (ed.), *Researching Social Life*. London: Sage. pp. 154–71.

Fischer, J. (1993) 'Empirically based practice: the end of ideology?', in M. Bloom (ed.), *Single System Designs in the Social Services: Issues and Options for the 1990s*. New York: Haworth.

Flick, U. (1998) *An Introduction to Qualitative Research*. London: Sage.

Fook, J. (1993) *Radical Casework: A Theory of Practice*. St Leonards, New South Wales, Australia: Allen & Unwin.

Fook, J. (1996) 'The reflective researcher: developing a reflective approach to practice', in J. Fook (ed.), *The Reflective Researcher: Social Workers' Theories of Practice Research*. St Leonards, New South Wales, Australia: Allen & Unwin. pp. 1–8.

Fook, J. (ed.) (1996) *The Reflective Researcher: Social Workers' Theories of Practice Research*. St Leonards, New South Wales, Australia: Allen & Unwin.

Fook, J. (1999) 'Critical reflectivity in education and practice', in B. Pease and J. Fook (eds), *Transforming Social Work Practice*. St Leonards, New South Wales, Australia: Allen & Unwin.

Fook, J. (2000) 'Theorising from frontline practice: towards an inclusive approach for social work research', paper presented at the Economic & Social Research Council-funded seminar series, 'Theorizing Social Work Research', Luton, July 2000.

Fook, J. (2002) *Social Work: Critical Theory and Practice*. London: Sage.

Foucault, M. (1978) *The History of Sexuality*. New York: Pantheon.

Foucault, M. (1980) *Power/Knowledge: Selected Interviews and Other Writings* (edited by Colin Gordon). New York: Harvester Wheatsheaf.

Frankenberg, R. (1993) *The Social Construction of Whiteness: 'White Women, Race Matters'*. London: Routledge with the University of Minnesota.

Fuchs, S. (1992) 'Relativism and reflexivity in the sociology of scientific knowledge', in G. Ritzer (ed.), *Metatheorizing*. Newbury Park, California: Sage. pp. 151–67.

Fuller, R. and Petch, A. (1995) *Practitioner Research: The Reflexive Social Worker*. Buckingham: Open University Press.

Galton, M. and Delamont, S. (1985) 'Speaking with forked tongue? Two styles of observation in the ORACLE project', in R.G. Burgess (ed.), *Field Methods in the Study of Education*. London: Falmer Press. pp. 163–89.

Ganguly-Scrase, R. (1998) 'The self as research instrument', in M. Crick and B. Geddes (eds), *Research Methods in the Field*. Geelong, Victoria, Australia: Deakin University Press.

Garfinkel, H. (1974) '"Good" organizational reasons for "bad" clinic records', in R. Turner (ed.), *Ethnomethodology*. Harmondsworth: Penguin. pp. 96–101.

Gelles, R. (1987) *Family Violence* (vol. 84). Newbury Park, California: Sage Library of Social Research.

Gibbs, L. (1991) *Scientific Reasoning for Social Workers: Bridging the Gap Between Research and Practice*. New York: Merrill.

Gilbert, N. (1993a) 'Research, theory and method', in N. Gilbert (ed.), *Researching Social Life*. London: Sage. pp. 18–31.

Gilbert, N. (1993b) 'Writing about social research', in N. Gilbert (ed.), *Researching Social Life*. London: Sage.

Gilman, S.L. (1992) 'Black bodies, white bodies: toward an iconography of female sexuality in late nineteenth-century art, medicine and literature', in J. Donald and A. Rattansi (eds), *'Race', Culture and Difference*. London: Sage with Open University Press. pp. 171–97.

Glaser, B. (1978) *Theoretical Sensitivity*. Mill Valley, California: Sociology Press.

Glaser, B. (1992) *Basics of Grounded Theory Analysis*. Mill Valley, California: Sociology Press.

Glaser, B. and Straus, A. (1967) *The Discovery of Grounded Theory*. Chicago, Illinois: Aldine.

Goffman, E. (1961) *Asylums: Essays in the Social Situation of Mental Patients and Other Inmates*. New York: Anchor Books.

Gold, R. (1958) 'Roles in sociological field observation', *Social Forces*, 36 (3): 217–23.

Gould, S. (1981) *The Mismeasure of Man*. New York: Norton.

Government Statisticians' Collective (1993) 'How official statistics are produced: views from the inside', in M. Hammersley (ed.), *Social Research: Philosophy, Politics and Practice*. London: Sage. pp. 146–65.

Graham, A. (1994) *Teach Yourself Statistics*. London: Hodder Headline Arnold, Teach Yourself Books.

Graham, H. (1993) *Hardship and Health in Women's Lives*. London: Harvester Wheatsheaf.

Greene, J. (2002) 'Mixed-method evaluation: a way of democratically engaging with difference', *Evaluation Journal of Australasia*, 2 (new series) (2): 23–9.

Gregory, R. (1997) 'The peculiar tasks of public management', in M. Considine and M. Painter (eds), *Managerialism: The Great Debate*. Melbourne: Melbourne University Press.

Griffin, J.H. (1961) *Black Like Me*. New York: Panther Books.

Griggs v Duke Power Co. (1971) 401 US 424.

Guba, E. and Lincoln, Y. (1982) 'Epistemological and methodological bases of naturalistic inquiry', *Education Communication and Technology Journal*, 30 (4): 233–52.

Hacking, I. (1990) *The Taming of Chance*. Cambridge: Cambridge University Press.

Hacking, I. (1999) *The Social Construction of What?* Cambridge, Massachusetts: Harvard University Press.

Hakim, C. (1993) 'Research analysis of administrative records', in M. Hammersley (ed.), *Social Research: Philosophy, Politics and Practice*. London: Sage. pp. 131–45.

Hall, C. (1997) *Social Work as Narrative: Storytelling and Persuasion in Professional Texts*. Aldershot: Ashgate.

Hammersley, M. (1995a) *The Politics of Social Research*. London: Sage.

Hammersley, M. (1995b) 'Theory and evidence in qualitative research', *Quality and Quantity*, 29: 55–66.

Hammersley, M. (1996) 'The relationship between qualitative and quantitative research: paradigm loyalty versus methodological eclectism', in J.T.E. Richardson (ed.), *Handbook of Research Methods for Psychology and the Social Sciences*. Leicester: PBS Books.

Harrison, L. and Cameron-Traub, E. (1994) 'Patients' perspectives on nursing in hospital', in C. Waddell and A.R. Petersen (eds), *Just Health: Inequality in Illness, Care and Prevention*. London: Churchill Livingstone. pp. 147–58.

Hart, E. and Bond, M. (1995) *Action Research for Health and Social Care: A Guide to Practice*. Buckingham: Open University Press.

Hartman, A. (1990) 'Many ways of knowing', *Social Work*, January: 3–4.

Hartman, A. (1992) 'In search of subjugated knowledge', *Social Work*, 37 (6): 483–4.

Healy, B. (1996) 'In doing you learn: some reflections on practice research on an advocacy project', in J. Fook (ed.), *The Reflective Researcher: Social Workers' Theories of Practice Research*. St Leonards, New South Wales, Australia: Allen & Unwin.

Hearn, J. (1996) 'Men's violence to known women: historical, everyday and theoretical constructions by men', in B. Fawcett, B. Featherstone, J. Hearn and C. Toft (eds), *Violence and Gender Relations: Theories and Interventions*. London: Sage. pp. 22–38.

Herrnstein, R.J. and Murray, C. (1994) *The Bell Curve: Intelligence and Class Structure in American Life*. New York: The Free Press.

Hill, A. and Jordan, E.C. (eds) (1995) *Race, Gender and Power in America: The Legacy of the Hill–Thomas Hearings*. New York: Oxford University Press.

Hollway, W. (1989) *Subjectivity and Method in Psychology: Gender, Meaning and Science*. London: Sage.

Holstein, J. (1988) 'Court ordered incompetence: conversational organization in involuntary commitment hearings', *Social Problems*, 35 (4): 458–73.

Holstein, J. and Gubrium, J. (1995) *The Active Interview*, Qualitative Research Methods Series. Newbury Park, California: A Sage University Paper.

Horne, D. (2001) *Looking for Leadership: Australia in the Howard Years*. Australia: Viking Press.

Hough, G. (2003) 'Enacting critical social work in public welfare contexts', in J. Allan, B. Pease and L. Briskman (eds), *Critical Social Work: An Introduction to Theories and Practices*. Crows Nest, New South Wales, Australia: Allen & Unwin.

Howe, D. (1997) 'Psychosocial and relationship-based theories for child and family social work: political philosophy, psychology and welfare practice', *Child and Family Social Work*, 2: 161–70.

Huberman, A.M. and Crandall, D.P. (1982) 'Fitting words to numbers: multisite and multi-method research in educational dissemination', *American Behavioral Scientist*, 26 (1): 62–83.

Huberman, A.M. and Miles, M.B. (1994) 'Data management and analysis methods', in N.K. Denzin and Y.S. Lincoln (eds), *Handbook of Qualitative Research* (2nd edition). Thousand Oaks, California: Sage. pp. 428–44.

Hudson, W.W. (1990) *The Clinical Measurement Package*. Homewood, Illinois: Dorsey Press.

Huggins, J. (1991) 'Theories of race and gender', *The Olive Pink Society Bulletin*, 3 (1): 6–15.

Huggins, J., Saunders, K. and Tarrago, I. (2000) 'Reconciling our mothers' lives', in J. Docker and G. Fischer (eds), *Race, Colour and Identity in Australia and New Zealand*. Sydney: University of New South Wales Press. pp. 39–58.

Human Rights and Equal Opportunity Commission (HREOC) (1997) *Bringing Them Home: National Inquiry into the Separation of Aboriginal and Torres Strait Islander Children from their Families*. Sydney: Sterling Press and Commonwealth of Australia.

Humphreys, L. (1970) *Tea Room Trade: Impersonal Sex in Public Places*. Chicago, Illinois: Aldine.

Humphries, B. (1994) 'Empowerment and social research: elements for an analytic framework', in B. Humphries and C. Truman (eds), *Re-thinking Social Research: Anti-discriminatory Approaches in Research Methodology*. Aldershot: Avebury. pp. 185–204.

Humphries, B. and Martin, M. (2000) 'Disrupting ethics in social research', in B. Humphries (ed.), *Research in Social Care and Social Welfare: Issues and Debates for Practice*. London: Jessica Kingsley. pp. 69–85.

Humphries, B. and Truman, C. (eds) (1994) *Re-thinking Social Research: Anti-discriminatory Approaches in Research Methodology*. Aldershot: Avebury. pp. 185–204.

Hyden, M. (1994) *Woman Battering as a Marital Act: The Construction of a Violent Marriage*. Oslo: Scandinavian University Press.

Ife, J. (2001) *Human Rights and Social Work: Towards Rights-based Practice*. Cambridge: Cambridge University Press.

Ife, J. (2002) *Community Development: Community-based Alternatives in an Era of Globalization* (2nd edition). Frenchs Forest, New South Wales, Australia: Pearson Education Australia.

IKE (1994) *Koorie Research Programme: Ethics, Protocols and Methodologies – A Discussion Paper*. Geelong, Victoria, Australia: Institute of Koorie Education, Deakin University.

Irvine, A. (1995) 'The social work role with personality disordered clients', in R. Fuller and A. Petch (eds), *Practitioner Research: The Reflexive Social Worker*. Buckingham: Open University Press.

Jacobs, S. (1997) 'Sociology as a source of anomaly in Thomas Kuhn's system of science', *Philosophy of the Social Sciences*, 27 (4): 466–85.

Jacobs, S. (2002a) 'The genesis of "scientific community"', *Social Epistemology*, 16 (2): 157–68.

Jacobs, S. (2002b) 'Polyani's presagement of the incommensurability concept', *Studies in the History and Philosophy of Science*, 33: 105–20.

Jayaratne, T.E. (1993) 'The value of quantitative methodology for feminist research', in M. Hammersley (ed.), *Social Research: Philosophy, Politics and Practice*. London: Sage. pp. 109–23.

Jenkins, G.D., Nadar, D.A., Lawler, E.E. and Cammann, C. (1975) 'Standardized observations: an approach to measuring the nature of jobs', *Journal of Applied Psychology*, 60: 171–81.

Jones, M. (1990) 'Understanding social work: a matter of interpretation', *British Journal of Social Work*, 20: 181–96.

Jones, M. (1999) 'Supervisor or superhero: new role strains for frontline supervisors in human services', *Asia Pacific Journal of Social Work*, 9 (1): 79–97.

Jones, M. (2004, forthcoming) 'Supervision, learning and transformative practices', in N. Gould and M. Baldwin (eds), *Social Work, Critical Reflection and the Learning Organization*. Aldershot: Ashgate.

Jupp, V. and Norris, C. (1993) 'Traditions in documentary analysis', in M. Hammersley (ed.), *Social Research: Philosophy, Politics and Practice*. London: Sage. pp. 37–51.

Kaufman Hall, V. (2001) 'Playing in the "mud" of government', in H. Byrne-Armstrong, J. Higgs and D. Horsfall (eds), *Critical Moments in Qualitative Research*. Oxford: Butterworth-Heinemann. pp. 115–27.

Kellehear, A. (1989) 'Ethics and social research', in J. Perry (ed.), *Doing Fieldwork: Eight Personal Accounts of Social Research*. Geelong, Victoria, Australia: Deakin University Press.

Kellehear, A. (1993) *The Unobtrusive Researcher: A Guide to Methods*. St Leonards, New South Wales, Australia: Allen & Unwin.

Kelly, L., Burton, S. and Regan, L. (1994) 'Researching women's lives or studying women's oppression? Reflections on what constitutes feminist research', in M. Maynard and J. Purvis (eds), *Researching Women's Lives from a Feminist Perspective*. London: Taylor & Francis.

Kemmis, S. and McTaggart, R. (eds) (1988) *The Action Research Planner* (3rd edition). Geelong, Victoria, Australia: Deakin University Press.

Kitzinger, C. and Wilkinson, S. (1993) 'Theorizing heterosexuality', in S. Wilkinson and C. Kitzinger (eds), *Heterosexuality: A Feminism and Psychology Reader*. London: Sage.

Kuhn, T. (1970) *The Structure of Scientific Revolutions* (2nd edition). Chicago, Illinois: University of Chicago Press.

Kumar, R. (1996) *Research Methodology: A Step-by-step Guide for Beginners*. Melbourne: Longman.

Lacey, C. (1970) *Hightown Grammar: The School as a Social System*. Manchester: Manchester University Press.

Lacey, C. (1976) 'Problems of sociological fieldwork: a review of the methodology of "Hightown Grammar"', in M. Shipman (ed.), *The Organization and Impact of Social Research*. London: Routledge & Kegan Paul. pp. 63–88.

LaPiere, R.T. (1934) 'Attitudes and actions', *Social Forces*, 13: 230–7.

Lee, R.M. (1993) *Doing Research on Sensitive Topics*. London: Sage.

Leininger, M.M. (1985) 'Nature, rationale and importance of qualitative research methods in nursing', in M.M. Leininger (ed.), *Qualitative Research Methods in Nursing*. Orlando, Florida: Grune & Stratton.

Leonard, P. (1997) *Postmodern Welfare*. London: Sage.

Levine, H.G. (1985) 'Principles of data storage and retrieval for use in qualitative evaluations', *Educational Evaluation and Policy Analysis*, 7 (2): 169–89.

Lofland, J. (1971) *Analyzing Social Settings: A Guide to Qualitative Observation and Analysis*. Belmont, California: Wadsworth.

Lorde, A. (1982) *Zami: A New Spelling of my Name*. London: Pandora.

Lucashenko, M. (1994) 'No other truth? Aboriginal women and Australian feminism', *Social Alternatives*, 12 (4): 21–4.

Lupton, D. and Najman, J. (1995) 'Sociology, health and health care', in G. Lupton and J. Najman (eds), *Sociology of Health and Illness: Australian Readings* (2nd edition). South Melbourne: Macmillan. pp. 3–26.

MacDonald, G., Sheldon, B. with Gillespie, J. (1992) 'Contemporary studies of the effectiveness of social work', *British Journal of Social Work*, 22 (6): 615–43.

Mackenzie, D.A. (1981) *Statistics in Britain 1865–1930: The Social Construction of Scientific Knowledge*. Edinburgh: Edinburgh University Press.

Manne, R. (2001a) *In Denial: The Stolen Generations and the Right*, The Australian Quarterly Essay. Melbourne: Schwartz Publishing.

Manne, R. (2001b) 'The stolen generations and the right', in R. Manne, *The Barren Years: John Howard and Australian Political Culture*. Melbourne: Text Publishing. pp. 151–63.

Markus, A. (2001) *Race: John Howard and the Remaking of Australia*. St Leonards, New South Wales, Australia: Allen & Unwin.

Marlow, C. (2001) *Research Methods for Generalist Social Work* (3rd edition). Belmont, California: Brooks/Cole.

Martin, M. (1994) 'Developing a feminist participative research framework: evaluating the process', in B. Humphries and C. Truman (eds), *Re-thinking Social Research*. Aldershot: Avebury. pp. 123–45.

Mason, J. (1994) 'Linking qualitative and quantitative data analysis', in A. Bryman and R.G. Burgess (eds), *Analysing Qualitative Data*. London: Routledge. pp. 89–110.

Mason, J. (1996) *Qualitative Researching*. London: Sage.

Maxwell, J.A. (1992) 'Understanding validity in qualitative research', *Harvard Educational Review*, 62 (3): 279–300.

McDonnell, D. (1986) *Theories of Discourse: An Introduction*. Oxford: Basil Blackwell.

Mickler, S. (1998) *The Myth of Privilege: Aboriginal Status, Media Visions, Public Ideas*. Fremantle, Western Australia: Fremantle Arts Centre Press.

Mies, M. (1993) 'Towards a methodology for feminist research', in M. Hammersley (ed.), *Social Research: Philosophy, Politics and Practice*. London: Sage. pp. 64–82.

Miles, M.B. and Huberman, A.M. (1994) *Qualitative Data Analysis: An Expanded Sourcebook* (2nd edition). Thousand Oaks, California: Sage.

Milgram, S. (1963) 'Behavioural study of obedience', *Journal of Abnormal and Social Psychology*, 67: 371–8.

Millen, D. (1997) 'Some methodological and epistemological issues raised by doing feminist research on non-feminist women', *Sociological Research Online*, 2 (3) (www.socresonline.org.uk/2/3/3.html).

Milner, J. (1993) 'A disappearing act: the differing career paths of fathers and mothers in child protection investigations', *Critical Social Policy*, 38: 48–68.

Morgan, D.L. (1998) 'Practical strategies for combining qualitative and quantitative methods: applications for health research', *Qualitative Health Research*, 8: 362–76.

Morgan, G. (1986) *Images of Organization*. Newbury Park, California: Sage.

Morgan, S. (2000) 'Documentary and text analysis: uncovering meaning in a worked example', in B. Humphries (ed.), *Research in Social Care and Social Welfare: Issues and Debates for Practice*. London: Jessica Kingsley. pp. 119–31.

Morrison, T. (ed.) (1993) *Race-ing Justice, En-gendering Power*. New York: Pantheon.

Morse, J. (1994) 'Designing funded qualitative research', in N.K. Denzin and Y.S. Lincoln (eds), *Handbook of Qualitative Research* (2nd edition). Thousand Oaks, California: Sage. pp. 220–35.

Moser, C.A. and Kalton, G. (1989) *Survey Methods in Social Investigation*. London: Gower.

Muetzelfeldt, M. and Briskman, L. (2000) 'Market rationality, organizational rationality and professional rationality: experiences from the "contract state"', paper presented at the conference 'Playing the market game? Governance models in child and youth welfare', University of Bielefeld, Germany, 9–11 March 2000.

Munford, R. and Sanders, J. (eds) (2003) *Making a Difference in Families: Research that Creates Change*. Crows Nest, New South Wales, Australia: Allen & Unwin.

NHMRC (1999) 'National statement on ethical conduct in research involving humans'. Canberra: Commonwealth of Australia.

Oakley, A. (1981) 'Interviewing women: a contradiction in terms', in H. Roberts (ed.), *Doing Feminist Research*. London: Routledge & Kegan Paul.

Oakley, A. (1999) 'People's ways of knowing: gender and methodology', in S. Hood, B. Mayall and S. Oliver (eds), *Critical Issues in Social Research: Power and Prejudice*. Buckingham: Open University Press.

O'Brien, M. (1993) 'Social research and sociology', in N. Gilbert (ed.), *Researching Social Life*. London: Sage. pp. 1–18.

O'Connor, I., Smyth, I. and Warburton, J. (eds) (2000) *Contemporary Perspectives on Social Work and Human Services*. Malaysia: Longman.

O'Connor, I., Wilson, J. and Setterlund, D. (1995) *Social Work and Welfare Practice*. Melbourne: Longman.

Okely, J. (1994) 'Thinking through fieldwork', in A. Bryman and R. Burgess (eds), *Analysing Qualitative Data*. London: Routledge. pp. 18–34.

Olesen, V. (1994) 'Feminisms and models of qualitative research', in N.K. Denzin and Y.S. Lincoln (eds), *Handbook of Qualitative Research* (2nd edition). Newbury Park, California: Sage. pp. 158–74.

Oliver, M. (1992) 'Changing the social relations of research production', *Disability, Handicap and Society*, 7 (2): 101–14.

OYA/SWPS (1984) *Income Support for Young People*. Canberra: Australian Government Printing Service.

Packham, C. (2000) 'Community auditing: appropriate research methods for effective youth and community work intervention', in B. Humphries (ed.), *Research in Social Care and Social Welfare: Issues and Debates for Practice*. London: Jessica Kingsley. pp. 102–18.

Parton, N. (1991) *Governing the Family: Child Care, Child Protection and the State*. London: Macmillan.

Parton, N., Thorpe, D. and Wattam, C. (1997) *Child Protection: Risk and the Moral Order*. London: Macmillan.

Patton, M.Q. (1987) *How to use Qualitative Methods in Evaluation*. Newbury Park, California: Sage.

Patton, M.Q. (1990) *Qualitative Evaluation and Research Methods*. Thousand Oaks, California: Sage.

Patton, M.Q. (1997) *Utilization-focused Evaluation: The New Century Text* (3rd edition). London: Sage.

Pease, B. and Fook, J. (eds) (1999) *Transforming Social Work Practice: Postmodern and Critical Perspectives*. St Leonards, New South Wales, Australia: Allen & Unwin.

Peile, C. (1988) 'Research paradigms in social work: from stalemate to creative synthesis', *Social Service Review*, 62 (1): 1–19.

Peile, C., McCouat, M. and Rose-Miller, M. (1995) 'Child abuse paradigms: an analysis of the basic theoretical and epistemological assumptions underlying child abuse literature', unpublished paper, Department of Social Work and Social Policy, University of Queensland, Australia.

Personal Narratives Group (eds) (1989) *Interpreting Women's Lives: Feminist Theory and Personal Narratives*. Indianapolis, Indiana: Indiana University Press.

Petr, C.G. and Barney, D.D. (1993) 'Reasonable efforts for children with disabilities: the parents' perspective', *Social Work*, 38 (3): 247–54.

Pithouse, A. (1987) *Social Work: The Social Organization of an Invisible Trade*. Aldershot: Avebury.

Platt, J. (1986) 'Functionalism and the survey: the relation of theory and method', *Sociological Review*, 34 (3): 501–36.

Polkinghorne, D.E. (1988) *Narrative Knowing and the Human Services*. Albany: SUNY Press.

Potter, J. (1996) *Representing Reality*. London: Sage.

Probyn, W. (1977) *Angel Face: The Making of a Criminal*. London: Allen & Unwin.

Procter, M. (1993) 'Measuring attitudes', in N. Gilbert (ed.), *Researching Social Life*. London: Sage. pp. 116–34.

Punch, K. (1998) *Introduction to Social Research: Quantitative and Qualitative Approaches*. London: Sage.

Punch, M. (1986) *The Politics and Ethics of Fieldwork*, Qualitative Research Methods Series. Newbury Park, California: A Sage University Paper.

Punch, M. (1993) 'Observation and the police: the research experience', in M. Hammersley (ed.), *Social Research: Philosophy, Politics and Practice*. London: Sage. pp. 181–99.

Rabbitts, E. and Fook, J. (1996) 'Empowering practitioners to publish: a writer's and a publisher's perspectives', in J. Fook (ed.), *The Reflective Researcher: Social Workers' Theories of Practice Research*. St Leonards, New South Wales, Australia: Allen & Unwin.

Reason, P. and Bradbury, H. (eds) (2001) *Handbook of Action Research: Participative Inquiry and Practice*. London: Sage.

Reid, W.J. (1994) 'Reframing the epistemological debate', in E. Sherman and W.J. Reid (eds), *Qualitative Research in Social Work*. New York: Columbia University Press.

Reinharz, S. (1992) *Feminist Methods in Social Research*. Oxford: Oxford University Press.

Renzetti, C. (1992) *Violent Betrayal: Partner Abuse in Lesbian Relationships*. Newbury Park, California: Sage.

Renzetti, C. and Curran, D.J. (1995) *Women, Men and Society* (3rd edition). Boston, Massachusetts: Allyn & Bacon.

Renzetti, C. and Lee, M. (eds) (1993) *Researching Sensitive Topics*. Thousand Oaks, California: Sage.

Reynolds, H. (2000a) *Why Weren't We Told?* (2nd edition). Ringwood, Victoria: Penguin.

Reynolds, H. (2000b) 'Indigenous social welfare: from a low priority to recognition and reconciliation', in A. McMahon, J. Thomson and C. Williams (eds), *Understanding the Australian Welfare State: Key Documents and Themes* (2nd edition). Croydon, Victoria: Macmillan Education Australia Pty Ltd. pp. 97–109.

Rhodes, M. (1986) *Ethical Dilemmas in Social Work Practice*. Boston, Massachusetts: Routledge & Kegan Paul. pp. 1–20.

Richards, T. and Richards, L. (1994) 'Using computers in qualitative research', in N.K. Denzin and Y.S. Lincoln (eds), *Handbook of Qualitative Research* (2nd edition). Newbury Park, California: Sage. pp. 445–62.

Richardson, L. (1994) 'Writing: a method of inquiry', in N. Denzin and Y. Lincoln (eds), *Handbook of Qualitative Research*. Newbury Park, California: Sage.

Riessman, C.K. (1993) *Narrative Analysis*, Qualitative Research Methods Series. Newbury Park, California: Sage.

Riessman, C.K. (1994a) 'Subjectivity matters: the positioned investigator', in C.K. Riessman (ed.), *Qualitative Studies in Social Work Research*. Newbury Park, California: Sage. pp. 133–8.

Riessman, C.K. (1994b) 'Narrative approaches to trauma', in C.K. Riessman (ed.), *Qualitative Studies in Social Work Research*. Thousand Oaks, California: Sage. pp. 67–71.

Rintoul, S. (1993) *The Wailing: A National Black Oral History*. Port Melbourne, Victoria: William Heinemann Australia.

Rojek, C., Peacock, G. and Collins, S. (1988) *Social Work and Received Ideas*. London: Routledge.

Rojiani, R.H. (1994) 'Disparities in the social construction of long-term care', in C.K. Riessman (ed.), *Qualitative Studies in Social Work*. Thousand Oaks, California: Sage. pp. 139–52.

Rose, N. (1989) *Governing the Soul: The Shaping of the Private Self*. London: Routledge.

Rose, N. (1998) *Inventing Ourselves: Psychology, Power and Personhood*. Cambridge: Cambridge University Press.

Rose, N. (1999) *Powers of Freedom: Reframing Political Thought*. Cambridge: Cambridge University Press.

Rowntree, D. (1981) *Statistics without Tears*. London: Pelican.

Royse, D. (1999) *Research Methods in Social Work*. Chicago, Illinois: Nelson-Hall.

Royse, D. and Thyer, B. (1996) *Program Evaluation* (2nd edition). Chicago, Illinois: Nelson-Hall.

Royse, D., Thyer, B., Padgett, D. and Logan, T.K. (2001) *Program Evaluation: An Introduction* (3rd edition). Belmont, California: Brooks/Cole.

Ryan, M. and Martyn, R. (1996) 'Writing about social work education: a content analysis of Australian journal articles 1983–1993', *Australian Social Work*, 49 (4): 19–23.

Ryan, M. and Martyn, R. (1997) 'Women writing on social work education: findings from a study of the content analysis of Australian journal articles 1983–1993', *Australian Social Work*, 50 (2): 13–18.

Said, E. (1978) *Orientalism*. Harmondsworth: Penguin.

Saleeby, D. (1994) 'Culture, theory and narrative: the intersections of meanings in practice', *Social Work*, 39 (4): 351–9.

Samuel, W.W.E. (2002) *German Boy: A Child in War*. London: Sceptre, Hodder & Stoughton.

Sanders, J. and Munford, R. (2003) 'Strengthening practice through research: research in organizations', in R. Munford and J. Sanders (eds), *Making a Difference in Families: Research that Creates Change*. Crows Nest, New South Wales, Australia: Allen & Unwin.

Sanders, W.B. (1973) 'Pinball occasions', in A. Birenbaum and E. Sagarin (eds), *People in Places: The Sociology of the Familiar*. London: Nelson.

Sapsford, R. and Abbott, P. (1996), 'Ethics, politics and research', in R. Sapsford and V. Jupp (eds), *Data Collection and Analysis*. London: Sage.

Sarantakos, S. (1998) *Social Research* (2nd edition). London: Macmillan.

Saunders, P. (2002) *The Ends and Means of Welfare: Coping with Economic and Social Change in Australia*. Cambridge: Cambridge University Press.

Sawicki, J. (1991) *Disciplining Foucault*. London: Routledge.

Scanlon, J. (1993) 'Challenging the imbalance of power in feminist oral history: developing a take-and-give methodology', *Women's Studies International Forum*, 16 (6): 639–45.

Scarborough, H. (ed.) (1996) *The Management of Expertise*. London: Macmillan.

Schofield, J.W. (1993) 'Increasing the generalizability of qualitative research', in M. Hammersley (ed.), *Social Research: Philosophy, Politics and Practice*. London: Sage. pp. 200–25.

Schon, D. (1983) *The Reflective Practitioner: How Professionals Think in Action*. New York: Basic Books.

Secretary of State for Social Services (1988) *Report of the Inquiry into Child Abuse in Cleveland*, Cmnd 412. London: HMSO.

Shapiro, E. (1973) 'Educational evaluation: rethinking the criteria of competence', *School Review*, 81: 523–49.

Shaw, I. (1996) *Evaluating in Practice*. Aldershot: Arena.

Shaw, I. (1998) 'Practising evaluation', in J. Cheetham and M.A.F. Kazi (eds), *The Working of Social Work*. London: Jessica Kingsley.

Sheldon, B. (1998) 'Social work practice in the 21st century', *Research on Social Work Practice*, 8 (5): 577–88.

Sheldon, B. and Chilvers, R. (2000) *Evidence-based Social Care: A Study of Prospects and Problems*. Lyme Regis: Russell House.

Shipman, M. (1988) *The Limitations of Social Research* (3rd edition). Harlow: Longman.

Silverman, D. (1993) *Interpreting Qualitative Data: Methods for Analysing Talk, Text and Interaction*. Newbury Park, California: Sage.

Silverman, D. (1998) 'Qualitative/quantitative', in C. Jenks (ed.), *Core Sociological Dichotomies*. London: Sage. pp. 78–95.

Silverman, D. and Perakyla, A. (1990) 'AIDS counselling: the interactional organization of talk about "delicate" issues', *Sociology of Health and Illness*, 12 (3): 293–318.

Sim, J. and Wright, C. (2000) *Research in Health Care: Concepts, Designs and Methods*. Cheltenham: Stanley Thorne.

Skeggs, B. (1994) 'Situating the production of feminist ethnography', in M. Maynard and J. Purvis (eds), *Researching Women's Lives from a Feminist Perspective*. London: Taylor & Francis. pp. 72–92.

Smart, C. (1988) 'Researching prostitution: some problems for feminist research', in Nebraska Sociological Feminist Collective, *A Feminist Ethic for Social Science Research*. Lewiston, New York: Edwin Mellen Press.

Smith, D. (1990) *Texts, Facts and Femininity: Exploring the Relations of Ruling*. London: Routledge.

Snizek, W.E. (1976) 'An empirical assessment of "sociology: a multiple paradigm science"', *American Sociologist*, 11 (4): 217–19.

Stanfield, J.H. (II) (1994) 'Ethnic modeling in qualitative research', in N.K. Denzin and Y.S. Lincoln (eds), *Handbook of Qualitative Research* (2nd edition). Newbury Park, California: Sage. pp. 175–88.

Stanley, L. (1992) *The Auto/biographical I: The Theory and Practice of Feminist Auto/biography*. Manchester: Manchester University Press.

Stanley, L. and Wise, S. (1990) 'Method, methodology and epistemology in feminist research processes', in L. Stanley (ed.), *Feminist Praxis: Research, Theory and Epistemology in Feminist Sociology*. London: Routledge. pp. 20–60.

Stanley, L. and Wise, S. (1993) *Breaking Out Again: Feminist Ontology and Epistemology* (2nd edition). London: Routledge.

Stark, E. and Flitcraft, A. (1988) 'Women and children at risk: a feminist perspective in child abuse', *International Journal of Health Services*, 18 (1): 97–118.

Steffenson, M.S. and Coker, L. (1982) 'Intercultural misunderstandings about health care', *Social Science and Medicine*, 16: 1949–54.

Stivers, C. (1993) 'Reflections on the role of personal narrative in social science', *Signs: Journal of Women in Culture and Society*, 18 (2): 408–25.

Strauss, B. (1987) *Qualitative Analysis for Social Scientists*. Cambridge and New York: Cambridge University Press.

Strauss, B. and Corbin, J. (1990) *Basics of Qualitative Research*. Newbury Park, California: Sage.

Tashakkori, A. and Teddlie, C. (1998) *Mixed Methodology: Combining Qualitative and Quantitative Approaches*, Applied Social Research Methods Series (vol. 6). Thousand Oaks, California: Sage.

Taylor, B. (1993) 'Phenomenological method in nursing: theory versus reality', in D. Colquhoun and A. Kellehear (eds), *Health Research in Practice: Political, Ethical and Methodological Issues*. London: Chapman & Hall.

Taylor, C. and White, S. (2000) *Practising Reflexivity in Health and Welfare*. Buckingham: Open University Press.

Teare, J.F., Peterson, R.W., Authier, K., Schroeder, L. and Daly, D.L. (1998) 'Maternal satisfaction following post-shelter family reunification', *Child and Family Forum*, 27 (2): 125–38.

Thomas, D. (2002) 'Evaluating the cultural appropriateness of service delivery in multi-ethnic communities', *Evaluation Journal of Australasia*, 2 (new series) (2): 50–6.

Thomas, R. (1996) 'Statistics as organizational products', *Sociological Research Online*, 1 (3) (www.socresonline.org.uk/1/3/5.html)

Thompson, E.H., Jr (1994) 'Older men as invisible men in contemporary society', in E.H. Thompson Jr (ed.), *Older Men's Lives*. Thousand Oaks, California: Sage. pp. 1–21.

Thomson, A. (1996) *Critical Reasoning: A Practical Introduction*. London: Routledge.

Thorpe, D. (1994) *Evaluating Child Protection*. Buckingham: Open University Press.

Thyer, B. (1989) 'First principles of practice research', *British Journal of Social Work*, 19: 4.

Thyer, B. (1993) 'Single system research designs', in R. Grinnell (ed.), *Social Work Research and Evaluation*. Itasca, Illinois: F.E. Peacock.

Trend, M.G. (1978) 'On the reconciliation of qualitative and quantitative analyses: a case study', *Human Organization*, 37 (4): 345–54.

Trinder, L. (2000a) 'A critical appraisal of evidence-based practice', in L. Trinder with S. Reynolds (eds), *Evidence-based Practice: A Critical Appraisal*. Oxford: Blackwell.

Trinder, L. (2000b) 'Reading the texts: postmodern feminism and the "doing" of research', in B. Fawcett, B. Featherstone, J. Fook and A. Rossiter (eds), *Practice and Research in Social Work: Postmodern Feminist Perspectives*. London: Routledge. pp. 39–61.

Truman, C. (1994) 'Feminist challenges to traditional research: have they gone far enough?', in B. Humphries and C. Truman (eds), *Re-thinking Social Research: Anti-discriminatory Approaches in Research Methodology*. Aldershot: Avebury. pp. 21–36.

Truman, C. (2000) 'New social movements and social research', in C. Truman, D.M. Mertens and B. Humphries (eds), *Research and Inequality*. London: UCL Press. pp. 24–36.

Truman, C. (2004, forthcoming) *Social Research and Social Inequality*, [provisional title]. London: Palgrave/Macmillan.

Truman, C. and Humphries, B. (1994) 'Re-thinking social research: research in an unequal world', in B. Humphries and C. Truman (eds), *Re-thinking Social Research: Anti-discriminatory Approaches in Research Methodology*. Aldershot: Avebury. pp. 1–20.

Tuhiwai Smith, L. (1999) *Decolonizing Methodologies: Research and Indigenous Peoples*. London and New York: Zed Books.

Van Maanen, J. (1988) 'Field work culture and ethnography', *Tales of the Field*. Chicago, Illinois: University of Chicago Press. pp. 1–12.

Verolme, H.E. (2000) *The Children's House of Belsen*. Fremantle, Western Australia: Fremantle Arts Centre Press.

Viswanathan, G. (1992) 'The beginnings of English literary study in British India', in J. Donald and A. Rattansi (eds), *'Race', Culture and Difference*. London and Buckingham: Sage with Open University Press. pp. 149–70.

Wadsworth, Y. (1984) *Do It Yourself Social Research*. Melbourne: Victorian Council of Social Service.

Wadsworth, Y. (1997) *Do It Yourself Social Research* (2nd edition). St Leonards, New South Wales, Australia: Allen & Unwin.

Wakefield, J.C. (1995) 'When an irresistible epistemology meets an immovable ontology', *Social Work Research*, 19 (1): 9–17.

Walker, J. (1991) *Australian Prisoners 1990*. Canberra: Australian Institute of Criminology.

Webb, E.J., Campbell, D.T., Schwartz, R.D. and Sechrest, L. (1966) *Unobtrusive Measures: Nonreactive Measures in the Social Sciences*. Chicago, Illinois: Rand McNally.

Weedon, C. (1999) *Feminism, Theory and the Politics of Difference*. Oxford: Blackwell.

Williams, M., Tutty, L.M. and Grinnell, R.M. Jr (1995) *Research in Social Work: An Introduction*. Itasca, Illinois: F.E. Peacock.

Windschuttle, K. (2002) *The Fabrication of Australian History: Vol. 1, Van Dieman's Land 1803–1847*, Sydney: Macleay Press.

Witkin, S.L. (1995) 'Whither social work research? An essay review', *Social Work*, 40: 424–8.

Wolcott, H. (1975) 'Criteria for an ethnographic approach to research in schools', *Human Organization*, 34 (2): 111–27.

Wolfe, R. (1992) 'Data management', in M.C. Alkin (ed.), *Encyclopaedia of Educational Research* (6th edition). New York: Macmillan. pp. 293–9.

Wooffitt, R. (1993) 'Analysing accounts', in N. Gilbert (ed.), *Researching Social Life*. London: Sage. pp. 287–305.

Woolgar, S. (1982) 'Laboratory studies: a comment on the state of the art', *Social Studies of Science*, 12: 481–98.

Yallop, R. (2003) 'Battle of the black armband', *The Australian*, 4 January.

Yeatman, A. (1995) 'Interlocking oppressions', in B. Caine and R. Pringle (eds), *Transitions: New Australian Feminisms*. St Leonards, New South Wales, Australia: Allen & Unwin. pp. 42–56.

Zapf, M. (1999) 'Barriers to the acceptance of indigenous knowledge: lessons from social work in Canada's north', *Rural Social Work*, 5: 4–12.

Index